IN PRAISE OF BOOKS

Middle East Studies Beyond Dominant Paradigms
Peter Gran, *Series Editor*

"Un poete (les Coptes dans la Hte Egypt)" by Melle. Browne, 1874.
Courtesy of Nelly Hanna.

IN PRAISE OF BOOKS

A Cultural History of Cairo's Middle Class,
Sixteenth to the Eighteenth Century

NELLY HANNA

SYRACUSE UNIVERSITY PRESS

Copyright © 2003 by Syracuse University Press
Syracuse, New York 13244–5160

All Rights Reserved

First Edition 2003
03 04 05 06 07 08   6 5 4 3 2 1

The paper used in this publication meets the minimum requirements of American National Standard for Information Sciences—Permanence of Paper for Printed Library Materials, ANSI Z39.48–1984.∞™

Library of Congress Cataloging-in-Publication Data
Hanna, Nelly.
In praise of books : a cultural history of Cairo's middle class, sixteenth to the eighteenth century / Nelly Hanna.— 1st ed.
p. cm.—(Middle East studies beyond dominant paradigms)
Includes bibliographical references and index.
ISBN 0-8156-3012-3 ISBN 0-8156-3036-0 (pbk.)
1. Middle class—Egypt—History. 2. Middle class—Books and reading—Egypt. 3. Middle class—Egypt—Intellectual life. 4. Egypt—Civilization—638–1798. I. Title. II. Series.
HT690.E3 I5 2003
305.5'5'0962—dc21
2003013954

Manufactured in the United States of America

Contents

Tables　vi

Foreword, PETER GRAN　vii

Acknowledgments　ix

1. Introduction　1
2. Society, Economy, and Culture　26
3. Culture and Education of the Middle Class　50
4. Books and the Middle Class　79
5. Shaping a Culture of the Middle Class　104
6. Radical Intellectuals: A Culture of Crisis　139
7. Conclusion　172

Notes　181

Glossary　195

Bibliography　197

Index　209

Tables

1. Number of Private Libraries and the Books They Contain   85
2. Total Value of Books in Given Years   86
3. Book Prices by Date from Probate Records   91
4. Professions of People Who Owned Libraries   99

Foreword

PETER GRAN

AN ASSUMPTION commonly found in social theory is that one of the distinguishing features of the West is that it is an integrated society. There is no great gap in language and culture between top and bottom. By way of contrast, the Orient, Egypt serving as an example, has long conjured up the idea of a dichotomy between high culture and low culture, making for what one could infer was a totally unintegrated society. Depending on the period in question, one could find this lack of integration manifest as a dichotomy between Ottoman Turkish and Arabic, between classical Arabic and colloquial Arabic, or even between French and English and colloquial Arabic. While there has been some sense of the inadequacy of this tableau on the part of scholars for many years, few works have attempted to confront this cultural model as a problem. In this work Professor Nelly Hanna explores a group of writers whose position is somewhere between the high culture of the Azharite *'ulama'* and of the state and the mass culture of the colloquial. They are, as she puts it, from the "urban middle strata."

To confront the prevailing model took years of empirical work. First there were the discovery and analysis of unknown works of literature and scholarship by heretofore unknown authors; then there were studies of their context, of the salon culture, of the evolving system of private libraries, this last studied in quite an original way from probate records; then there were studies of the paper trade as a part of the explanation for the financial feasibility for the growth of the number of books and of writing in this period, these studies too breaking new ground in more than one sense.

The work is further enriched by its recourse to comparative history, reflected in the sustained use of the important works of secondary scholarship on Mediterranean Europe as well as on the Ottoman Empire in this period. This dimension was especially important from my perspective as it solidified the idea of the broad comparability of Egyptian with early modern Mediterranean and European history.

Last but not least, works asserting the importance of Ottoman culture in Egypt naturally have as their foil the traditional idea of the Napoleonic-Muhammad 'Ali watershed. Professor Hanna goes a way toward making Egyptian literature of the Ottoman period a part of the modern Arabic literature of Egypt. This inclusion cannot help but attract the attention of scholars working in the "traditional" modern period.

Acknowledgments

IN THE COURSE of the five years that it took to write this book, a number of friends and colleagues have helped to bring it to the shape in which it stands today. Among these, Raouf Abbas, Asem Dusuqi, and Peter Gran read the manuscript and gave me helpful comments, some of which were incorporated in the text while others set me to rethinking the issues about which I had written. Amira Sonbol was always generous with her time and her ideas about the book, and our many discussions helped me to sharpen many of the arguments. Likewise Elizabeth Sartain, with her profound knowledge of medieval history, provided me much advice on various issues. My friend Jack Guiragossian read the manuscript at its different stages of progression and gave me very useful comments on how to improve the editing. T. J. Fitzgerald went out of his way when I needed help and pushed me to sharpen a number of the arguments in the book. Magdi Girgis was generous with his time, and I had to rely on his help on many an occasion. Nasir Ibrahim was likewise a great help. To all these friends and colleagues, I express my gratitude.

Acknowledgments are also due to the Ecole des Hautes Etudes en Sciences Sociales in Paris, where I was invited as a visiting scholar in May-June 1999 and where I had a chance to interact with French historians and to look more broadly at French scholarship. Last but not least, it would have been difficult to see this book out had I not had the benefit of release time from teaching at the American University in Cairo. The grant I received to research and then to write the book was indispensable.

IN PRAISE OF BOOKS

1

Introduction

THE IDEA FOR THIS BOOK came from an eighteenth-century literary text. Both the work, in manuscript form, and its author, Muhammad Ibn Hasan Abu Dhakir (born in 1106/1694), were unknown to modern scholars. Abu Dhakir appeared in no biographical dictionaries and has no other known work. His 250-folio book, whose title page is missing, is in fact a collection of short pieces that he wrote in the period between 1153/1740 and 1179/1765 on a large number of subjects and compiled in the form of a book. Its contents touched social, economic, and cultural issues; its style was sometimes autobiographical, at other times reflective or humorous; its language sometimes was grammatically correct and at other times was close to the spoken word.

The book was revealing in many ways as a document of the period, and its significance was multiple. On the one hand, Abu Dhakir wrote in an open, frank, easily accessible style. In many ways this was a personal narrative exposing his innermost feelings. It was also a social comment on what went on around him. On the other hand, his opinions—whether on *'ulama'*, on Mamluks, on the social structure, or on gender relations—often did not conform to the dominant view. As such his narrative offered an angle for understanding the eighteenth century from a viewpoint other than that of the establishment. Lastly, the comments that Abu Dhakir made on social issues such as poverty and money, and his comments on institutions such as the Azhar, give us an individual and personal reaction to the current issues and problems that his generation was facing. Thus, although the way he expressed himself— his openness and freedom of style—was unusual for his time, the content and the basic issues with which he was concerned were those of a generation who lived through this period of flux. At all these levels, the work stood in stark contrast to the better-known texts of its period, suggesting an innovative approach that had not been explored by modern research.

To fully appreciate its relevance, I had to understand the text in a broader social and cultural context that could allow me to explore the relationship between this literary work and the context that produced it. I therefore consulted many literary sources, belles-lettres, compilations of stories, and jokes and anecdotes, many of them still in manuscript form, as well as the better-known chronicles, dictionaries, and court records of the period, with the aim both of understanding the extent to which Abu Dhakir's work was unique or formed part of a trend that could be traced among his contemporaries and of placing him within the socioeconomic context of his period.

I did not examine the text in terms of its inherent artistic qualities, nor use it in the postmodernist sense of a discourse that had a life of its own independent of its social context. Instead, I examined this and other literary sources in terms of social history and of the general climate that produced them. I read them as an expression of a certain culture and a certain time, rather than as part of an inherited literary tradition or as an abstract construction. The contents were the expression of an individual author whose individuality, idiosyncrasies, and moods were felt by the reader, but at the same time they expressed a broader culture and a way of understanding the world and society. Consequently, the literary texts became meaningful when they were understood in relationship to the historical processes of the period, and they shed light on aspects of these processes that chronicles and biographies did not always show. This approach to the literary work as a cultural product was therefore in line with Raymond Williams's view that cultural activities should be studied in relation to other forms of social life because they are part of a context.[1]

The results indicated that much of what Abu Dhakir wrote had parallels among other writers, a few of them already known but many of them so far unknown, who had similar social concerns about the culture of a broad urban group that could be identified as middle-ranking or a middle stratum. Other writers and thinkers emerged in the course of the sixteenth to eighteenth centuries who expressed a middle-class culture that could be distinguished from that of establishment writers: middle-class culture was more inclusive in its concerns and in the way those concerns were expressed; scholarly culture was exclusive and comprehensible only to a few; one was an offshoot of institutionalized learning, the other was freer to express its views; finally, one was closer to morality and religiosity, the other to social realities and lived concerns.

In other words, my research suggested the existence of a category that does not have wide acceptance among historians of the period, notably a category of people who were educated without necessarily being scholarly, who may have been trained in religious institutions of learning but who had a realistic rather than an idealist view of the world. Although at first sight this category did not correspond to the dominant view that we have of the period, there was a certain logic to the fact that only few of the people who actually attended institutions of learning became professors and scholars or ended up as high '*ulama*'. Many more remained in middle- and lower-ranking positions. In addition, some people moved between religious professions and trades, sometimes keeping two jobs in order to make ends meet; sometimes too people with some college training subsequently moved into an economic or commercial activity. Therefore there was a large pool of people who received some education but who did not end up as scholars.

To fully understand the framework that allowed this kind of expression to emerge and develop, it became necessary for me to reconsider many issues that have been taken for granted, especially with regard to education and to other channels for the transmission of knowledge and culture, with regard to who had access to such channels, and finally with regard to the kind of person that the educational conditions of the period could produce. The study of these writings could thus shed light on both writing as a cultural phenomenon and the contents as social phenomena. In other words, these texts could enlighten us about society in the early modern period and allow us to explore the historical process through the optic of culture rather than exclusively through political, social, and economic dimensions. Consequently, by exploring cultural history, certain dimensions of the social history of the sixteenth through eighteenth centuries can be better understood, particularly important for a period and for a class that are in great need of exploration.

The works in question, moreover, showed a level of modernity that I had not encountered before and that to the best of my knowledge had not been studied by either historians or literary historians and critics. Their "modernity" was not in the sense of technology, of developed state structures, or of capitalism, but in the sense of an interest in the culture, the concerns and the forms of expression of a social stratum that was clearly not part of the elite and not part of the establishment. Modernity was manifested by an interest in the ordinary person and expressed in his everyday concerns, by an interest in real situations that were observed and analyzed with a realistic and empirical approach—people, in other words, who were outside the ruling establishment and the power structure, who were real rather than the exceptional or idealized man who stood out because of his deeds, his moral character, or his scholarly achievements. The simple style and language, close to the spoken word, were such that they were easily accessible to a reader who was not a scholar. Moreover, the analysis of social, personal, and intellectual situations was sometimes done from a religious angle but more often the angle was not religious but social.

The question this analysis raised was whether we could consider this culture to be an educated culture, a mass culture, or a popular culture. Cultural histories that group all nonelites, whether urban or rural, with "popular" culture do not sufficiently take into consideration the material and cultural differences between the rural population and the urban middle class—which included tradesmen, small-scale merchants, and craftsmen, some of whom enjoyed a level of material comfort—and the urban poor, who lived from hand to mouth: the thousands of carriers of goods, owners of donkeys, water carriers, street cleaners, entertainers of various kinds who roamed the streets and gave performances for a small fee, and many more people in a variety of professions. The culture in question was sophisticated; the people who wrote the texts were, for the most part, educated and well-read. There was no likelihood that they were living at subsistence level.

In short, these works expressed a culture of the urban middle ranks, different from that of scholars and princes, that is, from courtly or learned culture, but also different from popular culture or culture of the masses. This culture consequently does not fit into the social or the cultural categories that we usually use. We are in fact dealing with a social and a cultural category of people that have not usually been written about: the middle class. My exploration of the cultural production and intellectual contribution of this middle-class culture—which is not the culture of high-ranking *'ulama'* and courtly elites in the domain of education, learning, reading, writing, and books—suggested a more significant intellectual role than we thought and a need to consider this role more closely. The question was, notably, whether or not a dynamic role can be attributed to this class, whether or not this class could have an impact on society, and whether or not it could have an influence on the modern period—in other words, whether this class had a role in the historical process in the early modern or the modern period. The issue is controversial because it touches on the existence or absence of some sort of civil society. Opinions are divided.

One area of interest in Ottoman (and Egyptian) studies concentrates on various aspects of the ruling class. Ehud Toledano's book *State and Society in Mid-Nineteenth-Century Egypt*, for instance, explores the ruling elite in relation to the "rest of the population"; a role for the middle class is not apparent. Likewise, Jane Hathaway's study of the eighteenth-century rise of an elite household, the Qazdaglis, has shown the existence of close ties between the emergence of Mamluk elite households in Cairo and those in Anatolia. Her book explores an elite phenomenon, leaving much space for researchers to study other social layers with potential roles in the social dynamics of the period.[2] Other historians, like Suraiya Faroqhi and Abdul-Karim Rafeq, for instance, were interested in a potential role for those who were not part of the establishment and the power structure and tried to show that they were part of a historical process.[3]

Today, a generation of young scholars in Cairo is doing intensive work on the court records. Their research, regularly presented in the Ottoman Seminar of Cairo, sponsored by the Egyptian Society for Historical Studies, which has been active for some years now, is shedding much light on the social dynamics of the period in general and on the lives of ordinary persons. My own work has benefited greatly from discussions with some of these young scholars. The present book argues that a certain dynamism existed among those who were not at the top and were not part of the power structure. How to define this culture and its changing contours in relation to the rest of society is a subject that has not been explored. The present study is an attempt to embark on such a project.

The consequences of such a study are multiple. With regard to the modern period, the dominant trend in scholarship has been to find two sources for modern culture, one based on Western models and the other based on state policies of the nineteenth century. By contrast, the findings of the present study indicate that there were significant dimensions of modern culture that had their source in the two previous centuries. Moreover, an educated middle-class culture can be seen as constituting an important source for modern culture, a matter that has not as yet been explored.

Another important consequence of the study is that it showed a greater cultural diversity within the urban classes of the sixteenth through the eighteenth centuries than was thought, a diversity that has not been fully appreciated. As a result, any influence these urban classes may have had on the contemporary cultural scene or on nineteenth-century culture has passed unnoticed. It is important, therefore, to identify this culture, to analyze the conditions that favored its development, and to find out how it influenced modern culture. This study is a first attempt to provide this cultural identification and analysis. Finally, I had to identify the relationship of this trend to the historical context. For this culture to develop in the direction that it did and to be expressed in very articulate writing, certain developments had to have occurred both in terms of the material framework and of the level and type of education of those concerned. The pursuit of these goals and the elaboration of their ideas led to the exploration of three other directions: the link between economic and cultural conditions, the regional and local power structures, and the conditions that helped shape the nonreligious perspectives of the middle class.

The Economic and Cultural Contexts

The first direction for exploration was based on the premise that the culture of a particular group is linked to its economic conditions. This premise required searching for the material conditions that allowed a middle-class educated culture to come to the fore and to influence contemporaries. It required consideration of this culture in relation to economy and in relation to class dynamics, even though the absence of relevant studies, especially in the sixteenth and seventeenth centuries, proved to be a drawback. Little has been written on class dynamics with regard to most of the period. There were therefore many dark areas that I could at best make guesses about.

My study of cultural patterns of the middle class built upon the work of André Raymond, whose work on merchants and artisans in eighteenth-century Cairo explored the urban economy and those social groups who were part of it, both those who were actively involved in production, sales, and services and those who benefited from taxation of these activities. Using his work as a basis for the material conditions of the middle class, my research developed another dimension in their lives, the cultural dimension, showing some of the angles that were not explored by other historians. There was a particular advantage to working on the middle class in Cairo because its eighteenth-century economic history had been so thoroughly explored. It was possible, consequently, to link cultural history to the economy and to explore the way that material conditions could impact cultural trends.

The historical exploration showed that between the sixteenth and the eighteenth centuries, what we can call a middle-class culture developed, not in a linear way but with many ups and downs. The work of André Raymond showed an economic middle class that had a significant role to play in the history of the eighteenth century. The economic history of this class that Raymond explored was an essential element in understanding its culture. His work was, therefore, indispensable for the present study. His work drew the contours of this class, its position in the social structure, its relation to those in power, and the ups and downs of its fortunes. These people, who constituted an important and varied sector of the urban population involved in production, in trade, and in services, included craftsmen, middle-ranking merchants, and scholars. In terms of numbers, they may have made up about a third of the urban population.

As of the mid-sixteenth century or so, the expansion of international trade currents and of a commercial capitalism with a large demand for locally produced goods worked in favor of this class. Evidence from probate records as well as from multiple financial dealings show a middle class that had certain means. These conditions attracted them toward the marketplace as traders and producers, and as people in religious and military professions, on a temporary or permanent basis. In a society strongly embedded in guilds and professional structures, one can discern certain social and political concerns that cut across guild and professional lines. The middle ranks were thus both strata, in the sense of closed groups with a group interest concentrated on the guild or profession, and class, in the sense of the concerns that cut across these lines.

The term that is more often used to describe middle ranks prior to the Industrial Revolution is *stratum* rather than *class*. A dominant Marxist view considered the concept of class to have been a consequence of the Industrial Revolution, roughly at the end of the eighteenth century. Prior to that, one could refer to ranks, states, orders, or strata. Wealth and poverty, domination and subjection, property and lack of property, high and low prestige, all these were present both before and after the Industrial Revolution. The difference between the ruling class and the middle class was that before the Industrial Revolution, exploitation by ruling classes was guaranteed and legitimized, and people did not question the status quo; the Industrial Revolution abolished this system of norms and values.

In the context of early modern Cairo, there are arguments for or against the use of both *class* and *stratum*. I nevertheless chose to use the word *class* for a couple of reasons. Even though strongly embedded in guilds and professional structures, the group that I am talking about was not a closed order or estate autonomous from the rest of the social structure. In fact one of the main points of the study is precisely to show the conditions that shaped this group, the relevance of their links to the ruling class in this process, and the constant interplay and overlapping of interests or conflicts of interest between the middle class and the ruling class. The fortunes of the middle class were to some extent defined by this relationship, a dynamic relationship that underwent significant transformations in the course of the two centuries that the study covers.[4] Words like *stratum, estate*, and *order*, descriptive terms implying a static social order consolidated by privilege-creating religious or legal institutions, had some validity in the context in question but, given the state of flux with which the book is concerned, carried certain connotations that I preferred not to communicate to the reader.[5]

Thus the culture of the middle class is not studied in isolation, but in its relationship to the cultures of others: to the military ruling class because of the leverage it had on the economy, and to the religious establishment that had leverage on the cultural level. The middle class's relations with these two underwent significant transformations in the course of the period from the sixteenth to the eighteenth centuries. Hence, once we admit that the historical context shaped the way that culture developed, we can assume that the culture of the middle class was not a static and timeless block, but rather a changing and flexible body that interacted with its surroundings and that could develop or retract, shaped by the conditions of time and place.

Regional and Local Power Structures

This idea of the development of the middle class led to the exploration of a second direction, this time related to the power structure. I considered two significant channels. The first has to do with state and ruling structures, notably the local power structure (ruling class versus middle class) and the regional structure (Istanbul authorities versus local grandees). Among the factors that affected the development of middle-class culture was the level of tax exploitation that could, when carried out with impunity, suffocate the urban population and impoverish this class. To a large extent the issue was fought out between the local military (members of the *ujaqs* or Ottoman regiments and subsequently the Mamluk ruling class) trying to control the taxation system and the Ottoman state, which had the legitimate right to impose and control these taxes. The fluctuating relations between the central power and the provinces, and the growing weight of the local military or Mamluk groups in relation to the central authorities, opened up the way to numerous forms of exploitation of the urban population. Ironically, the balance in favor of the provinces, as the central power of Istanbul was becoming more diffuse, was a factor in the consolidation of a local culture, one that the urban middle class was familiar with and part of, and one that helped it to come to the fore.

The second channel was the local power structure. The extent to which high culture or establishment culture could monopolize or dominate society is fundamental to our understanding of cultural history. It is an issue for which there is a large divergence of views among scholars. On one side a Gramscian approach considered elites to have controlled populations through hegemonic cultures. Elites had the means to do so by their control of education and of information, thus forging a level of consensus for their rule among the populations that they exploited. On the other side of the spectrum, cultures were considered to be either a continuum, complementary to each other, or autonomous, a view characterized by the absence of conflict. To understand the way that this relationship worked, I had to pursue a number of further channels.

One of these channels was through consideration of the dominant religious structures. The preeminent position of the Azhar cannot be disputed. The Azhar dominated the scene in the sense that it was the most important educational institution, not only in Cairo but also all over Egypt and the Islamic world. People came from East and West to join the Azhar as teachers or as students. Its teachers had a prominent social position, and rulers respected its teachers. Its scholars played a prominent role as teachers, as *muftis*, as *qadis*, or in other such professions and acquired the recognition of their peers and their social surroundings for the breadth of their knowledge, for their writings, and for their social prominence. The Azhar and its *'ulama'* were, moreover, the guardians of an establishment culture that had as its aim to maintain a social and political status quo that was by nature conservative, that stood for social stability and for social harmony. They had the means through which to expose and diffuse their views, through the system of education, for instance. For example, key positions were only available to those who had been through the educational establishment, notably positions that could bring them in close touch with a wider public. Yet, in spite of the Azhar's weight on the cultural scene, both locally, regionally, and internationally, it was important to ask about the extent to which it monopolized all forms of learning or of transmission of knowledge.

Here, several issues were at stake. One of these was to challenge the application of the oriental despotism model to knowledge. In the same way as it is applied to society in general, when the paradigm of oriental despotism is applied to knowledge or to the transmission of knowledge, all is concentrated in the top establishment of the time; everything moves from this one source at the top along a set channel of transmission to the passive recipients below. Another issue, this time in the realm of methodology, had to do with cultural categories such as "popular culture" or "high culture" and whether or not these should be considered as fixed entities with clear-cut borders. Cultural studies by major scholars have frequently used a two-tiered division, *high culture* and *popular culture*. A number of prominent cultural historians, such as Peter Burke and Robert Darnton, have offered variations of this division. Peter Burke's influential book *Popular Culture in Early Modern Europe*, for instance, developed the idea of society's having what he called a "great tradition" to refer to the culture of learning and of the establishment and a "little tradition," an unofficial culture of nonelites, that was a shared culture in which elites also participated. The little tradition included the culture of peasants, artisans, and tradesmen. Society was made up of a minority of people who could read and write and a majority who could not, a two-layered definition that many other cultural historians used.[6] Robert Darnton used this two-layered definition, the upper one dealing in matters of the mind, notably formal thought and philosophy, and the lower one dealing in the way that ordinary people made sense of the world, not in logical propositions but with things that their culture made available to them such as stories or ceremonies.[7]

In neither Burke nor Darnton was there a distinct culture between that of formal thought and philosophy and that of ordinary people, nor a clearly defined middle-class culture. Thus neither had a place between the high culture of the rich and educated and the popular culture of the masses. The culture of the urban middle class was integrated into a "popular culture" that was essentially an oral culture. Often, by implication, the incorporation into an oral culture was linked to illiteracy, the understanding being that oral culture was the domain of those who could not read or write. They best expressed their culture through varied and numerous collective festivities and ceremonies, religious and secular, picturesque sometimes, burlesque at others, in which license was tolerated.[8]

On the other hand, the elite mass approach dominated historical studies for a long time, whether in the field of social, economic, or political history. Society was seen as divided between rulers and ruled, and nothing intervened between these two categories. The establishment consisted of political rulers associated with a courtly culture and a religious judiciary establishment associated with a religious or academic culture. The urban population that did not form part of the political or religious establishment was associated with a popular culture. This approach, sometimes referred to as the oriental despotism model, considered that all dynamism was concentrated at the top and that below the top was an undifferentiated and passive mass that formed society.

Although the two-tiered model has strongly persisted, there have been some shifts in its framework. At the present time, a trend to move from the higher levels of culture and cultural production to the lower levels or to popular culture has emerged. This trend was part of a general shift from the study of elites to that of masses. European cultural studies, for example, have been moving away from the culture of great men such as the philosophers of the eighteenth-century French Enlightenment, and going beyond the learning and scholarship of their academies and institutions. These studies explore other social groups and their relationship to literacy, to learning, to the book, and to forms of transmission other than those linked to the establishment. Peter Burke, in his recent work *A Social History of Knowledge*, proposed to consider the Renaissance, the Scientific Revolution, and the Enlightenment as no more than the surfacing into visibility of certain kinds of popular or practical knowledge and their legitimization by the academic establishment.[9] More and more, the European Enlightenment is being studied in terms of the total picture rather than solely in terms of the scientists and philosophers at the top, whose names dominated the field for many decades. French historiography, for instance, rather than concentrating only on the achievements of great men, has dwelled extensively on the spread of reading and writing, on what it meant to different social groups to be literate and on the way they approached the written word. A parallel development is taking shape in the study of Ottoman history. After decades of concentration on courtly culture and the culture of the religious establishment, the culture of the common man is making its way into historical scholarship. Suraiya Faroqhi's recent book *Subjects of the Sultan: Culture and Daily Life in the Ottoman Empire*, for instance, pays attention to townspeople and to everyday culture, to the way they understood the world around them.[10] In the present study I preferred to move away from the notion of static entities that the dominant culture could at all times fully control and to use a more nuanced approach to the culture of the middle class, one that is shaped by historical conditions and by the changing relationships between the various social groups.

The study explores the conditions that shaped the relationship between middle-class culture and establishment culture and gives consideration to the way the borders between them were constantly in a state of flux. Establishment culture maintained its dominant position in society by a variety of mechanisms: through the system of education, through the written word, through its attempts to spread and control certain kinds of knowledge, and through the social prominence of its proponents. At certain times the grip of this culture on others was tight, at other times less so. Under certain conditions, common interests brought these classes closer together so that the element of conflict was more diffused. At these times, the climate was favorable enough to allow a middle-class culture to flourish. At other times, less favorable conditions could lead to a retraction. The development of a book culture, for instance, and the greater presence of the middle class as consumers as well as producers of the written word, meant that a certain part of book production fell outside the domain of the dominant culture.

The Nonreligious Perspectives of the Middle Class

The third direction was to find explanations for the nonreligious perspective of middle-class culture and to explore the conditions that helped to shape this perspective. A persistent view has held that prior to the modern period culture was dominated by religion and that only after the nineteenth century was a secular culture introduced. In the first place, the presence of a nonreligious dimension in middle-class culture did not make it a secular culture. Their culture was many-sided. The study assumes that individuals as well as groups had more than one cultural dimension, that they could move between one and another with a certain ease, and that this many-sidedness applied to people who devoted their life to learning as well as to merchants, craftsmen, and tradesmen. As a matter of fact, it is misleading to consider *'ulama'* solely in their religious dimension. *'Ulama'* culture, although essentially academic and scholastic, and although much too specialized to reach a broader public, was nevertheless a complex culture.

The religious dimension of the middle class was an important part of their culture, as can easily be seen by the spread of Sufi *tariqas* or brotherhoods among craftsmen and tradesmen, and by the voluminous production of saints' lives and Sufi works. It is not always possible to make a clear distinction between what was religious and what was not. A look at the books that members of this class owned shows beyond doubt that, for the vast majority, it was religious works, lives of saints, and Sufi works, for instance, that they were interested in.

In the second place, because modern scholarship on culture has put so much emphasis on *'ulama'* and on their institutions of learning, it has tended to overlook other significant cultural dimensions. One cannot understand the total cultural picture exclusively through this religious establishment culture. One has only to think of the men in the bureaucracy, whose administrative culture was highly developed. Muhammad Hakim has done some work on what he called the "political arithmetic" of Coptic scribes, who worked for Mamluk beys in the eighteenth century and for Muhammad 'Ali subsequently. Highly trained in mathematics, in accounting, and in auditing, these men had a well-developed political sense of the power that their knowledge gave them vis-à-vis the power structure.[11] Likewise, there was a form of scientific culture that in the eighteenth century centered around the field of astronomy. Al-Jabarti mentions a group of astronomers who were particularly active, like al-Khawaniki for instance. The training that they had, the methods of its transmission, the books that guided them, all these are subjects about which there is a complete blackout, mainly because this culture was transmitted outside institutions, in homes or in workplaces, from father to son, or from administrator to trainee. What these subjects show is that there were ways of obtaining knowledge other than the religious colleges. Thus there was a context allowing the development of a nonreligious culture that was highly educated.

In the third place, within its own culture the middle class had a significant social and intellectual dimension. Its members had a rich literary culture, both oral and written. They were exposed to a commercial culture with a practical outlook, one that emphasized this world, not instead of but together with the next, one that emphasized mundane matters and social issues, a culture that was concerned to protect its interests by the means available to it. A significant dimension of middle-class makeup was influenced by this commercial culture.

It was therefore evident that there were forms of education and culture among social groups other than high *'ulama'* and Azharites, and that it is useful to explore these others rather than to be restricted to the top layer. The cultural and educational influences these groups were subject to were multifaceted and complex. In other words, the fact that they may have been the products of a religious education, whether at the primary or higher level, could not fully explain the middle-class phenomenon. We have to, on the one hand, understand the limits and the possibilities of the *madrasa* differently, and on the other hand look for forms of transmission of knowledge other than institutional ones.

The implications are significant. Firstly, there were forms of education and channels for the transmission of knowledge not necessarily linked to educational institutions and consequently less subject to the restraints that institutions could impose. Secondly, the end product of the colleges of religious education were not as homogeneous as they were thought to be.

The culture of the middle class, or even that of the educated middle class, was potentially less concerned with the perpetuation of institutional norms and might have been more open to new ideas and practices. This study opted for a wider and more inclusive approach to education, one that includes various forms of transmission, not just those within educational institutions. It argues for a greater diffusion than is usually thought, as well as for greater diversity of the end product. This diversity and diffusion can in part be explained by the diverse forms existing for the transmission of learning and knowledge—such as the spread of a book culture, the coffeehouse, the literary salon—and their significance for our understanding of the way that the middle-class culture was shaped during the period under study.

Both institutional and noninstitutional forms of education had a role to play, a situation that unintentionally led me to write an intellectual history of people who were not usually considered as intellectuals. By bringing these forms into the picture, one can gain an understanding of the diversity and the complexity of the cultural scene at a given moment, an understanding that a concentration on scholars and institutions could not achieve.

Two major difficulties of the study were, first, the absence of a parallel study of middle-class culture in the early modern period in another region that could have been used as a model to build upon; and second, the fact that for the period covered, neither the social history nor the evolution of knowledge can be said to be established. Consequently, to undertake such a study on the culture of the urban middle class, to suggest that such people may have been educated without belonging to the scholarly community or that their culture may have had an impact on the culture of the upper strata, or that there was a distinct culture linked to this class, meant feeling my way around, with all the risks that this entails. It also meant exploring the various levels of reality of a middle-class culture, in terms of its nature and its manifestations, as well as in terms of where it stood in the total social and cultural scene at a particular moment in time.

The Broader Issues

There was a broader significance to the study of middle-class culture that went beyond the particular group that the culture touched most and beyond the confines of the geographical area where they lived. The work ended up by questioning a number of givens about the period, about the region, and about the study of culture. The study can be placed in different contexts.

At the level of methodology, as the study progressed it became increasingly clear that a number of important trends observed in Cairo were in fact evident in other European and Ottoman regions. A comparison with these was a way of reinforcing the arguments. I used studies undertaken in other regions, mainly in Syria and Anatolia for the Ottoman part and in France and Italy for the Mediterranean part, to compare and to reinforce the significance of these trends as regional phenomena. The numerous works on cultural history in Europe and the Mediterranean provided a comparative framework with which to understand what was going on. Thus, some historical developments could only be understood by taking into consideration broad geographic regions. For some issues it was more relevant to integrate the northern Mediterranean, for others, the Ottoman lands.

Some of the economic factors that helped to shape this culture were broadly diffused geographically, and consequently the study of this aspect allows us to perceive common grounds between the north and the south of the Mediterranean. The commercial capitalism that partly helped to shape the culture of the middle class of Cairo was at the source of many aspects of the culture of urban groups in Venice, for instance. Likewise, economic factors suggest common grounds between regions within the Ottoman empire that had similar conditions.

As a regional phenomenon, the rise of northern European states linked to Atlantic trade and the shift of dynamism from south to north, emerging in the sixteenth century, are considered to have ushered in the cultural decline of the Mediterranean region. There was thus an argument based on both a regional and a local basis to support the idea of decline. At present, the idea that there could be more than one dynamic center functioning at the same time, that the dynamism of one did not necessarily lead to a decline of all others, is being developed both on the theoretical and the empirical level. Peter Gran has argued for the coexistence of multiple centers. He used this concept in relation to the study of world history, arguing for social history rather than a Europe-centered world history and consequently for a variety of possible patterns and social structures.[12] Yet the concept may well have some relevance in a Mediterranean or an Ottoman context because it can be used to argue that the rise of one region did not necessarily lead to the decline of another one. Peter Gran's approach can with some adaptations be applied to the present context insofar as the different regions of the Mediterranean and Ottoman worlds, in spite of their common patterns in economy, trade, and social structures, had different social dynamics and consequently different cultural patterns.

Some studies on the Mediterranean at the period of their "decline" (that is, after the center of international commerce and finance moved northward toward Antwerp and London) show how certain regions maintained their dynamism. Seventeenth-century Spain, for instance, long after the peak of its glory, played a dominant role in the formation of Baroque culture, as José Antonio Maravall indicates in his book *The Culture of the Baroque*, producing such giants as El Greco and Velasquez and significant innovations in literature.[13] In other words, even if new centers had become very influential, it did not necessarily have to follow that the old ones died off or had nothing more to offer.

Another issue, rather more complex, related to the somewhat artificial divisions that are made with regard to the Mediterranean. There is evidence that in the period from the sixteenth to the eighteenth centuries, neither the north/south nor the Christian/Muslim divide across the Mediterranean was as clear-cut as we sometimes assume. I have already suggested in an earlier work the relevance of this Mediterranean context in the domain of trade and commerce.[14] The present book explores this context somewhat further by its consideration of cultural trends that could potentially have a bearing on a broad geographical region. It shows, for instance, that there could be a link between the spread of literacy and the growth of trade regardless of whether they occurred in an Italian city like Venice or Florence or in a city like Alexandria, Damietta, or Aleppo. Likewise, the relatively cheap paper that was being produced in Europe in answer to the growing needs created by the printing press could have had an impact in any Mediterranean region, whether on the European side or on the Ottoman side. The logic of trade and profit pushed merchants importing European merchandise to purchase this inexpensive paper. As a result, the production costs of books were reduced. The list of parallel developments south and north of the Mediterranean could be longer. We are still awaiting more studies that identify and explore them more fully.

In relation to the Ottoman context, the study addressed a number of issues and debates, and built upon the work of a number of scholars and historians. One fundamental issue has to do with the way that historians integrate the study of a particular region to the larger Ottoman context. My comments deal with the Arab-speaking lands, although they could probably also be relevant to the Balkan lands. Major works of Ottoman history have appeared in recent years in which the Arab world is either absent or given marginal interest. This region has not really been integrated into Ottoman history, although it covered about two-fifths of the Ottoman state and contained about half of its population, not to mention its resources, trade routes, and religious centers. It is sometimes subsumed in the appellation of "Ottoman" and sometimes appears in a separate section or chapter that does not quite show the weight it had in the Ottoman Empire or explore the dynamic relationship between them. There is a methodological problem here because such studies are, in a sense, ahistorical if they do not sufficiently take into account the significance of the sixteenth-century incorporation of Arab lands into the Ottoman state, or the nineteenth-century ceding of these lands to other powers. Not to recognize the two-way impact of such factors, as political, as economic and commercial, and even as cultural phenomena, is problematic to say the least.

For decades, historians of the Middle East in general and of Ottoman studies in particular have been challenging Orientalist history that placed Europe in a position central to the understanding of Islamic, Arab, or Ottoman societies. Orientalist history put these societies in a position of being passive and often unsuccessful recipients of European models. Many alternative solutions were offered in writing the history of former colonized regions without using Europe as a primary point of reference. Today we need to develop methods that allow us to understand the history of the Ottoman state, with all its diversities, complexities, histories, without falling back to the methods of Orientalist or colonial history. One needs alternatives to certain trends that are emerging in the field. One dimension of the problem involves the use of "Ottoman" when in fact the research is clearly placed in Istanbul or Anatolia. The assumption is sometimes that the results of research undertaken in one region can be applicable to other regions. To understand the history of Cairo, Aleppo, or Damascus only in terms of what was taking place in Istanbul may be misleading insofar as it may presume that a region like Egypt or a city like Cairo is a bad copy of the original. This may or may not be the case, but certainly it cannot be taken as a given. Such generalizations, moreover, may miss important dimensions: firstly the importance of the local dimensions in shaping the broader historical process, and secondly the dynamic relationship between local forces and regional or international ones. The marginalization of the Arab-speaking region in the field of Ottoman studies has created, in my view, an impediment to a real understanding of the Ottoman world and of the process of change in the region as a whole.

Another potential form of marginalization emerged in some recent scholarship. The fact that many localities have turned out to possess court records has been both a blessing (insofar as provincial histories could for the first time be written, showing the specificities of their culture and their history) and a problem (insofar as it could bring out minutia that was interesting for itself only). For people who work on these court records, the sheer volume of material may sometimes push scholars in the direction of minutia. Thus, although local in-depth history of specific localities may avoid the dangers of generalization, this approach too has its dangers if one does not make the research relevant to a larger context and consequently tends to marginalize these localities. Local histories may tend to emphasize small and medium localities as isolated entities, their relationship to the larger picture left unclear and their consequence for any understanding of the larger context not shown. Avoiding this problem means writing a history of the region that takes local structures into consideration without losing sight of the larger picture, and that shows common patterns but that also considers the great diversity that existed between different geographical entities.

Writing this kind of history is no easy task, and we need to formulate new methodologies or adapt existing ones that can be applied to this particular region. This kind of history is still in the making, and a number of scholars are experimenting with various kinds of comparative history,[15] including methodologies developed in the field of world history. Joseph Fletcher, in a study of global history, asked not only if there were parallels between one history and another, or one region and another—in China, the Middle East, Central Asia, and Europe—but also if there were a general history that one could call global history. In other words, he was interested in finding similar patterns in different regions that could have the same explanation or that were related.[16] Likewise, Peter Gran, in his attempt to challenge the writing of world history that uses Europe as the center of the world, proposed a model that took into consideration the social structures of particular regions to explore the way that they impacted political structures. His method meant that it was possible to study large geographical areas to analyze specific trends and to explore the way these trends were molded by social conditions. In this way he could affirm that, instead of one single center, one could analyze a wide region in terms of multiple centers.[17]

My own concern was multiple. I tried to integrate phenomena taking place in Cairo with other parts of the Ottoman Empire. For me, it was particularly important in relation to cultural history to recognize that one had to go beyond the strict borders of one's primary sources—in my case, Cairo—in order to understand the larger context. Moreover, if the writing of national history had a particular significance with regard to the nineteenth century when the nation state was in the process of formation, this significance was less so in relation to the seventeenth and the eighteenth centuries. Finally, because many of the trends affecting the middle class in Cairo had their parallels in other cities of the Ottoman state, it was particularly important to try to find parallel causes or common factors, even if the chronologies for their emergence was different. The studies on literacy, on books, and on reading, for instance, all suggest the existence of trends that went beyond national borders. The objective was to suggest a way of studying the relationship between the Arab world and the Ottoman world as a dynamic one, affected by geopolitics, by the economy, by the power structure, and so on, rather than as a static relationship of dominators and dominated.

Using this approach, one could argue that within the regions of the Ottoman state, different centers could have had their own dynamism. Courtly arts, for instance, flourished in Istanbul, nourished by imperial patronage, financed by a prosperous ruling class: illuminated manuscripts of high quality, a jewel industry, luxury textiles, and so on. That the vernacular language, including the dictionaries of the colloquial of the early seventeenth century, had a fuller and more dynamic development in Cairo may be because Egypt had a long association with the written word, because the colloquial in written form had antecedents that went back to the early centuries of Islam, even if its history was not continuous or linear.

Even more relevant would be to study common trends within the Ottoman state, even if they emerge with different chronologies in different parts of the empire and if they appear in somewhat different forms or manifestations. One important issue in this regard was the spread of cheap European paper, a trend that affected certain regions more than others, probably reached certain areas before it did others, and may have had different consequences depending on many variables.

Thus one needs to keep in mind the common parallels, especially insofar as cultural trends were concerned, while at the same time not forgetting that local factors may have had a significant bearing on the current scene.

Sources

I first undertook this analysis of the culture of the middle class by means of an empirical study that included the discovery and analysis of a number of works of literature and scholarship by heretofore unknown authors. This discovery led to an exploration of their context, notably of the salon culture and of the evolving system of private libraries, which were studied from probate records. It also led to an examination of the paper trade as a part of the explanation for the financial feasibility of the growth in writing and the number of books in this period.

A number of different types of sources were used for the study, from the court records and *waqf* deeds that are well known to historians to the standard biographical sources such as those of al-Jabarti and al-Muhibbi and the many secondary works dealing with the subject upon which this work builds. In addition to these were some sources that are less well known but that form an important part of the present study, notably literary sources such as the book written by Muhammad Ibn Hasan Abu Dhakir.

Court records are essential for any understanding of the material conditions of the middle class. Not only do they provide us with voluminous information about their businesses and their finances, but we also get to see the houses where they lived, their wives, and their families. Transactions for goods or for property, disputes among neighbors or guild members, marriage contracts, appointments of guardians for minors, and many more kinds of cases fill the registers of the *qadi*. A careful reading of these records can tell us where this social group stood in relation to those in power and to the religious establishment. It can also tell us how their economic conditions fared, through their probate records, for instance, over a given period. Cairo has a particularly rich collection of these records between the early decades of the sixteenth century up to the nineteenth century, with very few lacunae. There are also rich court records for Alexandria, Rashid, and Damietta, which are now starting to be explored by a number of young scholars. This fact makes it possible not only to form an accurate picture of this social group at a given moment in time but also to observe its development over a longer period. André Raymond's pioneering work in this field has been an example for many scholars interested in this field of study. It has formed the basis for much research, including the present work.

Studies that try to explore the social history of Egypt mainly by a consideration of sources in Istanbul, state sources for the most part that are obviously written with certain objectives in mind, may get an incomplete or a distorted picture. State archives are important and shed light on relationships between the capital and the provinces. They are particularly useful for those regions that do not possess significant archives before the nineteenth century (Tunis, for instance). Alone, however, they cannot serve to write about the social dynamics of Aleppo, Damascus, or Cairo, because their emphasis lies with the state, its administrators and representatives, its orders. The emphasis on political layers to the detriment of an understanding of social dynamics, the writing of history from the top down, the implicit use of the capital as a model by which to measure the provinces, all tend to marginalize societies in the provinces. At best, it is difficult to see how internal dynamics can be studied at such a distance or from the perspective of an authority issuing orders. At worst, the methodology of writing about a province from the optic of the center may produce a kind of history that takes us back to the colonial history of the last century, to history from the rulers' perspective, or to some form of "great men" history. In any of these cases, it is a history that cannot go much beyond the top layers.

Chronicles and biographies have formed the basis of many studies on learning and education. The biographies of learned men, of their teachers, their writings, their students, have provided generations of scholars with the basic material for understanding institutions of education and the people associated with them. Biographies are plentiful in Islamic history. To a certain extent, the approach that concentrated on high *'ulama'* can be explained by the number and type of available sources (especially published sources) and by the way they are used.

However, these sources have their shortcomings. First, the biographies tend to concentrate on certain set bits of information at the expense of others, notably that information which fits in with the projection of a certain public image: his shaykhs and students, his educational biography, his books. The biographies in al-Muhibbi and al-Jabarti, for example, provide us with a dimension about learned people, that dimension which in the view of contemporaries would be the most significant. They consequently sometimes give a mistaken impression of homogeneity among scholars. Modern historians have sometimes been misled into exaggerating this level of uniformity among the graduates of the educational institutions. Doubtless, the *'ulama'* were also concerned about perpetuating the dominant image of their institution and of themselves. They had many means at their disposal to do this. One of them was through the biographies of *'ulama'* such as those of al-Jabarti for Cairo and al-Muhibbi for Damascus. By looking at a major teaching institution, the *madrasa*, not from the inside nor as seen by its own *'ulama'*, which is the angle we usually get from reading the biographies of learned men, but from the outside, as seen by those who did not belong to it, we can see another angle. Second, for a study of learning or education of lesser-known people, of middle-ranking scholars, of people educated but not linked to institutions, biography is a less useful source. The chronicles of al-Jabarti, al-Damurdashi, and Ahmad Shalabi, or the biographical dictionary of al-Muhibbi, tend to concentrate on prominent or powerful people and on important events. The ordinary person was, for the most part, left out. To explore the culture of the urban middle class, other sources have to be used.

We have two important sources that give us information on book culture: the private libraries of deceased persons in court records and catalogues of Arabic manuscripts. The records of the courts of Qisma 'Askariyya and Qisma 'Arabiyya contain probate records. I have used the records from these two courts, with samples of ten-year periods, to identify all legacies that included books in order to determine how extensive book ownership was. The objectives were to identify who were the people who owned books and to find out the spread of a book culture among social groups who were not directly or primarily linked to religious or educational establishments. I used catalogues of Arabic manuscript collections in various libraries in Egypt and Europe containing manuscripts written or copied in the seventeenth and eighteenth centuries to indicate the volume of books this period produced, whether composed or copied, as well as the type of work that was prevalent. These catalogues can be used as primary source material to show a number of points.

First, the number of copies of some works can be used to indicate the popularity of a particular work. Second, the number of manuscripts copied at any one time can be indicative of demand for certain works. The fact that innumerable manuscripts of works written in different periods were copied in the eighteenth century is an indication of significant cultural dynamism during that period.

There exist a number of literary texts written between the sixteenth and the eighteenth centuries. They are significant in number and diverse in subject matter and genre. There has been a complete neglect of the literary sources of the Ottoman period, the large majority being in manuscript form and dispersed all over the major Arabic manuscript collections, some by known, many others by unknown, writers. Because the enormous body of literature has remained in manuscript form, it is mostly unavailable to students and researchers. Some of these sources are known because they were reproduced in biographical works such as those of al-Muhibbi and al-Jabarti, but the bulk are yet to be explored. Subsequent to Muhammad Sayyid al-Kilani's work—important but necessarily limited—no significant studies on the literature of the period were published; the period on the whole is generally considered a "literary desert."[18]

The value of these texts has yet to be explored by social historians. Too often, scholars have classified them as worthless literary writings. Among these is J. Heyworth-Dunne, who should be given credit for seriously considering the literary production of the eighteenth century. Nevertheless, he was dismissive of its worth, describing it as a literature for members of "higher society" who wanted to have an "acquaintance with one or two of the favorite poets and the learning by heart of some verses and proverbs which could be used in polite conversation."[19] These literary works were therefore considered as devoid of content, concentrating on literary tricks but having nothing of significance or of depth. Certainly some of the written production may well fit this description.

Modern criticism has tended to look at the negative side of this production: panegyrics with flowery, unrealistic language. One part of the literary production did correspond to this description. But it does not represent the totality of the literary production of the seventeenth and eighteenth centuries. We must turn our attention to these other texts. The manuscripts of the period are in fact much more various and diverse than is generally believed. In terms of genres, we have autobiographical texts; books of conduct; compilations of anecdotes and stories; books of jokes; and various works that escape classification within the standard genres, referred to in some catalogues as belles-lettres or *adab*. As an expression of social and cultural trends, some of this written production offers much material that a historian can use.

The literary production relevant to the study of middle-class culture, with a few exceptions, has been insufficiently explored and much of it is still unpublished. Yet it contains important indications that historical chronicles and biographical dictionaries often neglect. These literary texts, important for themselves, can also be used as a source for history. More specifically, they can shed light on many aspects of culture that are still unexplored. The use of literature to understand history is not new. In the last two to three decades, a trend has spread to consider literary texts not as ahistorical texts with universal values, but rather as being rooted in historical contexts. A series published at Reading University in England, called Early Modern Literature in History, specializes in studies that combine culture and literature and that study the text in its historical context. Scholars analyzed these texts not for literary value but for issues such as race, class, and gender, and discussed subordinate or marginal groups. The literary text was, in other words, used as a source for social analysis.[20]

Peter Gran, in his *Islamic Roots of Capitalism, Egypt, 1760–1840*, is one of the few scholars who have used literary texts as a source for intellectual and social history, but this methodology is still largely unexplored in Middle Eastern history. Moreover, in the field of literary studies, Sabry Hafez has looked at modern literature from a social perspective, considering literary works in their sociocultural context rather than in terms of the genealogy of any particular genre. In his study of modern Arabic literature, he relates the emergence of the short story in the early twentieth century to the newly educated middle class, which in terms of power, recognition, or status remained a fringe. In other words, he was suggesting that this genre became important not because of the earlier works it could have been influenced by but because of the contemporary social conditions that gave rise to it.[21]

The present study considers a number of texts in order to understand the cultural context in general and as the expression of a specific social group. By looking at some of the literary texts of the sixteenth through eighteenth centuries, one can observe a democratization of culture through the language and style used. The spread of the colloquial or semicolloquial in literary and other texts, and the ample use of popular proverbs, indicate that the culture from below was coming to the fore in the written word. Moreover, some of these texts focus on particular social groups, with ordinary people and ordinary events, and use a realistic approach based on empirical observation. These literary sources are a clear indication that the biographical dictionaries upon which we rely, important as they are as historical sources, do not give us the whole picture.

Academic religious production was the most voluminous. It is in fact so voluminous that its extent is not yet known. It has not, moreover, to the best of my knowledge, been catalogued or studied in historical perspective. But it is on the nonacademic production, including religious works not primarily for the academic community, that we will focus our attention. For the most part, this production is in manuscript form and has been explored neither in the domain of literature and belles-lettres, nor in the field of historical studies as the cultural expression of a given period. My exploration of this production is therefore a beginning.

I explore this nonacademic literary production at a number of levels. In contrast to works in the religious sciences that were primarily produced as guides to students, teachers, *qadis*, and so on, some of the literary production could be aimed at wider audiences and readers. It can therefore be seen as a mirror of sorts, to a certain extent reflecting the concerns, the viewpoints, and the tastes of people in certain socioeconomic categories. This written production, diverse in style and content, can thus be seen as an expression of these groups that few other sources can provide. As literary historians have pointed out, there is a lot of literature in which writers show their language skills, their ability to manipulate words and letters. There is also a lot of *adab* with flowery language in formal tradition. Going through the written production, we nevertheless find that we can discern trends other than these in the writings of the sixteenth through eighteenth centuries that are significant even if they do not represent a voluminous production. They indicate a trend in thought, approach, and style that needs to be understood in a historical context. It is these trends that I am concerned with.

2

Society, Economy, and Culture

AT THE BASE of a middle-class culture were material conditions that allowed it to develop, that gave its members a share of resources and consequently space within which to develop. The study of these conditions entails finding out what allowed a middle class to make profits and to maintain them in a context in which they were outside of power structures. For them to make such profits presumed an intricate balance between their access to financial gain, dependent on various local and regional factors, and the interests of the tax-gathering class that could curtail these gains. In other words, this culture was consolidated by a certain economic framework and by class dynamics that are not always clear to us, especially with regard to the sixteenth and seventeenth centuries.

Two factors were of particular significance. On the regional level was the spread of commercial capitalism and the way it was applied; at a local level were the dynamics of taxation and relations with the power structure that either allowed or restricted the middle class from making and keeping the benefits it made. A stronger central state, for instance, with a measure of control over the taxation system, could limit the excesses of local grandees. During the early period, an active production and trade of local goods, and a relatively low taxation rate, were among the major factors that allowed those who were not part of the ruling structures a degree of economic well-being and social prominence. As a result, the sphere for cultural expression was broadened.

The framework and the direction in which the culture of the urban middle class was shaped can thus be understood in the context of the urban economy of which it was part. For much of the period under study, the middle class was living well beyond subsistence; it could afford a certain measure of leisure and indulge in spending on nonessentials, which indicates a level of economic well-being. These conditions came about first because of the conditions of commercial capitalism, which brought economic benefits to this class, and second because of their relationship to the ruling class, which controlled the taxation system and which could potentially use it either in a balanced way or as a mechanism to exploit the taxpaying class.

At different dates, conditions changed with regard to taxation, to production, and to trade. A slow process had loosened the centralized power structure of the Ottoman state, with local military rulers gaining more control over resources. At first, these military groups were loosely structured and in constant conflict among themselves over the control of resources. As of roughly the middle of the eighteenth century, the loose local power structure started to give way to a more structured and eventually more centralized local military power structure in the Mamluk households, which eventually became the virtual rulers. The elites in the religious and educational establishment became closely associated with the rising Mamluk households, thus consolidating their own positions in society and expanding the opportunities for personal gain.

Economic changes of the latter part of the eighteenth century did not work in favor of the middle class. Whether through their profits from the importation of European textiles or their expansion in abusive taxation, the ruling class created new forms of control on economic activities; the result was the impoverishment of many urban dwellers. The cultural sphere of the urban middle class, which for some time had flourished and had attained a social prominence and a recognized legitimacy in various forms (see chapter 3), was reduced and its sphere of movement restricted.

One important economic factor in developing the culture of the urban middle class was the benefits it obtained from commercial capitalism, or more specifically from the way that commercial capitalism was implemented. When conditions of commercial capitalism were favorable to the production of urban wealth, when they allowed wealth to filter down to other than merchants, notably tradesmen and producers, the culture of the urban middle class was given an impetus to emerge, develop, and gain a level of legitimacy and prominence within the social body. Toward the end of the period, sometime in the mid-eighteenth century, when conditions became less favorable, the adverse effects of the economy also had a negative impact on the dynamism of this culture.

Time, Place, and the Economy

This study takes as its starting point the period when major transformations in world trading patterns brought about an intensification of trade and a broadening of trading networks during the sixteenth century. New trade routes across the Atlantic and beyond the Indian Ocean had opened immense commercial possibilities, which the Dutch, then the British, turned to their advantage.[1] A dominant paradigm in economic history has suggested that the intensification of trade and the benefits thereof, which were channeled to major trading centers in Europe—to Venice, then to Antwerp and London—led to a decline of trading in the southern Mediterranean. The picture is of a neat and symmetrical move from south to north. The reality, however, is more complex. There was a loss to local commerce as a result of European conquest and settlement in Asia. The merchants of Cairo in the fourteenth century, for example, had practically monopolized the spice trade in the Mamluk period. This monopoly was no longer the case in the sixteenth and seventeenth centuries. But from this to conclude that the whole region had declined economically is a far step. Statements like these justify neglect of academic studies on the Mediterranean subsequent to the northern "takeover." The implication is that nothing important happened from then on. Rather, one can approach the matter by trying to find out the way that the social groups that were affected by such changes reacted, given certain conditions and restraints.

Although the economic history of the eastern Mediterranean is yet to be written, work done so far shows that there is no reason to believe that the developments in that region were uniform or homogeneous, that transformations taking place in Anatolia necessarily took place in Cairo, and that when parallel changes occurred they did so at the same time everywhere. One scholarly trend, for example, suggested that the economy of parts of Anatolia was incorporated into European capitalism as early as the sixteenth century, a process that continued into the seventeenth and eighteenth centuries.[2] Anatolian raw materials such as raw silk and cotton tended to be exported to Europe, while silk weaving in Bursa and woolen production in Salonica ceased to be remunerative, or at least as remunerative as they had been earlier.[3] Studies on Egypt in the same period show another picture, one in which increased world trade brought about increased demand for certain important commodities produced locally, notably sugar and textiles, and a growing demand for goods, notably coffee, that were controlled by merchants in Cairo. No historian has yet been able to show any major signs of a peripheral economy in 1600, or even in 1700. More significantly, historians have yet to explore the reasons for this difference in chronology between Anatolia or the Balkans on one hand and Egypt on the other hand. The reasons why conditions that pushed the spread of European capitalist economies in Anatolia about 1600 only started to appear in Egypt well after 1700, close to the mid-eighteenth century, are unclear. It is clear that the periodization that we can use for one region does not necessarily apply in others, even if many common trends can be observed.

Thus, although on the one hand certain losses resulted from the major trade transformations of the sixteenth century, on the other hand factors such as the intensification of trade, the increase for demand in certain goods, and the opening of new markets brought with them new possibilities for commercial gain. For some time, European merchants were mainly interested in procuring goods they could sell in Europe. Europeans were, in other words, becoming important consumers. Consequently the concern of merchants was to provide goods for local customers whose standard of living was rising from the sixteenth century onward. Europe was at that time more a consumer than a producer. Only later, in the eighteenth century, did their higher production rates require new markets for their goods, thus coming into competition with locally produced goods.

It is likely that these profits may not have reached the levels they had had before the development of the Atlantic trade. But the significance of their volume and their socioeconomic impact cannot be denied. Rather than creating a peripheral economy, these conditions of world trade were, for a certain period, an incitement to greater production in a certain number of local commodities, which in turn meant that the producers of these commodities could play an important role in this activity.

Cairo stood on a number of important trade routes, and its merchants, as the work of André Raymond has shown, prospered enormously from these activities, accumulating large fortunes. Their prosperity was in part due to the power structure. The Ottomans rapidly abandoned the policy of state intervention in international trade and of trade monopolies practiced by the Mamluk state during most of the fifteenth century. The first beneficiaries were the merchants, who no longer had to share benefits with the state. The possibility of these profits filtering down to others was consequently widened. How much profit actually reached the middle ranks was a function of various factors that changed over time and that will be considered below.

The theory of the peddler traveling with as much merchandise as he could handle, developed by Van Leur and elaborated by Neils Steensgaard, hardly seems applicable to such large commercial centers as Cairo, Aleppo, or Istanbul, or to the merchants there, whose trading ventures were extensive.[4] Many of the conditions of commercial capitalism that historians observed with regard to other periods or regions, in the Italian port cities of Venice and Genoa, for example, were in fact prevailing in Cairo and Aleppo. Merchants in these cities made use of multiple financial mechanisms (notably loans, credit, and partnerships to fund trading ventures) that helped them to accumulate individual wealth, trading on a wide scale through complex networks, dealing in luxury and in bulk merchandise. Numerous institutions—especially the courts where deals were legalized; legal tools such as partnerships, loans, and credit; and the network of commercial warehouses where goods were stored and sold wholesale—helped merchants to organize their trading activities and provided them with the facilities that could handle large ventures.[5]

Most of these conditions predated the sixteenth century. The Karimi merchants, who during the fourteenth and fifteenth centuries controlled the Red Sea trade and whose commercial networks extended over Asia, Africa, and the Mediterranean, had complex and sophisticated business dealings; they made use of numerous institutions to help them carry out their trading activities. With certain ruptures, especially in the first half of the fifteenth century when Sultan Barsbay (1422–38) instituted state monopolies on major commodities, one can still see their continuity with merchants in the sixteenth century in terms of the breadth of the network and the institutions that helped merchants consolidate their trading ventures.

Yet to see historical development only as a straight line is misleading. The sixteenth century had created conditions that were quite different from those of the preceding period. An intensification of trading relations, linked to world conditions, was taking place. As far as Egypt was concerned, these conditions manifested themselves in two ways. The first manifestation was the trade in bulk rather than luxury items. Trade in precious stones, for instance, hardly played the same role in the sixteenth and seventeenth centuries that it had in the fourteenth and fifteenth centuries. Moreover, pepper, considered a luxury commodity in the fourteenth century, had become a bulk item by the sixteenth century. Finally, the goods produced in Egypt and exported to the Mediterranean, the Red Sea, and Africa were not luxury items but mainly textiles of varying quality and sugar.

The second manifestation was in the intensification of trade during this period. This could be part of the trend in the development of cities in many parts of the Mediterranean, north and south. It could also be part of a greater level of wealth, which we know to have been the case in many parts of Europe. One of the major commodities in demand during this period was sugar, of which Egypt was a major producer. In Europe, sugar had been transformed from a luxury item, very expensive and difficult to get before the sixteenth century, to an item found on everyone's table.[6] It had become a bulk item, much in demand from then on, a situation that was particularly favorable for Egyptian trade for over a century.

The number of persons involved in production and trade was considerable. The population of Cairo in the seventeenth and eighteenth centuries was estimated by André Raymond, on the basis of data provided by the Turkish traveler Evliya Chelebi around 1660 and by the *Description de l'Egypte* in 1798, to be about one-quarter to one-third of a million inhabitants. André Raymond found about 38 percent of the working population involved in artisanal activities, 33 percent in commercial activities, 20 percent in services, and 6 percent in entertainment. Of the people involved in artisanal activities, the most important, in terms of both number and their material level, were those in textile production, because textiles constituted about a fifth of all exports.[7] An important textile production took place in the provincial and rural areas of Egypt, but the history of this production has yet to be fully explored, and until that is done, little can be said about it.

The study of probate records suggests that for a good part of the seventeenth and eighteenth centuries, merchants in Cairo were keeping much of the profits of this trade. Only toward the end of the eighteenth century did the ruling class stand in the way of their accumulation of profits, as did the appearance on the local scene of European merchants supported by the military rulers. André Raymond's book *Artisans et commerçants au Caire au XVIIIe siècle* explored the fortunes of coffee and spice merchants from the end of the seventeenth to the end of the eighteenth centuries. Accumulation of great fortunes was accompanied by a luxurious lifestyle, much like that of the members of the ruling class with whom they were associated in their commercial activities. A coffee merchant such as Qasim al-Shara'ibi left a fortune of over twelve million paras in 1148/1735; another, Muhammad al-'Arayshi, left close to fourteen million paras in 1203/1788—immense fortunes for their times.[8]

Closer to the concerns of the present study is the issue of whether these commercial activities that allowed merchants to accumulate large fortunes were in any way linked to the economy as a whole, or whether they benefited only a restricted class of people. On a broader level, the question investigates the link between commercial activities and economy as a whole. Historians are in fact divided as to whether long-distance trade, which greatly enriched those who undertook it, had any significant impact on strata other than those with a direct involvement in it. In practice, whether or not international commerce impacted the economy depended on various factors. Generalizations are difficult to make, and what was true of one period or locality did not necessarily apply to all. In other words, commercial capitalism could have different forms that were shaped by historical factors and that had diverse consequences and varying degrees of impact. K. N. Chaudhuri's work on the Indian Ocean trade, for instance, indicates that merchant capitalists were kept, either by individual preference or by social, legal, or political traditions, separate from other groups in society.[9] Likewise, Halil Inalcik explored the close relationship between the merchant class and the state, and between their commercial activity and political structure, as well as what he saw as "popular hostility" to the merchant class. He considered the merchant class to be a social group isolated from the broad social context.[10] Others argue that international trade had little impact beyond enriching merchants and providing rulers with the goods they needed, because much of the commerce was concentrated on luxury goods and consequently affected only a few.

Subhi Labib, presenting another point of view, considered trade to have been quite closely related to the economy. For instance he does not hesitate to use the term *capitalism* in relation to the activities of medieval merchants. He notes that although long-distance trade did not change the social structure of society, it had a considerable effect on capital accumulation and on production. Even state factories, such as those of Fatimid Egypt that produced luxury textiles for the private needs of rulers, also had excess production for trade.[11]

A major issue that concerns the present chapter has to do with the link between commercial capitalism and a group other than the merchants who had reached the top of the hierarchy, in other words, a link to people belonging to the urban middle class of artisans, tradesmen, middle-ranking merchants, or others. This subject has attracted the attention of scholars, both those studying Europe and those studying the Middle East, to a much lesser degree than the relationship between merchants and the ruling class or that between merchants and the state bureaucracy.[12] Consequently, the features of commercial capitalism that have to do with relations among merchants, elites, and states are more or less explored; merchant-artisan relations have been studied in some detail only in relation to the putting-out system in early modern Europe (particularly prevalent with textile production) whereby a merchant ordered certain goods he needed for his trade and provided the raw material, usually to a rural artisan who earned less than an urban one, thereby gaining a level of control over production. We know much less about textile workers who worked independently of merchants, or of sectors other than textiles.

Conditions Around the Mediterranean

One way of dealing with the link between commercial capitalism and the middle strata is by a comparative approach with Mediterranean cities where commercial capitalism flourished. This regional framework has some significance here for more than one reason. Economic trends do not follow political borders; thus, to understand the consequences of commercial capitalism in Cairo, a comparative approach with other trading cities sharing similar conditions can shed light on the subject, especially in view of the absence of scholarly works to serve as guidelines. The importance of Mediterranean trade and the intensity of commercial exchanges make such comparisons between north and south even more relevant.

From what we can glean in studies on Mediterranean commercial centers between the sixteenth and eighteenth centuries, it appears that an urban middle class took an active part in certain capitalist activities such as investment, financial operations, and commercial operations, on a scale more modest than that of the elite merchant but nevertheless significant when considered globally. We can, moreover, surmise that the trend was Mediterranean rather than specifically European or Ottoman, from the fact that it can be detected in Italian cities like Venice as well as in cities like Istanbul, Aleppo, or Cairo in the Ottoman state. The regional nature of this trend suggests an important point: that certain regions north and south of the Mediterranean, regardless of political borders, were undergoing similar or parallel economic trends, and that potentially these could be accompanied by similar cultural trends. It also suggests that the division used by some scholars of the Mediterranean into a Christian space and an Islamic space can be misleading insofar as it does not give economic realities the weight that they deserve.

The impact of commercial capitalism on the medium-scale tradesman and producer, and the potential benefits that they could reap from their links to commerce and could maintain for themselves, depended on different factors. Thus the wealth that commerce engendered to elite merchants could under certain conditions and in varying degrees filter down to the strata below, to tradesmen, producers, middle-ranking merchants, or others. It is therefore important to identify what some of these conditions were. On the empirical level, the application of these theoretical criteria depends on the existence of in-depth studies, which in many cases have not yet been undertaken. We know next to nothing about the textile industry in Egypt during this period except that it was very important and that Egyptian textiles were much in demand as an export item. We are in the dark about the mode of production, the urban-rural relationship, and the impact of guilds on this product.

One important factor that potentially allowed the urban middle class to be part of commercial capitalism was the presence of a significant production center. Chaudhuri has shown that certain commercial centers along the Indian Ocean, convenient stopping points for maritime traffic, were in fact isolated from any other economic activity and that their importance was based entirely on their position on the trade routes.[13] They had no hinterland and they had no production. Such centers would obviously fall into the category of cities where trade only affected merchants and their auxiliaries. On the other side of the spectrum, in cities like Cairo, Aleppo, Istanbul, Venice, and Marseilles, where significant production took place and where this production either relied on imported raw material or was in excess of local consumption and was exported (as was the case with textiles produced in Cairo), the links between international trade and local production could be very significant. As a consequence, members of the urban middle class—producers of goods, tradesmen, shopowners—could be linked to the activities of long-distance trade.

Another important factor that regulated the participation of the middle class was the degree of involvement of merchants in craft production of the goods they needed for their trade. This involvement could take a number of forms, from hiring of labor with wages, advancing the craftsman money, or using the putting-out system by providing a weaver who used his own loom with raw material. The preference of merchants to disregard urban production in favor of rural production, which was usually much cheaper, was obviously harmful to tradesmen and artisans. The Bursa silk industry of the seventeenth century used a putting-out system whereby a merchant used the textile weaver as a wage earner, providing him with raw material and taking from him the finished product, which the merchant then sold—a system similar to that in contemporary Europe. Suraiya Faroqhi indicates that a strong merchant presence in textile production can be observed in Bursa, Ankara, and Aydin.[14] Fernand Braudel likewise found that many urban industries moved to small towns and villages around the Mediterranean in the seventeenth century.[15] This trend could severely limit the benefits that the producer received, potentially entailing impoverishment of the artisan in some degree or other. The empirical study of these trends and of their historical development, especially with regard to the major sectors of production such as textiles, is still to be undertaken in relation to Egypt and Syria. Some work on the sugar industry in early seventeenth-century Egypt suggests a system of merchant financing of a rural industry. We know neither the development of this trend in the later period nor its extension to other products.

Cairo, like many of the cities on the Mediterranean, was involved in major trading activities, both as a center for the transit of goods and as a center for production. The resumption of Red Sea activity in spices, thought to have been interrupted by the presence of the Portuguese in India, was in fact reactivated as early as the mid-sixteenth century, when pepper again started flowing in through this waterway; moreover, toward the end of the century, coffee was emerging as a commodity that, within a few decades, was to multiply in importance and volume. Thus, as a center for the international transit trade, Cairo remained a central part of the network.

Another factor linking the urban middle class to commercial capitalism was regional or international demand for locally produced commodities. Egypt was exporting considerable amounts of raw material such as rice and grain, but it also exported a significant volume of its locally produced products, notably textiles and sugar. There has been some debate about production activity during this period. André Raymond wrote in *Artisans* that artisanal activity was stagnant, its tools unchanged for centuries, a view that he later reconsidered somewhat.[16] Yet, for the rate of production to keep up with the new level of demand in world markets, producers needed to make certain adjustments to increase its volume. Textile exports to France, for instance, reached great heights in the mid-eighteenth century; they were shipped to Marseilles and from there reshipped to Spain and Holland.[17] On the whole, the textile industry was one of the most important, providing a major export item to Mediterranean and Red Sea ports and to Black Africa. Because, as indicated, this industry has not been studied in Egypt, either in its rural or its urban settings, any discussion of textile production before the nineteenth century remains fragmentary.

Local Elites versus the Middle Class During the Early Period

In the decades that followed the conquest of Egypt in 1517, the authority of the Ottoman ruler was generally recognized. The Ottoman conquest brought a reshuffling of the power structure that severely curtailed the power of local groups, notably the emirs who had served the Mamluk state. One of the important objectives of curtailment was for the Ottoman state to maintain, through its representatives, control over the taxation system. The early period is not well studied in this regard, but it would appear that taxation levels were kept within reasonable limits. These limits could potentially work in favor of an urban middle class. The social dynamics of the late sixteenth and the seventeenth centuries, unlike those of the eighteenth century, have not been studied. We can only look at manifestations. A major manifestation is in the probate records of this class.

Level of material comfort was to a significant degree dependent upon the level of taxation imposed by the ruling class. In other words, the benefits from production and trade could only be maintained if taxation did not swallow them all up. Taxation was a significant mechanism whereby the ruling class could accumulate money from rural or urban populations. The abusive taxation that potentially befell the ordinary urban dweller was a very common way to curtail his earnings. Whereas during the seventeenth century the level of taxation was not excessive, it became so in the eighteenth century. Exploitative taxation was a consequence of the empowerment of local elites who abused the *iltizam* system, using it to their private benefit at a time when the authorities in Istanbul were losing their power to regulate it. Taxation was therefore a major issue in shaping the fortunes of the middle class. When taxation rates were low it could flourish; when they were high or exploitative, it could become impoverished. The relationship to the ruling class, who was actively involved in both commercial activity and tax collection, was consequently a vital factor in shaping the material conditions of the middle class.

Although the members of the middle class stood outside the power structure, under certain conditions they could maintain some links of common interest with the ruling class. The level of shared interests, essentially based on the commercial and tax concerns of the ruling class, was more solid at times, less so at others. The middle class either produced goods and services that directly served the ruling class as consumers, or they produced commodities such as textiles, sugar, or leather for international trade in which the ruling class was involved.[18] Because the significant portion of the tax revenues of the ruling class was made up of urban taxation, moreover, it was important for them to keep the flow of taxes steady by maintaining a level of economic urban stability. Thus, when the urban middle class was an important part of the economic network, and when the ruling class deemed it important to maintain the urban middle class because it provided necessary goods and services, this class prospered. When the emphasis of the ruling-class economy shifted more toward rural concerns at the expense of its urban concerns, it was deemed less important to maintain or protect the concerns of the urban middle class.

During the early period members of the middle class could dispose of some resources, as can be seen by their involvement in financial operations and in financing commercial ventures large or small, an activity that has not yet been fully explored by historians. The existence of loans, credit, and partnerships as legal tools is well established. Their use in trade can also be seen from numerous court record cases. This practice was spread out over a wide region along the Mediterranean. Fernand Braudel, for instance, has shown that in sixteenth-century Venice, large commercial ventures of great merchants were often made up of numerous sums put up by small investors. He writes that in the trading voyages, "the names of lenders, when we have them, reveal a wide range of 'capitalists' or so-called capitalists, some of whom were men of very modest substance." He suggests that the entire Venetian population can be seen as having advanced money to merchant ventures, thus creating a sort of commercial society that embraced the whole town. Braudel considered that this constantly available and spontaneously offered supply of credit made it possible for merchants to operate alone as individuals, without the long-term trading companies that provided the structure and funding that characterized the more advanced commercial activity of Florence. In the case of Venice, funding was large-scale but short-term.[19] The involvement of an urban class in finance, credit, and loans is likewise apparent in other Arab cities in the Ottoman state, suggesting a spread of commercial capitalism over towns and cities of a large region. Sevket Pamuk's study of the evolution of the monetary system in the Ottoman Empire shows that there was an expansion in the demand and use of money among both rural and urban populations during the sixteenth century as a result of worldwide economic and monetary transformations.[20] Studies on individual cities in the empire confirm the trend. Bruce Masters has demonstrated this trend in relation to Aleppo (1600–1750). His study of this city showed that all Aleppines with any excess capital were engaged at one time or another directly in trade or in credit relationships involving commerce, regardless of class, gender, or ethnic origin. The findings of Colette Establet and Jean-Paul Pascual are similar in relation to Damascus.[21] Likewise, in his study of seventeenth-century Kayseri, Roland Jennings estimated that about a third of the population of the town was involved in some form of loan or credit, usually of modest amounts of money.[22]

Cairo followed a similar pattern during the seventeenth century. The court records of this period show innumerable merchants, artisans, tradesmen, and ordinary people in a multitude of professions engaged in small investments, loans, and credit operations. Finance, in other words, was not a specialization carried out only by bankers or financiers, but an activity diffused over a large number of people whose primary economic activity was in diverse other domains. Many of the loans are recorded as transactions, and many more emerge in court records when disputes arise between the partners, such as when Hajj Muhammad, *kayyal* (weigher of goods) in al-Rumaila district, brought an accusation against Hajj 'Umar, *mugharbil* (sifter of flour); he had sold him six *qintars* of Maghribi oil for sixty qirsh on credit and asked to get the payment now. Loans appear in the form of written agreements, as the one between Shihabi Ahmad and Ahmad Khattab al Ruwi'i, *qahwaji* (coffeeshop owner), which stated that the small sum of 135 *nisfs* was to be repaid to the first party.[23] These cases in court records show that the investments were often modest or very modest, perhaps representing all the savings that a small tradesman or artisan owned or could risk. The bottom line as far as the middle class was concerned was the existence of a certain amount of extra cash beyond what was needed for subsistence. The cases also show that these craftsmen and tradesmen were not necessarily investing their money in an activity related to their own profession. Finally, they show that this financial activity cut across professional lines, meaning that it went beyond those whose profession was moneylending or those who were directly involved in large commercial ventures. This factor is significant for our understanding of some of the ways that, in a society strongly embedded in guild and professional structures, a common social, economic, and then political dimension cut across these professional lines.

We have records of much larger loans that passed between the hands of important personages and those of merchants trading in international commodities, running into the tens of thousands of *nisfs* and sometimes more. Occasionally too, women were involved in some of these loans, sometimes to a relative, such as in merchant families where a sister with money of her own lent her brother sums with which he would be trading, probably with the expectation of some sharing in the returns.

For members of the middle class to participate in such operations, moreover, we have to assume that their economic activity, in production or services, gave them enough extra revenue that they could spare some funds to dispose of in the form of loan or credit. Potentially, therefore, the urban middle class could play an important role in these trading operations. Firstly these people were a middle stage in networks for the distribution of goods, between the merchant who imported merchandise and the consumer, on a small scale but with the potential to be essential for the network that could extend outside the urban center to the periphery or to rural areas. These people could reach areas that were perhaps out of the reach of the important merchant, who might consequently rely on them for this purpose. Therefore, even though their activity might be on a small individual scale, it was significant to the local economy. Secondly, the small or modest investor or moneylender had a potentially important economic role in the redistribution or accumulation of cash.

Trade and industry were major activities in the economic life of Cairo, and consequently the bulk of the population of the city was made up of artisans and tradesmen with a variety of skills and specializations, very varied in their fortunes and in their relation to commercial capitalism. Many of these tradesmen and artisans were among the members of the middle class. André Raymond included in his "middle-class" bracket people whose inheritances fell between 5,000 and 50,000 *nisfs*.[24] The range is wide, but it meant that many of them had comfortable living conditions. A study of middle-class housing, for instance, showed that many lived in individual houses they owned in full or in part, with a variable number of facilities in terms of the number of rooms, the toilets, occasionally storerooms, and courtyards. We know for instance that a miller, a sugar producer, or a shop owner could be living in a stone or brick house, which for many was made up of a ground and upper floor. They could thus dispose both of living units and of a certain number of services. Almost all of them had toilets but not bathrooms. Some had a storeroom where cereals could be stored. We know from the few houses that have survived, even though their size is not comparable to the better known palaces of the ruling class, that there was nevertheless a comfortable space and a certain amount of decoration such as a stone-carved entranceway or a window with colored glass.[25] They owned or rented their shops and workshops where they exercised their professions and the storerooms for their merchandise; they owned the equipment with which they produced their goods. At their deaths they left inheritances that included money, goods, merchandise, and sometimes urban property.

Contours of the Middle Class

These conditions cut across guild lines and professional lines, and consequently included a variety of different professions and skills. Many of the people within this bracket were merchants, but formed a category different from that of the elite merchants who accumulated large fortunes—running sometimes into the millions—who were involved in the international coffee or spice trade and who can be considered as part of the ruling class. The middle-ranking merchants were closer to those that Terence Walz studied, involved in the less lucrative Africa trade, importing black slaves and gold from Bilad al-Sudan.[26] The middle class included people involved in commercial services, weighers of goods, for example, who often figured among the wealthiest of the middle class, their wealth directly linked to the existing level of commerce. The same is true for middlemen (*simsar, dallal*) who brought together buyers and sellers, taking a commission on sales.

The middle class included the craftsmen whose goods were in demand in international markets, such as textile producers and sugar producers. If times were good, their earnings were significantly higher than those of other artisans and craftsmen. Those in textile production stood out by their number and by their level of wealth. Textile workers in the period 1624–36 left an average inheritance of 58,615 *nisfs*, while shaykhs of guilds for the same period left an average inheritance of 68,561 *nisfs*. By the end of the century, 1679–1700, the average inheritance for all artisans was 48,845 *nisfs*, still a considerable figure. A century later, between 1776 and 1798, it had decreased to 29,644 *nisfs*, indicating a dramatic impoverishment among these people.[27]

The Core and Periphery of the Middle Class

The terms *core* and *periphery* of the middle class are used with somewhat different meanings here than those which are generally applied to the system whereby the expansion of European capitalism created core areas—strong, dynamic areas that controlled peripheral economies by creating the structural changes necessary for such a control to be effective. *Core* is applied here to that sector of the middle class that was involved directly in trade and commerce, their involvement depending on a certain social and power structure, while *periphery* is used to refer to that sector of the middle class that was linked to the core either indirectly or directly on an occasional basis.

The people involved in economic activities of trade, industry, and services, the producers of goods, and the tradesmen dealing in them formed the core of the middle class, the core being the decisive element in the group. If things went well in the core, the same was likely to happen in the margin; if things went bad, if a crisis occurred, the margin was also affected. Who then was on the margin of the middle class, in the sense that their fortunes were tied to the middle class, benefiting from good times and suffering from bad times? Many people in the military and religious professions were directly involved insofar as they practiced an economic activity either on the side or as their primary activity.

The word *'ulama'* is sometimes used to refer to scholars who have reached a high level of knowledge and social prominence or who occupy positions of importance in the educational or judiciary establishment. It is sometimes also used to refer to the totality of persons employed in such establishments regardless of their position in the hierarchy, or to persons who have been educated in establishment institutions. In this case, a distinction is usually made between the "high" *'ulama'* and the "other" (middle- and low-ranking) *'ulama'*, the people sometimes referred to as *sighar al-'ulama'*. It is with the latter that we concern ourselves here. The middle- or low-ranking *'ulama'* were those people who occupied positions as teachers in colleges, as court employees, as *waqf* employees, as mosque employees, or in a series of nonreligious jobs that required a certain amount of education, like librarians or bookshop owners or accountants.

André Raymond has shown that many of these *'ulama'* were involved in economic activities, a fact that we know was true among the *'ulama'* of the fifteenth century, working part-time as merchants or craftsmen.[28] In addition to their primary jobs, the *'ulama'* of eighteenth-century Cairo undertook a multitude of second jobs to increase their salaries, for example as copyists, like Husayn al-Mahalli (d. 1171/1756–57), a scholar of Shafi'i jurisprudence, who had a shop near the Azhar where he sold books; or Ahmad al-Sanablawi, a professor of jurisprudence (d. 1180/1766), who had a shop in Suq al-Kutubiyyin (the book market). Many others held secondary professions that were completely unrelated to their primary activity, like a certain Shaykh Mustafa al-Falaki (d. 1203/1788), an expert in astronomy and in composing calendars who also worked as a tailor. He cut and sewed clothes surrounded on one side by other tailors working on garments and on the other side by students discussing learned matters with him.[29] Al-Muhibbi shows that the same thing was taking place in Damascus. He tells us about Muhammad al-Hariri, a scholar and a poet who earned his money as a silk weaver; many of his students came to his shop for their lesson.[30]

These examples could indicate a movement toward certain crafts or services that were more lucrative than others and could absorb a larger number of persons at a certain moment in time. A growing book trade in the eighteenth century, for instance (see chapter 4), was sure to attract a larger number of persons involved in some aspect of this trade, as booksellers, as copyists, and so on. Like many other people, the middle-ranking *'ulama'* were involved in credit and loan operations. They also participated or invested in commercial activities. Thus, although often salaried in one *waqf* or another, a significant dimension of their economic life was part of the larger economy.

These people were therefore on the one hand linked to the religious hierarchy, where they stood on the middle or lower scales, and on the other hand to whatever profession or craft they were exercising and which linked them to others involved in the same activity. As part of the religious or educational hierarchy, they had a dependence on those at the upper end of the hierarchy. Potentially they could be candidates for *waqf* positions and salaries; such positions were provided by the people who founded a *waqf* or by the supervisors of such *waqfs*. This situation made the ordinary or middle-ranking *'alim* dependent on either the property-owning class who founded *waqfs* or the higher-ranking *'ulama'* who could have some form of say in them. As part of a craft or trade, they had to have links with others in the same trade in order to survive.

A similar trend is evident among soldiers. A number of reasons were behind the trading activities of soldiers, among which was the net decrease of salaries occurring as a result of the money devaluation at the beginning of the seventeenth century. This devaluation led troops to look for other sources of income. It was also part of the phenomenon whereby various members of the urban population were taking part in production and trade in ways often unrelated to their own profession. André Raymond's work indicates that the military had shops; Hasan Mutafariqqa, for instance, was a silk merchant; another officer was a saddler; Muhammad 'Ali al-Jawli, member of the troops of Suez Citadel, had a store (*hasil*) in Wikalat Mustafa al-'Attar in Cairo. Soldiers in fact could be found among many professions, as moneychangers, merchants, goldsmiths, coffeehouse owners, and tobacco sellers.[31] Likewise, these activities involved levels of wealth from modest (with inheritance worth less than 5,000 *nisfs*) to inheritance close to half a million *nisfs*. As for the *'ulama'*, soldiers' interests were partly tied to the military from which they received their salaries and got their promotions and partly tied to economic life in the city.

This possibility of moving into and out of a particular craft raises questions about our understanding of the way that guilds functioned, more specifically about the control of guilds over their artisans and about the ability of a guild to monopolize a particular economic activity. In the past, the dominant view in scholarship was that the guilds restricted their membership, and that they could restrict nonguild members from practicing a particular activity. If such restrictions were actually put into practice, the result would be that certain economic activities were divorced from market forces. The examples just mentioned suggest a more flexible situation in which some movement between different crafts and professions was possible. The examples of troops and of *'ulama'* moving in and out of certain crafts, and of the participation of a broad urban population in retail sales, credits, and loans suggest a picture of guilds that at some level took into account market forces.

A second feature created close links between soldiers, religious scholars, and the middle class. Interactions of various kinds took place between the middle class proper and the soldiers and middle-ranking religious professions. Those sharing a similar socioeconomic level had ties and associations in terms of marriage alliances and family ties, in terms of business and financial deals, and in terms of living quarters. Marriage in Cairo, for instance, did not usually take place among cousins, as seems to have been the case in some other regions, in certain parts of Syria, for instance; marriage between members of a single profession occurred but was far from being the only or the most dominant type of alliance. Much more common was marriage among people of similar socioeconomic level. Shaykhs, for instance, often intermarried with families of craftsmen. It was common for craftsmen and tradesmen to marry off their daughters to shaykhs, or for professors in the Azhar to marry into trading and commercial families.[32] Marriage alliances could thus create common material interests between families in different professional groups. Likewise the innumerable cases of large or small loans, credit, or other financial dealings can be said to have followed the same rough pattern, taking place sometimes within a family or profession and sometimes within a class. One should add that it was highly uncommon for the well-off to marry into poor classes. One does not find, among the hundreds of marriage contracts in the court records of the period, alliances between the urban poor (for instance, the unskilled workers, carriers of goods, owners of donkeys, and water sellers) and members of the middle class.

Conditions of the Later Period

This study takes as its terminal point that time in history when dramatic changes occurred in trading patterns. In the early decades of the eighteenth century, the Egyptian economy was starting to face a threat to the demand for its local products. Sugar exports, so important until then, began to suffer as a result of competition from sugar-growing areas in the Americas. Textiles, also a major product, began to suffer competition from imported European textiles in the local market. The middle class was adversely affected as the trading patterns were undergoing transformation. It became more profitable to import the European goods that competed with local products.

At the end of the seventeenth century emerged the Mamluk households that eventually came to control the economic resources of Egypt by laying their hands on the taxation system, a process that allowed them to divert the revenues theoretically due to the Ottoman state to their own pockets. These local military elites came to dominate more and more state resources through their control of the *iltizam* (tax-farming) system and the large benefits it offered. The loosening of control of the central Ottoman state on the system of taxation adversely affected the fortunes of the middle class.

The loose power structure gave way to a more structured and hierarchical structure. The consolidation of the Mamluk households and the resulting polarization led to a polarization within the *'ulama'* community, the top ones getting more and more benefits through their connections with Mamluks. A more centralized form of power emerged as the Mamluk households consolidated their hold on the economic resources. In the early eighteenth century one household comes to dominate the scene: the Qazdughli household, to which were attached most of the important political figures of the eighteenth century. Eventually, by the time of 'Ali Bey al-Kabir (d. 1773), who physically eliminated other households and gained control over the other members of his own household, this process of centralization came to a peak. Wealth accumulated from the tax revenues that should have been sent to Istanbul but were kept by these Mamluks, and from the imposition of legal and illegal taxation on the rural and urban population. The absence of regular or systematic checks from the central administration of Istanbul facilitated these activities.

For most of the seventeenth century, the wealth of the military class, which was slowly coming to dominate the system of taxation, had remained limited, and, with few exceptions, the grand lifestyles of the later emirs had not yet fully emerged. In the eighteenth century, this situation was changing. The rise of these households was accompanied by conspicuous consumption, as many Mamluks acquired large palaces, numerous slaves, and concubines. Many more undertook the construction of public buildings such as mosques and schools, for example 'Uthman Katkhuda's (d. 1736) development of the southern part of Birket al-Azbakiyya. Only as the eighteenth century progressed did the Mamluks start to live in great luxury and to construct monumental buildings on an extensive scale, such as those of 'Abdul-Rahman Katkhuda (d. 1776), whose construction program was unmatched through all the period of Ottoman domination. The wealth they accumulated through taxation of the population allowed them to spend lavishly on their lifestyles and to indulge in extensive purchase of slaves and Mamluks in order to consolidate their households. The consequence was the impoverishment of those that their taxes stifled.

The late Ottoman period likewise witnessed a significant enrichment and empowerment of elite *'ulama'*, a trend closely linked to the rise of Mamluks and beys. Some of the prominent *'ulama'* were closely linked to the power structure, a relationship that helped them to accumulate large fortunes. High *'ulama'* of the eighteenth century consequently emerged as wealthy men. Afaf Marsot has shown the level of wealth of the elite *'ulama'*, the way they obtained their money, the diversity of their investments—in short, their conduct as businessmen. They owned urban and rural property, slaves, large palaces. They became involved with major *iltizams* (tax farms). In other words, the elements of their wealth were not much different from those of the ruling Mamluks with whom they enjoyed close links. Shaykh 'Abdalla al-Sharqawi, Shaykh al-Azhar from 1208/1793 to 1234/1818, for instance, started life in dire conditions, then became one of the wealthy men of his time. Shaykh Muhammad al-Mahdi (d. 1814), who befriended many of the important Mamluks, had *iltizams* in the provinces of Bihira, Munufiyya, Jiza, Gharbiyya, and Fayyum. He, like Shaykh al-Sharqawi, received a salary of some quarter of a million *nisfs* a year from the *waqf*s of the Holy Cities; he possessed houses in Cairo, Bulaq, and Azbakiyya.[33]

In practical terms this empowerment of the elite *'ulama'* meant that more and more of the *waqf* benefits, of the lucrative positions, were being channeled toward a few people at the top. The lower ranks of the religious structures, like their lay counterparts, were the ones who felt the consequences. These changes were accompanied by a level of polarization, not only in society in general but also within the learned or educated community, privileges and benefits being more concentrated at the top. Among those to suffer the immediate effects of this trend would be the lower- and middle-ranking *'ulama'* to whom some of these benefits would normally have gone. More and more they would feel that they were being deprived of what was potentially theirs. It was becoming more obvious to this generation that they were being marginalized from potential benefits, salaries, and positions that were more and more being concentrated in the hands of fewer people.

The ruling classes in Cairo were involved in the urban economy at several levels. From early on, for example, we know that the governors of Egypt were directly involved in major trading activities. Yet controls from Istanbul and the fact that their appointments rarely exceeded two or three years limited their ability to form power bases. Subsequently, as the seventeenth century progressed, the lucrative customs tax farms were held by members of the local ruling elites, who also came to control the taxation on urban activities, production, services, and transport of merchandise; much of the taxation thereof filled the pockets of the members of the militias and the Mamluk beys. André Raymond has shown that during much of the seventeenth and eighteenth centuries, this class depended as much on its urban revenues as it did on its rural revenues. The middle class, which was the object of much of this taxation on production, service, and transport activities, was therefore potentially at risk of overtaxation. Moreover, as a result of the tremendous importance of the customs as a source of revenue, it was customs that those in power counted upon to accumulate wealth. Stanford Shaw has suggested that the various customs houses in Egypt in the seventeenth century produced something like four times the revenue of the taxation from urban (trading and production) activities.[34]

Finally, because the ruling class had interests and concerns in international trade, it attempted to keep satisfied urban classes who produced the merchandise for export and who were also consumers of imported goods. André Raymond's work has shown the importance of urban wealth in the revenues of the ruling class. Until the late eighteenth century, he saw what he called a "partnership" between these classes and the military rulers. The importance of the urban sector's revenues is estimated to be as high as the rural *iltizam*, those controlling it therefore having a great political weight.[35]

As a result, there were close links between the military rulers and their subjects; horizontal links of common interests sometimes came to smooth the edges of the more dominant vertical ones that brought about a level of exploitation. For this reason, and because exploitation of urban activities was so important, the *iltizam* holders, the Janissaries, had to negotiate a kind of partnership with the urban population. But by 1760–70, conditions changed drastically. The power of the Mamluk beys became much more dependent on the exploitation of rural wealth through *iltizam*, and the partnership between the ruling class and the urban population was dissolved. Moreover, 'Ali Bey al-Kabir's interest in trade with Europe and his protection of European merchants were indications that the ruling class was shifting its interests to the import trade, presumably making more money from these imports than it did from exporting local products. This is another aspect of a rift in the "partnership" between the ruling class and the productive class. Thus the extra revenues that ordinary people had used in modest investments were no longer available on the same scale. One consequence of the investment of Mamluks and wealthy merchants in land was that the city of Cairo became less important to them economically and was left to deteriorate.[36] By the last years of the eighteenth century, the former urban wealth of Cairo had thus given way to the deterioration of its public buildings. The only quarters that maintained their previous beauty were those, like Azbakiyya, where the ruling class had built their palaces. André Raymond found a dramatic decrease in the price of shops that indicated a flow away from urban investment and a lack of funding for commercial activity.[37]

Reactions from the Population

André Raymond has studied some of the ways that the urban population reacted to the adverse conditions they faced in these times of crisis. The "popular" classes—variously called by establishment writers like al-Jabarti *zu'ar* (good-for-nothing), *ghawgha'* (populace), *awbash* (low people)—assembled in times of crisis and filled the streets, often marching to the Citadel, where the governor resided, to express their demands. Tradesmen, merchants, artisans, and craftsmen, many of whom played a more passive role in these events, joined in, generally closing their shops to express their dissatisfaction. During the events of 1146/1733, silk weavers (*haririyyin*) and tassel-makers (*'aqqadin*), who were among the more prosperous traders, joined the marchers who occupied the Azhar and then marched to the Citadel.[38] In other words, members of the middle class, not only the urban poor, undertook the demonstrations against authority.

The present study is not so much concerned with these events as it is with analyzing through their writings the way that some of the educated people reacted to them.

The Culture of the Urban Middle Class

During the period between the major transformations in world trade, in which a decentralized power structure was eventually replaced by a centralized one, the urban middle class experienced a level of material comfort; their culture was consolidated and received a certain level of recognition. The combination of factors formed a basis for an urban middle-class culture to flourish materially. During those times when this group formed an essential part of urban wealth, its social prominence came to the fore and the legitimacy of its culture was more broadly recognized.

The importance of urban wealth to the ruling class had created common interests with the urban population, bringing about a more open interpenetration of interests and consequently a greater flexibility of the culture of the rulers and the culture of urban dwellers. The consequences were complex. The cultural sphere of the middle class expanded. Its members could participate more actively in cultural production; they could spend more money on nonessentials like books, thus opening up new avenues of learning and education. Their culture consequently came more to the foreground, with a marked impact on the written word in subject matter, in style, and in language. At times when economic conditions allowed them to have a social weight, their culture gained legitimacy among various social groups, including the *'ulama'*. One can in fact discern among them a few people who were educated without being scholars or academicians, people who were erudite, who read, who wrote, but whose vocation was not in the field of scholarship but in broad social concerns. Moreover, one can detect the self-assertiveness of a distinct culture emerging.

The period during which shared interests created a link between the ruling classes and the urban middle class had, in fact, allowed for a flexibility of the borders between establishment culture and the culture of the middle class, and allowed for the latter to be more visible and more prominent in the total cultural scene, bringing about a democratization of certain aspects of learned culture, the manifestations of which will be considered in some detail in later chapters.

As conditions changed and the interests of the ruling class and the middle class diverged, the culture of the middle class reflected this dissociation with the ruling class and the establishment. The cultural sphere that the urban middle class had enjoyed for many decades was subsequently sharply reduced under the changing conditions of the later period and the economic hardships that hit the urban population at large. The shifting of the social structures and the greater social polarization of the last decades of the eighteenth century brought about the impoverishment of the middle class. Their numbers, after having increased for more than a century, may be presumed to have fallen as more and more people moved below the poverty line.

In this period a political dimension emerged in the writings of certain members of this class. Experiences of dissociation and of difference were expressed in written texts. Thus, at a time that the legitimacy and prominence that they had gained were fading away, and their cultural sphere was defined by more rigid boundaries, their cultural expression was also gaining a new dimension.

3

Culture and Education of the Middle Class

TO UNDERSTAND the culture of the middle class a number of economic, social, and historical factors that potentially had a bearing on it need to be explored. Middle-class culture cannot be considered as a residue or as a diluted form of scholarly culture. Nor do terms like "religious" culture and "traditional" culture give it the credit it deserves. These views presume that because all education, whether at the primary or upper level, was of a religious nature, middle-class culture resembled a simplified form of religious culture shaped by the guidelines of establishment scholars. The reality was more complex. In fact, this culture has its own cultural and intellectual history developed in relation to the particular context and conditions prevailing in the sixteenth through eighteenth centuries.

Many members of the middle class could in fact read and write, they owned books, and they were heirs to an important literary culture. However, the issue of interest here is how their relation to the oral culture and the written word differed from that of the academic community, of the scholars whose voluminous production dominated the intellectual scene, as well as how it differed from popular culture.

Whatever training people obtained from institutions of education cannot fully explain their cultural makeup. Even if institutions formed the core of the educational setup, noninstitutional channels of learning (such as the book) also need to be considered. Moreover, although those who attended these institutions were essentially searching for a religious education, religion may not have been their only objective in joining. In some ways, the culture of the middle class had important links to the dominant religious culture, but in many other ways it was a distinct culture with features that were peculiar to it.

Among the factors that had a bearing on culture are the economic conditions that had created common interests and concerns among middle-class individuals and families whose livelihood was more or less dependent upon production, services, and trade. A commercial dimension, with its focus on the here and now, formed part of their culture, as opposed to *'ulama'* culture, focusing on religious ideals and morals (see chapter 2).

This does not mean the middle class had a homogeneous culture. Quite the contrary, there were considerable differences. Not everyone, for instance, had equal access to education. A large number of people had access to basic literacy through the *kuttab* (elementary school) system. The number of elementary schools in Cairo, about three hundred for a population of around 260,000 at the end of the eighteenth century, suggests that about a third of the male population had attended an elementary school.[1] What kind or level of education a pupil reached is much less quantifiable. A few had exposure to a more or less prolonged college education and were erudite, well read, articulate, and productive, and consequently had the potential to be the intellectual elite of the middle class, regardless of their position within this class. Their erudition could suggest, in other words, a hierarchy of education among the middle class quite distinct from the hierarchy of scholars. It could also suggest that this educational hierarchy within the middle class was different from whatever socioeconomic hierarchy existed.

These views raise a number of questions and challenge a number of paradigms that have dominated the history of this region for a long time. Yet they help to answer many questions for which we so far have had no answer. One of these questions is in relation to the before/after approach usually applied to education. Too often, views on education before the reforms of Muhammad 'Ali (1805–48) are based on a black-and-white picture, or a before-and-after, with 1800 or thereabouts as the cutting line between modern and traditional or between the religious education of the early period and the secular education introduced in the nineteenth century. This viewpoint not only reduces the importance of the historical forces that could have a bearing on the educational scene at any one period, but it also tends to pile a few centuries together under the appellation of "traditional," a term that can efface significant social and economic realities. Muhammad 'Ali has, moreover, been closely associated with the education of the middle classes by his introduction and spread of a modern school system, a view that implicitly rejects as a valid form of learning the traditional elementary school education current in the sixteenth through eighteenth centuries.

The approach used here proposes that education, even within the "traditional" system dependent on religious institutions, can be understood in both a social and a religious context. It challenges the view that explains everything through Islam and that thus gives little weight to regional differences, to historical development. Within the before/after approach, what was true for one time and place was necessarily true for others and what was applicable to the early period was, in broad terms, given some ups and downs, applicable to a later period as well. The blanket descriptions of "Islamic education" overlooked regional and class differences, and tended to portray "Islamic" societies as an undifferentiated mass, timeless and spaceless. Regional differences between large cities like Cairo, Aleppo, or Istanbul, or between larger and smaller urban agglomerations for instance, were rarely part of the picture, important as they may have been. Socioeconomic conditions were likewise totally absent or largely ignored.

The present approach in no way reduces the importance of religious factors in education, but attempts to put them in a larger context. Religious factors can explain why literacy had a centuries-long existence over many parts of the Islamic world. The religious attitude toward learning in Islamic societies can explain the spread of elementary education among their civilian population at an early date. Islam in fact encouraged education and enjoined Muslims to search for it. By contrast, the Catholic Church during the same period stood against the spread of learning, taking steps to limit its diffusion, an attitude that tended to delay this spread among the majority of the population. Thus, whereas in the European context broad literacy appeared among minority populations—Protestants for instance—before it did among the majority, in Islamic societies, on the contrary, Muslims were encouraged to learn in order to be able to understand their religion. Therefore in theory learning had a positive value.

In practice, from very early on, mosques undertook the function of teaching the basics of learning to Muslims who were not essentially interested in pursuing academic careers. This teaching took place in Cairo as it did in other cities in Egypt and in other Islamic countries. In cities in the Ottoman world elementary education was available to a large number of people. Robert Mantran's study of sixteenth-century Istanbul maintains that elementary education was a widespread phenomenon in the city.[2] Likewise, in his book on eighteenth-century Aleppo, Abraham Marcus noted that the children attending Quranic school never had to go far from their houses because most neighborhoods offered some kind of educational facility.[3] The pupils were usually taught free of charge, although remunerated education was also available. *Waqf* deeds indicate that in addition to free schooling, they also received benefits such as clothing on special occasions, an enticement to social groups that were not privileged.

The same kind of education applied to non-Muslim children, notably the members of the Coptic and Jewish communities. Their numbers in Cairo are estimated to have been, at the end of the eighteenth century, about ten thousand Copts and three thousand Jews, out of a total population of about a quarter of a million people. Both had their own *maktab* where children were taught more or less the same basic education as Muslim children, notably reading, writing, and arithmetic. Rather than teaching them Islam, their teachers, themselves members of their communities, taught them the basics of their own religion.[4] Women also had some access to education, although sources of the period are too scant for us to try to quantify its extent. Certainly, they did not reach the level of men either in terms of numbers or in terms of depth or variety of exposure. Some had tutors at home, others paid a schoolteacher to teach them. The statements made by Muhammad Abu Dhakir in 1173/1759 on this matter probably reflected the view of many people: Husbands should teach their wives to read so that they might learn their religious obligations, but they need not learn to write.[5] On the other hand, we occasionally find women who owned books, as the following chapter will suggest. It would certainly be enlightening to pursue this matter further on the basis of literary works, court records, or other sources.

If, then, the education of these people was inevitably linked to institutions that were essentially religious in nature, the issue at hand is how did their culture evolve in other directions? How to explain that middle-class culture was a potential source for "modernity"? In other words, we need to ask how a traditional culture could help to create rather than to stop modernity and how it developed an "educated" as opposed to a "scholarly" culture, a culture defined by them rather than for them. This entails questioning many of the "givens" that have for long dominated the field of Middle East history.

To answer these questions entails taking a broader view that can encompass trends that spread beyond political borders. Because there are still many blanks in our knowledge, our approach could benefit from comparing neighboring Mediterranean regions that had similar or parallel conditions and that could shed some light on the issue. Finding answers also entails broadening the framework that is used to explore education so as to identify and explore factors that could potentially have a bearing on the subject. It entails moving from the formal to the informal. The assumption is that not all education took place in institutions and that we need to look beyond in order to get a better idea of how culture or knowledge could be transmitted and developed. It also entails consideration of an oral culture rather than solely a written one.

To understand the complexity of middle-class education, various religious, historical, geographical, and economic dimensions were considered. These dimensions showed that, firstly, the educational culture of the middle class in Cairo was as rich as it was complex; on the one hand it was broadly based, with a large number of people able to use the written word, and, on the other hand, a few of its members were highly educated. Secondly, it had the potential to create "modernity," to create intellectuals. Thus the end products of the religious institutions of education were not identical nor did they conform to a single standard type. Some of the great thinkers and writers of the nineteenth century—like Rifa'a al-Tahtawi (1801–73), 'Abdalla Nadim (1845–96), or 'Ali Mubarak (1823–93), and many others—were students in religious elementary schools, not only in Cairo but also in remote villages where outside influences would tend to be more limited. They nevertheless subsequently developed in a number of directions, as people also developed in the seventeenth and eighteenth centuries. These features constituted part of the cultural and intellectual history of the middle class and made it distinct as a culture.

A History or "Histories" of Middle-Class Education?

Part of the complexity of middle-class culture lay in the fact that it was the result not only of "traditional" education or "religious" education, but of a number of elements that helped to shape that culture. Access to literacy through the system of religious education was a fundamental aspect of middle-class culture. It was also one of the important factors that led to a broad use of reading and writing among the urban middle class. Many historians have written about the history of "elementary" education in Islamic societies. Its contours are well known to us. In these schools (called *maktab* or *kuttab*), young boys were taught the basics of education: how to read, perhaps how to write; they could also be taught to recite parts of the Quran and the basics of Islam. Mosques performed the same function of teaching young boys the basics of their religion and enough literacy to perform the necessary religious functions. The school was also a tool for the socialization of a new generation, where youths were taught certain social values, exposed to the social ideologies regarding their place in society, with the aim of making them good Muslims and good subjects. The *waqf* of 'Uthman Katkhuda (d. 1149/1736), for instance, specifically required that the boys attending the school he had founded be instructed to recite verses from the Quran (*yahduna thawab qiratihim*) with blessings aimed at the Prophet, his companions, his relatives, at *'ulama'*, and at *uwliya* (holy men) and the four *imams*.[6] These boys, who generally had not yet reached puberty, thus learned from early on the place that *'ulama'* should hold. Thus certain social ideals were passed on to the new generation.

Important as elementary religious education was, however, it constituted only one of the "histories" of middle-class culture and did not represent the whole picture. Other important dimensions enter in, of which some have a local bearing and a local history, and others have a regional significance. In either case, these other dimensions brought into the middle-class culture of Cairo between the sixteenth and eighteenth centuries certain realities that we cannot ignore, or certain "histories," each with its own source and trajectory as well as its own geographical boundaries. Each of these other "histories" could be more or less dominant at certain points in time or among certain individuals. To study them as "histories" rather than as a single "history" not only suggests a greater complexity than is usually attributed to these people, but also brings to the fore certain contradictions and tensions within this culture.

History of the Written Word in Egypt

The use of the written word in Egypt, for which we have ample evidence over a long period, constitutes one of these "histories" that in one sense seem to have evolved independently and yet which may have had an important bearing on middle-class culture for a number of reasons. There is a historical dimension to the use of the written word among those that were not in scholarly professions, at the same time suggesting a different attitude toward writing, one with a certain pragmatism.

From a fairly early period, evidence indicates that writing was used for a number of purposes, in official documents as well as in private deeds and in letters. In Egypt, probably more than in the neighboring regions, there existed a long tradition of the written word. The archives that have reached us indicate that this tradition was neither limited to a scribal class nor to the religious establishment. Even though the history of writing up to the sixteenth century, which this study takes as a starting point, has yet to be written, we have clear indications that the written word had a long, if intermittent, history in Egypt. Certain periods, such as the period of the Arab papyri, contain tens of thousands of written papers, private and public, dating from the first centuries of Islam, and more than one hundred thousand papyrus and parchment documents excavated in Fayyum in 1877–78. Some of the documents date as early as the ninth century, going up to the thirteenth century.[7] Nearly three hundred thousand written papers from the Geniza, covering roughly the tenth-eleventh to the thirteenth-fourteenth centuries, were the documents of a specific community, the Jewish community of Fustat. Yet they reflected the traditions of the context from which they came. Jewish communities did not leave us anything on a similar scale in other lands.

Other finds are those from the excavations of Qasr Ibrim in the south of Egypt and the port of Tur in the Red Sea, where several thousand documents were excavated by a Japanese expedition, of which about a thousand fragments are dated to the period between the mid-fifteenth- to the mid-sixteenth centuries, presumably with commercial concerns an important part of their subject matter.[8] A systematic exploration of these bodies of archives of the centuries that preceded the sixteenth century, in terms of their geographical location; the kind of deed, document, or letter; and the social categories involved can shed light on the use of writing; such a study as yet has not been done.

The various caches of documents and manuscripts found in different parts of Egypt for different periods have so far only been considered in the context of new sources or new archives to be used by scholars. Their social significance has not been explored, nor has the history of the written word so far been written. Even so, one can clearly see that there was a long history of the use of the written word before the sixteenth century, and that even if we cannot, on the basis of research done so far, consider all the implications of this phenomenon, what clearly appears to be the case in many of these archives is that the written word was neither limited to professional bureaucrats nor to professional scholars. These archives indicate a close relationship with the written word not only in the capital city but also in provincial towns, not only among elites but also among middle classes. As such, these documents and archives had a bearing on what we can call the history of middle-class education in Cairo. At the same time, this "history" could be a significant factor in explaining the immense regional differences within the Ottoman state.

Trade and Literacy

Another "history" is the history of a literacy that was connected to trade and commerce, a literacy that aimed to protect the interests of tradesmen and merchants. Here again, this literacy had a bearing on the culture of the middle class; at the same time, its geographical boundaries were different from those of other "histories." These boundaries could follow those of the regions where commercial capitalism was a significant force.

The link between trade and literacy can be made at many levels. It has been some time since European scholars made a link between the spread of literacy and trade. The Italian historian Carlo M. Cipolla, for instance, suggested a close association between literacy, mercantile development, and urban life in medieval southern Europe.[9] The logic behind this link was evident: to undertake certain dealings, a person needed a basic knowledge of how to read or write in order to protect his interests, and he needed basic mathematics in order to do essential calculations. Thus it was essential for him to have a basic education in order to carry out his economic activity.

One would like to see if the link that Cipolla made between trade and literacy in the Italian context has some applicability to other regions that shared comparable economic conditions, to see if one can make a parallel between north and south and apply the same reasoning. There are, in fact, a number of arguments that suggest the validity of such a comparison.

One could apply the same reasoning to the countries of the southern Mediterranean, which were linked by more or less intensive commercial currents. Not only were there historical parallels between north and south, created by a long history of trade and exchange, but also, at the level of historical methodology, certain methodologies applied to European history can be meaningfully applied to our context. This is one way of moving away from the Orientalist paradigms that have dominated the study of Islamic societies, with their notion of a dynamic north and passive east, or of a north understood via historical process and a south through static religion.

In the same way that an elementary education protected a tradesman's interests in Italy or France, it did so in Egypt, Syria, and Anatolia; and in the same way that a trading community in Europe was more likely to be literate than a fishing, hunting, or pastoral community, the same applied to the countries of the south. Consequently, similar commercial conditions in different geographical areas can lead to parallel consequences as far as education is concerned. Seen in these terms, the divisions between southern and northern Mediterranean areas appear not to be as rigid as modern academic studies sometimes suggest. If commerce were a factor behind the spread of literacy in Cairo, then it is likely to have been one of the factors behind literacy in other commercial centers around the Mediterranean and in the Ottoman world—in Anatolia, Syria, France, and Italy—especially at times of economic prosperity, which we know to have been the case. Studies on many other cities in the Ottoman world have confirmed this view.[10]

In fact, roughly around the sixteenth century, the dissemination of learning and the spread of literacy were observed over a large Mediterranean area, long before state policies were set up to combat illiteracy and schools founded for this purpose. Historians dealing with the sixteenth and seventeenth centuries have noted a rise in literacy, or, more accurately, in certain forms of literacy, in France and in Italy as in Istanbul and Damascus. Carlo Ginzburg's study of a sixteenth-century miller, Menoccio, living in Montereale, shows that, in a small provincial town, a person in a trade that was not highly lucrative owned a few books on various subjects.[11] Ginzburg's study indicates that there was a spread of books not only in provincial towns but also among the middle and lower class. One cannot make the same comments for provincial towns in Egypt and Syria (in any case, no studies have been undertaken), but with regard to the social level of those who own books, work done in Cairo and in Damascus shows that the higher members of the middle class were among the book owners. Recent scholarship has uncovered the importance of literacy around some parts of the Mediterranean basin roughly around the sixteenth century. French historians have done extensive work on early modern France, both about literacy and the spread of a book culture. There are parallels for these trends in the southern Mediterranean region.

This situation suggests two points: that certain common factors were behind these trends that affected a large region, and that at certain levels the north-south differences in the Mediterranean area were not as wide in the sixteenth century as has sometimes been thought, but rather became so at a later date, probably sometime in the eighteenth century. In other words, the regions where commercial capitalism flourished were affected by some of its indirect consequences. This idea is worth pursuing, but has been somewhat thwarted by the paradigm of a division between a passive south and a dynamic north.

This link between literacy and trade may shed light on our understanding of the diversity within the Ottoman world. Recent research has suggested that Jerusalem, for instance, a place of pilgrimage, a center of religious significance not particularly involved in major trade or industry, may not have had a large literate population. Probate records show that in Jerusalem, unlike in some other cities in the region, only elites were literate and only *'ulama'* and bureaucrats owned books.[12] The same could be true of other villages, towns, and cities in Egypt, Syria, or Anatolia. A recent study, for instance, has suggested that even up to the nineteenth century the large majority of the Muslim population of Salonica was apparently illiterate.[13] What this information indicates is that different factors could emerge to either encourage the spread of literacy or, on the contrary, to limit it. One would like to be able to mark on a map the agglomerations where educational facilities were offered in order to see spatial patterns that would suggest where and why variations existed. It seems very likely, for instance, that educational facilities for children were available in large cities in the Ottoman state. It is less clear what facilities existed in medium-size or small towns that may have developed around certain functions, and unclear what was available in rural areas. Moreover, one might, when such studies are sufficiently advanced, be able to identify certain types of cities or urban agglomerations that were more likely to emphasize child education, commercial cities, cities with strong religious functions or which were places of pilgrimage, cities with administrative functions. This direction has the advantage of offering a way out of a tendency that has developed in Ottoman studies in recent years, which, in my view, has been detrimental to the field: Scholars talk of "Ottoman" when they really mean Anatolia. From there they generalize to all the Ottoman state, without regard to variations, to cultural specificities, or to historical dimensions.

The link between trade and literacy in Cairo can also be made at the level of chronology between certain trading upheavals and the evidence available about the spread of literacy, either by the number of schools built or by other means. In other words, periods of more intense trading were accompanied by a greater spread of literacy, and the other way around.

Cairo was an important commercial center throughout the Mamluk period (1250–1517), being on the crossroads of several major trading routes and being a center for the Red Sea trade as well as for Mediterranean trade and trade with Africa. The end of the fifteenth century brought in a period of crisis, due to various factors such as the Portuguese disruption of trading with India and internal economic conditions in Egypt. As of the middle of the sixteenth century, the Red Sea trade picked up again. Frederic Lane has shown that by the second half of the sixteenth century the activity of the Red Sea trade had become intense, restoring what it had lost in the opening years of the century when some of the Asiatic merchandise for Europe was channeled by means of the Atlantic Ocean.[14] The repercussions of this intensification may be surmised from a little-known and unpublished text that was written in 975/1550 by an eminent and highly respected scholar called Ibn Hajar al-Haythami.[15] It falls chronologically in the period in which Frederic Lane sees a revival of the Red Sea trade after a few decades of crisis resulting from Portuguese settlement in Goa.

This text by Ibn Hajar al-Haythami addresses a number of concerns that schoolteachers face in dealing with their pupils, some of them concrete daily issues, others matters of principle: among them was the way to deal with gifted pupils. Should they get special treatment and be singled out? Was that detrimental to those who did not have special gifts? He was concerned, moreover, with what to do in case a pupil was absent as well as with more abstract matters such as who had the right to physical punishment, and if it were proper conduct to take money for teaching because learning was a religious duty.

Were there particular conditions at this time that pushed Ibn Hajar al-Haythami to write a treatise to guide teachers? His view could be a reflection of an actual situation in mid-sixteenth-century Cairo during a period that experienced an increase in trade. This situation might have resulted in al-Haythami's lifetime in a greater demand for elementary education, leading to an increase in the number of pupils and teachers. Or there may have been an increase in the more structured elementary schools (*maktab*) as opposed to mosque teaching, about which we know little but which was not as regulated by *waqf* provisions as was the *maktab*. In fact one of the concerns that he addressed in this text was precisely the issue of whether a teacher could allow more pupils to attend schools than the number that was mentioned in the *waqf* document for the school. Normally the *waqf* of an elementary school gave precise numbers of pupils who could be attending, providing them not only with lessons free of charge, but with clothes, food, and gifts for special occasions. Normally the stipulations in *waqf* deeds had to be strictly observed. Yet Al-Haythami was quite flexible on this issue. He considered that the teacher could allow a larger number of pupils to attend the lessons if they did not incur any additional expense to the foundation.[16]

He was also concerned about issues related to the boys' education and their relationship to their teacher. If a boy were absent from school, did the teacher have the right to send another pupil to look for him? No, said al-Haythami, not unless he was paid a wage, because this was a service, not a duty. Could the teacher beat a disobedient boy? No, said al-Haythami, unless the boy's father explicitly allowed him to do so, and if the student were an adult, only with the permission of the *qadi*. Such matters covered the day-to-day problems that many schoolteachers presumably faced among their students. It is relevant that these questions should be asked at that particular moment in time.

Another piece of evidence that links literacy to trade is the construction of elementary schools. The number of elementary schools constructed in the course of two centuries is relatively high. André Raymond identified 118 *sabil-maktabs* that were built in Cairo between the sixteenth and eighteenth centuries, although he admits that this figure is far below the actual situation.[17] These figures do not take into consideration the schools already existing from the previous period, nor are any figures available for pupils who attended their lessons in mosques. But even so, the increase in new schools founded in this period of trade intensification opened up new facilities for a significant portion of the population.

The chronology of school construction and trading conditions can be linked even more specifically. A clear curve can be detected that followed commercial conditions of the eighteenth century. The number of new schools constructed in Cairo in the eighteenth century rose significantly during the first few decades as the coffee trade was growing, then fell sharply at the end of the century. Thirteen new schools were constructed during the first quarter of the eighteenth century, nineteen during the second quarter, twenty-two in the third quarter, and a mere six (or 10 percent of those constructed during the eighteenth century) in the last quarter, or one-half to one-quarter the number of other twenty-five-year periods during that century.[18] The impoverishment of the people in crafts, for various reasons such as a more intense flow of European goods, taxation that was becoming more abusive and exploitative, and natural causes, presumably reduced the number of pupils attending school, as the ruling class turned its attention to rural rather than urban resources, and as fewer impoverished middle-class families could afford to spare a child (see chapter 6). Impoverishment was also related to the concerns of the ruling class. As long as they depended on urban wealth for their revenues, they helped develop urban infrastructures. When they turned to rural wealth, they lost interest in urban structures.

Another important piece of evidence links literacy to trade, notably an evolution of the way that courts were used. A significant difference can be observed between the court records of about 1550 and those of 1600. This difference may be attributed in part to the courts themselves and the ways of recording cases. However, we can also observe an increasing number of tradesmen and craftsmen who brought to court the daily cases related to their business dealings, such as sales on credit, even for relatively small sums, and debts. A look at court registers indicates an extensive use of the written document for everyday dealings. The period 1550–1650 sees a steady growth in use of court records by a broad public for private and public purposes. A comparison of the early records with those of the later ones shows the extent to which there is an enormous increase, both in the number of people in the trades coming to record their daily transactions and in the details that each case is provided with. What clearly emerges from this comparison is that, more and more, the written word came to be a part of the lives of urban middle-class tradesmen. During this period, many more members of the middle class took to the court questions related to their daily activities: a sale on credit, a loan, a receipt for goods given in safekeeping. The striking feature about many of these questions was the humble nature of the dealings and the relatively small sums that were sometimes involved. Thus, by the end of the sixteenth century, 1580 or 1590, an ordinary tradesman who had a shop in the market could be regularly making use of the court for any concerns that might protect his interests.

And we know from the way that court procedures were followed that, for the payment of a small sum of money, he could get a copy of whatever deed was registered in the records. The copy of the deed that claimants took with them was a protection of their interests, a deed that could be used if their interests were at risk. Thus one can see through these cases the usefulness, for many merchants and craftsmen, of the written word, and of the benefits they could get from a certain familiarity with the written word, from the ability to read and perhaps write as well. This was one of the incentives for many people working in the marketplace to gain some reading and writing abilities.

In addition, business was also undertaken informally between partners without going to court. The manuscripts Saad El Khadem published are of particular significance in view of the fact that they are informal papers that are written by those concerned, as compared to the deeds in court records, written in legal language by specialists. One of them is a receipt by Khawaja Shams al-Din al-Faraskuri for some textiles; the wording is brief, unlike the legal documents issued in court; the receipt could serve as an aide-mémoire. This informal way of doing business without passing through the court was probably widespread.[19] Likewise the note listing copper kitchen utensils, written by an artisan that Saad El Khadem presumed to be an engraver, who carved people's names and personal insignia on their utensils, illustrates some of the practical applications in which people used writing in their work.[20] Likewise, merchants who could read and write could maintain a correspondence with their agents, a fact that unfortunately we know little about. Yet André Raymond in his work on merchants and artisans indicates that the archives of Vincennes include some of the business correspondence exchanged between merchants in Cairo and Damascus.[21]

For traders with dealings of a certain significance, daily affairs may also have been rendered more difficult by the existence of a complicated monetary situation. This complexity was a result both of the great fluctuations in the value of the local currency used in Cairo, studied by André Raymond, and of the number of imported currencies that were used in the market in addition to the local currencies, such as the Dutch and Venetian coins, the Spanish piaster, and the German thaler, each with its own exchange rate and its own fluctuations in value.[22] These currency issues did not simplify people's daily dealings and may have been a further incentive to putting them down in writing.

The complexity of trading relations may also be behind the extensive use of courts in these dealings, a fact that constituted a significant difference between the way that business was carried out in the Geniza period (tenth-twelfth centuries) and in the seventeenth century. The informality that characterized business dealings in the earlier period seems to have been replaced by a more formal approach. We know about the complexities with which merchants and tradesmen carried out their daily dealings not from informal letters they wrote each other but from legal deeds recorded in court.

The vaster and more complex a business was, the more the need for written documents. At the same time, the elite merchants who ran these vast businesses often employed scribal help, using literate scribes, often Copts, to run the administrative and accounting part of their work. The Copts were known for their skills in accounting and in auditing, skills that they presumably learned on the job and were eager not to divulge. With them, an important merchant could run important dealings while he himself was illiterate. But for smaller businesses, for middle-ranking merchants or for a shop owner running a more restricted venture, for instance, some literacy gained importance, because the employment of persons specialized in scribal affairs was unlikely at that level.

The Oral Culture of the Middle Class

The oral culture available to the middle class constitutes another of its "histories," one that has not been well studied. The culture of the middle class combined a written culture with an oral one. This duality of oral and written requires some explanation. Little has been written about this dimension of culture, and the comments that follow attempt to consider its relevance without claiming to be exhaustive. They explore certain aspects that were evident in the sources consulted.

As described above, the urban middle class had a written culture linked to the marketplace, whereby small deals of various sorts were recorded on paper, dictated by need to protect material interests. Another dimension of their cultural makeup remained oral. Therefore, although a relatively high proportion of the urban male middle-class population had some familiarity with the written word, these people were also closely linked to an oral culture that could take various forms and that developed along different lines. Thus need created a duality between written and oral. One could in fact argue that the oral tradition was so strong and so rich as to allow for a certain type of person who, in spite of the absence of reading or writing skills, might have a broad culture obtained through the various and diverse forms of oral transmission. One often reads about blind scholars and blind Quran reciters whose acquisition of their skills depended entirely on what they heard rather than on what they read. Al-Jabarti's necrology of the great scholar Shaykh 'Atiya al-Ajhuri (died 1190/1776)—a jurist proficient in jurisprudence, *hadith* (prophetic tradition), and instrumental sciences, and the author of several works in the religious sciences—is an example of a blind scholar, not unique but part of a phenomenon.[23]

One needs to understand these two types of culture as not being opposites: oral linked to ignorance and literacy to education. Thus orality was part of a social context. Within this social context, being articulate and capable of manipulating language was given a positive value, as was the ability to recite texts. Certain skills such as memorization, considered negative in the modern context because it is seen as the opposite of rational thought, as discouraging a student from thinking and teaching him to repeat what he was told with no mental requirement on his part, were, on the contrary, highly regarded.

Therefore, a distinction is necessary between the oral culture of those that were illiterate and for whom this was the only form of expression available, and between those who were educated, erudite, well-read, but for a number of reasons also found oral culture an appropriate means for expression. As a matter of fact, oral transmission was part of the system of education in *madrasas*. Thus books were studied with a shaykh, perhaps read out loud, in some cases memorized and recited. In fact, although the *'ulama'* dealt extensively with books—composed them, read them, owned libraries, and so on—there was a strong element of orality in their approach to knowledge and in their teaching method. In private gatherings, the practice of reciting memorized texts was frequently practiced and appreciated; the feats of a person who recited al-Bukhari, a recitation lasting for several hours, or a Syrian poet who memorized the *maqamat* (narratives) of al-Hariri, were greatly admired and those who undertook them were held in esteem.[24]

Scholars like Elizabeth Eisenstein draw a very clear line between a literate culture and an oral culture; they see an enormous gulf between oral and literate cultures, with significant differences of mentalities shaped by reliance on the spoken word as opposed to the written word.[25] Yet it is problematic to apply a view like Eisenstein's without considering the cultural specificity of different regions. Given the importance of the oral tradition in early modern societies in general and in Arab and Islamic ones in particular, this specificity cannot be dismissed lightly. During the period between the sixteenth and the eighteenth centuries, two contradictory trends were occurring at the same time in relation to the oral and the written.

The prevailing conditions had led to the development of the oral tradition. One dimension of this development has to do with the urban spaces that emerged in this period and that had a bearing on the oral tradition. Of these, the coffeehouse had a significant role to play. Coffeehouses, which were starting to become popular in the cities of the Ottoman Empire as of the middle of the sixteenth century, became widespread in Cairo. Coffeehouses could be found in all the parts of the city and drinking a cup of coffee was within the means of many of its inhabitants. Nevertheless, to a large extent, this public space was linked to the middle class. For the poor of the city, living at subsistence level, it was a luxury that they could not afford; spending money on nonessentials was not an option. Likewise, the members of the ruling class were unlikely to frequent this public space, preferring the privacy of their homes and palaces for socializing and entertainment.

The coffeehouse has not been given the consideration it deserves as a cultural forum. In the first place, because of its association with oral culture it has fallen victim to our clear-cut division between the oral—associated with illiteracy and by association with ignorance—and the written, which we associate with learning and education. The coffeehouse was, moreover, relegated to the domain of popular culture or mass culture, associated with entertainment such as games with animals, vulgar displays, male dancers dressed up as females, drugs such as hashish and opium. Descriptions by travelers give us an idea of what went on there. They talk of monkeys and bears, of animal trainers. Certainly this entertainment was an important aspect. However, other activities also took place in the coffeehouse, and even though what we know is limited, it is significant.

And yet, one could argue that the coffeehouse gave an impetus to the development of certain literary forms, like storytelling and certain kinds of poetry. It thus provided a new forum for such activities that had previously been part of street performances. There was in fact a guild of storytellers in coffeehouses and other locations, indicating some significance to this profession.[26] Some of these storytellers were employed by coffeehouses. Presumably this employment gave them a certain level of financial security, because employment could mean having a salary on a regular basis rather than being paid wages or receiving a payment by the piece. This situation, in any case, is what is suggested in some court cases, where a person is identified as being a storyteller or *hakawati* in a particular coffeehouse, as with a certain Salama b. Shihata, who in 1068/1657 was a storyteller in the Sulimaniyya coffeehouse of Bulaq.[27] Certainly there must have been many more like him. Humorous shows and farces also took place in the coffeehouses. Johann de Wild, who travelled to Cairo between 1606 and 1610, talks of burlesque farces commonly played out in coffeehouses and of "comedies" that were acted out in street performances.[28]

The degree of specialization among these storytellers is indicative of a fairly high level of sophistication in their art. Some storytellers specialized in the epic of Abu Zayd al-Hilali; others specialized in the epic of al-Dhahir Baybars, the Mamluk sultan who fought the Crusaders; still others specialized in the story of Antar. Their numbers, which Edward William Lane provides, are also indicative: fifty poets specialized in Abu Zayd, thirty in the Baybars epic, and six in the story of Antar.[29]

Within the space that the coffeehouse offered, where a literary culture flourished and the clientele could hear the dramatized recitation of *siras*, another dimension can also be considered. The coffeehouse provided a space free of the restraints of institutions or of formal gatherings. More specifically we find indications not only of professional artists who came to perform for a fee or salary, but a space where the clients of the coffeehouse could themselves find a forum for what they wished to express. For some people, this meant conversing about religious matters, as was the case in a coffeehouse owned by a Sufi shaykh in Suwayqat al-Mahruqa in Damascus, which became the meeting place of his friends and disciples.[30] For others, going to the coffeehouse provided different kinds of entertainment, notably musical performances. In 1744, we are told, three Jewish musicians from Aleppo with a high command of their repertory and great expertise in their instruments arrived in Damascus and performed their music in the various coffeehouses of the city, entertaining both the high and the low.[31] The coffeehouse also served as a place where one could be heard reciting one's verse to a friend or companion. The well-known poets of the period are known to have frequented coffeehouses, as we are told by al-Muhibbi with regard to Damascus. In fact the most prominent poet of Damascus, Abi Bakr al-'Umari, who had the title of *shaykh al-adab bil Sham* (head of the poets of Damascus), for one, wrote a poem in the Jadida coffeehouse below the Citadel of the city, where he went with his friend al-Shamsi Muhammad 'Ayn al-Mulk, not in his capacity as a professional poet reciting verse for which he would be paid, but because he was inspired at that particular moment to write verse and found a listener who could appreciate or comment on it. In other words, this was an appropriate space for him to be at ease, to express himself, and to be heard.[32]

People could take their ease in what they did and in what they said, an absence of restraint that must have bordered frequently on the absence of respectability. Coffeehouses were linked to hashish consumption. The funny stories and poetry recited there were often, in the critical eyes of a contemporary scholar, full of lies, and those who recited them did not deserve to be paid a fee for telling these lies.[33] The coffeehouse was also a space that provided a certain equality of exchange, an impression one gets from a court case dated 1655, brought against a court employee who upon entering the coffeehouse removed his turban, indicative of his social condition, and remained bareheaded, to the horror of his superior, the *qadi* of Qanatir al-Siba' court.[34] Coffeehouses were, as a result, often severely criticized by the members of the religious establishment as dissolute. Such criticism can be put in the context of a social space with rules of conduct that may have been different from those in the place of work or in a family context.

The richness of this oral literary life went beyond the coffeehouse to other public and private spaces in the city. Popular literature was kept alive and developed by professional storytellers, poets, and reciters who performed their arts not only in coffeehouses but as street entertainers or in private dwellings. Popular literature was also kept alive within small groups who met informally to enjoy it. Muhammad al-Muradi's biography of Ahmad al-Kiwani, a Damascene poet, tells us that he had literary sessions, which the most prominent literary figures attended, regularly taking place in his shop in one of the city's markets, Suq al-Darwishiyya. By its very nature, this kind of session, like that of a coffeehouse, provided a meeting point for people who were not part of the elite.[35] Neither could it have attracted a clientele among the urban poor living on subsistence. Here again, by exclusion, private spaces emerge as a meeting place for those in the middle ranks.

The duality of oral and written culture was influenced by the developments of the seventeenth and eighteenth centuries. As a result of broad literacy combined with the material comfort that allowed the middle class to spend money on nonessentials, coincident with the spread of cheap paper came a trend to write on paper what had been an oral literature. The examples of writings that had a long history in the oral tradition and then appeared in written form during the period are many. Stories of al-Sayyid al-Badawi, for instance, which circulated by word of mouth for centuries, first appear in writing in short notices in the fourteenth and fifteenth centuries, the full biography of this holy person only appearing in the sixteenth and seventeenth centuries.[36] The bearing that this trend had on the written word is discussed in chapter 4.

These developments indicate that oral culture had multiple dimensions. Heroic epics and stories of saints formed an important aspect of this culture, but there were other aspects too that reflected a more down-to-earth reality. Saad El Khadem mentions a manuscript containing a poem by and for artisans that well illustrates this matter. Unfortunately he does not provide the Arabic text, but only his French translation of the original. The poem starts off with "If you love me, buy me a garment," and continues with a choice of textiles available in the market that the beloved can ask for, upon which choice the lover will comply to satisfy her. He reveals the soft cloth from which he can make a costume for her and the bracelets and earrings she might want to have. He is willing to go to Khan al Khalili to buy what she needs.[37] Thus the writer expresses his love in a poem but writes from a down-to-earth perspective, with a touch of humor and a heavy reliance on the local, both with regard to the place to which he was referring and with regard to the closeness to the spoken word. His setting is in the area of the city with which everyone involved in its commercial activity was familiar.

Given this multiplicity of currents and trends that made up middle-class culture, it emerges as a more complex and diverse culture than it has been made out to be. To understand the factors underlying its potential to produce educated persons with cultural contours that were not identical to those of scholars, its potential to create intellectuals, and finally its potential to create "modernity," we need to turn our attention to other dimensions of this culture.

Potential for Intellectual Leadership

The potential for an intellectual leadership within the middle class is an important concept. It suggests that a leadership could emerge from within the middle class and that this leadership shared in its complex religious, commercial, and literary culture. It was an intellectual leadership that did not consist of great men. As such, it suggests a kind of leadership that was distinct from that of the high *'ulama'* who were the guardians of religion and who regarded themselves as guiding the morals of society—a kind of leadership that is closer to the idea of "organic" intellectuals that Antonio Gramsci developed.[38] This potential came into existence when social, economic, or other factors were favorable. On a broad level, this meant that at certain times and under certain conditions, the intellectual and moral leadership that the *'ulama'* had of all classes of society was not the only kind of leadership, even if it remained the strongest and most permanent. Other less conspicuous, less powerful forms of leadership had their following and were consequently of some significance. We know, for instance, the role played by the shaykhs of the various Sufi *tariqas:* they also formed parallel forms of religious leadership of their respective brotherhoods, which multiplied during the eighteenth century. Thus we can see the leadership of the intellectual leaders of the urban middle class as part of a trend that colored the eighteenth century.

One important factor in creating this potential leadership was the vast differences in the level of education among the middle class, between those with enough basic literacy to make use of a receipt or to acknowledge a debt, and those with a great erudition, familiar with a vast literature, who had exposure to higher education but who for various socioeconomic reasons were not scholars, or not primarily scholars. The potential existed for an elite different from the *'ulama'* elite to arise from among the latter group.

This exposure to higher education of significant numbers of young men was the consequence of the historical developments of the sixteenth century. In the course of the Mamluk period (1250–1517), colleges had received immense funding through the pious foundations of the sultans and their emirs. By the end of the period, Cairo had been endowed with dozens of *madrasas*, many of them with generous funding to support teachers and students. The complex and extended bureaucracy of the Mamluk state, in the capital and in provincial cities in Syria, offered these college graduates a better chance to be integrated into the administration than in the subsequent period. The Ottoman administration in Egypt following the conquest of 1517 was incomparably simpler than that of their Mamluk predecessors. Numerous government departments were closed, the chanceries and the army department, for example, no longer having any role to play. These functions were centralized in Istanbul. As a result, many college graduates were deprived of positions that they might have had in the administration.

The result was a discrepancy between college students and available positions. It appears that *waqf* initiatives in favor of higher education were not in proportion to actual needs, a condition apparently prevalent in various regions of the Ottoman state in the sixteenth and seventeenth centuries. Scholars such as Karen Barkey and Cornell Fleischer in his study of Mustafa Ali describe similar conditions. Fleischer's work suggests that by the middle of the sixteenth century, the ranks of *'ulama'* and students were severely overcrowded, and that the standards of education had declined,[39] while Karen Barkey found that students, fearful of not obtaining job positions, were involved in the Jilali revolts.[40] The phenomenon apparent in Cairo, where the Mamluk sultans and emirs had constructed tens of *madrasas* in the fourteenth and fifteenth centuries, may well have been part of a more widespread trend linked to the overextension of *waqfs* on *madrasas*. The approximate figures available indicate a fairly large college population. James Heyworth-Dunne reviews the available estimations of Azhar students: In 1835, Lane estimated their number at fifteen hundred, but stated that some put the figure at one thousand and others at three thousand. In 1838, Rifa'a al-Tahtawi gave the figure of twelve hundred, adding that the student body had been twelve thousand in the past.[41] The length of time a student spent in the institution was not defined; a student could stay as long as he wished. Ahmad 'Izzat 'Abdul-Karim suggests that it took eight to ten years of study to become a shaykh or an *'alim*, but many students left after two to three years.[42]

If we take the conservative figure of fifteen hundred students in al-Azhar at a particular moment and an estimated average five to six years' stay, it means that every year two hundred fifty to three hundred graduated. Over a generation of thirty years, then, seventy-five hundred to nine thousand graduated from the Azhar alone, not to mention many other institutions of higher education still functioning in Cairo. In reality, we could multiply this figure many times for the number of *madrasas* functioning in Cairo for which we do not have any indication of the number of students. In fact, Heyworth-Dunne counted some twenty *madrasas* mentioned in al-Jabarti and as many mosques where students attended courses, a total of some forty institutions of higher learning.[43] It is therefore a very conservative figure to say that we can triple or quadruple the number of educated: nine thousand times 3.5, for instance, and talk of thirty thousand. Of these an unknown number left Cairo for the provinces or for other regions, mainly Syria and North Africa. This figure cannot be more than conjectural. But suffice it to say that even with a conservative estimation, we find a fairly large number of people who had had exposure to college learning. It is likely that these persons moved to different professions; only a few would end up in an academic profession. The *'ulama'* teaching in the Azhar are variously estimated at forty to fifty, according to Chabrol, sixty according to Chauvin,[44] and at sixty to seventy according to Gamal El-Din El-Shayyal.[45]

Therefore many more people had spent some time in *madrasas* than those who eventually became part of the educational or judicial establishment. These people, many of whom moved to nonreligious professions, were perhaps, in times of high commercial activity, integrated into trading jobs as craftsmen, tradesmen, or merchants; others might have copied manuscripts. In some periods, a number of people trained in religious sciences, whether in an institution or through a private relationship with a shaykh for either short or long periods, ended up working in economic rather than intellectual or academic activities. If certain trades were doing well at a particular moment, as for instance textile production, prosperous until the last part of the eighteenth century, that trade might attract more people, especially if religious positions became scarce. Muhammad Khalil al-Muradi, the eighteenth-century Syrian historian, for instance, talks of an *'alim* who did not have an appointment, so in spite of his profound knowledge of Islamic sciences, he earned his living from weaving textiles.[46]

The college thus had an important role in producing not only the socially respected scholars that became prominent in the religious scene, but also a large number of people who eventually did not pursue religious study or necessarily take up religious or judicial positions. Sometimes they entered professional life in one trade or another. Sometimes, too, they maintained their two careers, one in economic life and the other in religious life, either at the same time or at various times of their lives. Thus the line between religion and economy was far from clear-cut for a large number of people. These conditions could leave people with links to the academic world in an ambivalent position, their interests linked to the educational or religious institution and their earnings linked to the marketplace. Their intellectual and cultural leadership role has been almost entirely neglected by modern scholarship in favor of the more prominent *'ulama'*.

The emergence of a middle-class cultural elite can also partly be attributed to other factors, notably to exposure to various forms of knowledge and culture that were taking place outside of institutions. In addition to the coffeehouse and the comedies and farces, the seventeenth and eighteenth centuries witnessed a multiplication of the *majlis* (pl. *majalis*). *Majalis* were salons, usually taking place in people's homes, where people met in informal gatherings to discuss specific or general matters. The *majlis* has been a feature of cultural life for a long time; works have been written on the *majlis 'ilm*, where discussions took place around religious matters, and *majlis adab*, where literature was the main focus, in the Abbasid period. The issue to explore is how the *majlis* was shaped during each period and what people did in it.

These *majalis* are well documented in the chronicles and biographies of the period. Was their function a purely religious exercise—for prayers, recitations, or Sufi *dhikrs*, an extension of the religious activity taking place elsewhere? Or were they essentially for entertainment, *lahu*, as al-Jabarti described in the house of Ridwan Katkhuda? In other words, should these *majalis* be considered by historians in the context of cultural history, as they have in cultural histories of France and Germany, to be a place for the exchange of ideas, a forum for debate, or should we consider them as part of the world of entertainment? There are no simple answers. This, like any other social body, responded to the demands of its period and to the context within which it was functioning. The functions of the *majlis*, an old institution in Islamic societies, were not rigidly defined by an outside force but changed in time and place according to social or economic circumstances. It is to these circumstances that our attention should be drawn.

The sources of the period indicate clearly that the *majlis* was very widespread in the late seventeenth and the eighteenth centuries, and that it covered a great variety of concerns. It is erroneous to consider it as being solely Sufi, religious, or even entertainment. The *majlis* was in fact used for a large variety of purposes. Al-Nabulsi and al-Muhibbi, whose works repeatedly refer to these social gatherings, give us an idea of the breadth of concerns they covered. A strong Sufi element was present in many salons where the *dhikr* was practiced. At other gatherings, those that the sources call *majlis adab*, the literary element dominated: people recited literature, composed poetry, improvised verses, and read books out loud.

Sometimes a *majlis* was mainly for entertainment, with musical instruments, singing, and games of chess (*shataranj*). Al-Jabarti points out that the *majlis* at the house of Ridwan Katkhuda al-Jalfi (d. 1754) was licentious and that the behavior of those who went tended toward impropriety. But when this same Ridwan attended the *majlis* of Khawaja Ahmad al-Sharaybi, a merchant known for his concern with propriety, he modified his behavior to comply with the tone of that *majlis*, only taking with him those of his friends who could behave properly. And, of course, the more serious *majalis* focused on scholarly issues, with the participants discussing *fiqh* or *tafsir*.[47] Some salons were concentrated upon a particular individual. The famous ones are those of Ridwan Katkhuda al-Jalfi, Murtada al-Zabidi, 'Abdul-Ghani al-Nabulsi, and Hasan al-Jabarti. Al-Nabulsi's many references to the salons he attended during his visit to Cairo show that they potentially involved more than entertainment. In the *majlis* that he described, the participants were introduced to new books; these were read out and discussed. Occasionally an author was invited to come introduce his work. On 2 Jumada II 1110/1698, in the *majlis* of Shaykh Zayn al-'Abidin al-Bakri, they read a work entitled *Al-Fath al-Rabbani*, written by Shaykh Ibrahim al-'Abidi al-Maliki, after which they decided they wanted to meet this person, living in al-Buhayra, and wrote him a letter asking him to join their *majlis*. Al-Nabulsi indicates that discussions and readings of specific works seem to have been common. Other matters of concern were also discussed: Nabulsi says that in the *majlis* of the pasha, which took place once a week, the people attending debated matters of religious and worldly concern, "*al umur al jaliyya lil manafi' al-diniyya wal dunyawiyya 'ind al-jamhur.*"[48]

Given the multiplicity of concerns that these *majalis* dealt with, one would be inclined to think that among their activities would be some that had a bearing on the intellectual life of the period. Some direct evidence of this fact can be found in statements made by writers who admitted to the influence of *majlis* discussion on the way that they formulated their thoughts. The development of various forums for exchange such as the coffeehouses where storytelling and poetry reciting were important activities and the *majlis* or literary salon where a variety of activities took place sometimes had a direct bearing on the book, as is told by Yusuf al-Shirbini, author of *Hazz al-Quhuf*. Shirbini clearly points out that the work he was writing had been discussed in the *majlis*, a fact that is supported by the oral quality that scholars have noted about his work.[49] Thus, in a very direct way his book was thought out in a *majlis* and developed from the discussions therein. Likewise, Yusuf al-Maghribi shows how the issues discussed in a *majlis* helped form his ideas that were eventually incorporated in his dictionary of Egyptian colloquial, *Raf' al-Isar*. In his discussion on the word *qahwa*, coffee, he explicitly indicates that the word had been discussed in a *majlis*.[50] Thus the formulation he used in his book was in fact the result of his discussion with others in one of these forums as well as of his own reflection.

This association between what took place there and what the participants wrote suggests that these gatherings could be a dynamic cultural influence on religious and nonreligious culture. Potentially they were freer and more flexible, in terms of their content or concerns and in terms of who could participate, than the more institutionalized forms of transmission of knowledge.

Majlis and the Middle Class

The *majlis* was an elite phenomenon linked to high culture or courtly culture. In late sixteenth-century Istanbul the *majlis* included poetic sessions attended by the most cultured class, who could express themselves in Persian, the language of high culture; in Arabic, the language of scholarly and religious sciences; and in Turkish.⁵¹ The various components of the ruling class in Cairo likewise held such literary sessions, including the Ottoman pasha or governor, who occasionally held his *majalis* in his residence in the Citadel in the south of the city, to which he invited important personages. This kind of forum was also fairly spread out among both the religious scholars and the military emirs and Mamluks. Prominent shaykhs, emirs, and Mamluks held *majalis* in their homes.

Yet available evidence suggests that toward the end of the seventeenth century the *majlis* was becoming accessible to some members of the middle class. Different pieces of evidence seem to indicate that even people who were not part of the elite were attending these sessions. There are indications of literary salons intended for the *a'yan* (elites) and others for people who did not form part of these *a'yan* groups. Muhammad Abu Dhakir hurled criticism at certain types of *majlis* in which some of the people who attended were often made to feel unwelcome because they were poorly dressed. (By "poorly dressed" we have to understand "middle ranking" as there is no way that he can be referring to the real poor.) Citing the way that people behaved in a *majlis* salon, he says that if somebody who was well dressed walked in, he was showered with praise and compliments.⁵² There were exclamations of how eloquent (*fasih*) he was, how knowledgeable (*fahim*). On the other hand, if someone dressed modestly or poorly showed up, even if he had the brains of a genius, the moment he left the room he was heaped with criticisms and people were eager to make fun of him. Once he was outside the *majlis*, their comments started. They made fun of what he was wearing; they said he dyed his moustache, that his beard was filthy, and that he lived in Harat al-Fahhamin (that is, the district where coal sellers lived—another way of saying that he or his clothes were as dirty as coal).

Finally, the occasional remarks we find in texts here and there on how to behave in a *majlis* constitute an additional piece of evidence that "newcomers" were penetrating this forum. Such remarks can be interpreted as having parallels with the books of conduct that Norbert Elias used as the basis for his work on the "civilizing process." These were intended to show people who were being integrated into a "civilized" society the proper way to conduct themselves in eating and in sleeping. The model for proper conduct was that of the civilized upper classes; the lessons were for the bourgeois and middle class who wanted to pattern their table manners after those of the ruling class. The civilizing process was in fact a process whereby the culture of the court, polished and refined, sank down to other classes who, as they became integrated into a certain form of conduct, had to learn its rules.[53] The books of conduct can thus be interpreted as symptomatic of a society in flux, in a period of shifting social structures.

It is along these lines that we can interpret texts such as those of Abu Dhakir, who gave his reader advice on how to behave in a dignified way in a *majlis*. People who attended were advised not to talk too much (*la yatakkalam illa itha nuqish*), not to boast (*la yaftakhir*), and not to flatter (*la yatamallaq*).[54] Other texts are almost like etiquette books that tell beginners how to conduct themselves.

In an anonymous manuscript datable to the seventeenth century, *Kitab Nuzhat al-'Ashiqin wa Ladhat al-Sami'in*, a father advises his son (*ya ibni*, or *ya waladi*) on how to behave in a gathering, how not to quarrel with others who were there, how to speak, and how to listen carefully.[55] These texts may be interpreted as evidence that newcomers were penetrating into a forum such as the literary salons that had been a prerogative of elite shaykhs and members of the ruling class, and that to be accepted by those who were already part of such forums, they had to follow some rules of behavior that were new to them.

The Middle-Class Elite

Conditions had thus created a broadly literate middle class as well as a well-educated middle-class elite that could potentially provide leadership among this class. But it was an elite of a certain kind, with no formal structure, whose role in relation to others was shaped by conditions, without necessarily having permanency. Unlike the elite *'ulama'*, who were often close to the power structure, this was a cultural elite that stood for the most part outside of the power structure. It could express, articulate, and put in writing issues and concerns that were distinct from those of the traditional *'ulama'* elite. It could also sometimes assume the role of spokesmen for this class, in a time of crisis for instance, as some of them did in the eighteenth century when their writings came to voice the social concerns of an urban middle class in crisis (see chapter 6).

In terms of the larger social structure, there were therefore two forms of leadership: this educated middle-class elite and the scholarly elite of *'ulama'* who held the primary positions of leadership and who regarded themselves as the guardians of religion for all the society, not only for segments of it. The blurring of the line between those who were leaders and those who were not but claimed to be so, between the "real" scholars and those who were educated in colleges but had not taken the scholarly road or those with claims to education, resulted in tensions. These tensions were reflected in a number of texts written in this period that criticized, in serious or humorous modes, those who claimed to be knowledgeable. Deploring the conditions of his time, the great Hanbali scholar Mari'i al-Maqdisi wrote at the beginning of the seventeenth century that the ignorant boasted of their large libraries, and wore large head shawls and expensive clothes with long sleeves, while the really deserving ones went unnoticed.[56]

With his well-known humor, Yusuf al-Shirbini, writing along the same lines at the end of the seventeenth century, stated that only those with a thorough knowledge of a particular question or issue should be allowed to give an opinion about it. He advised people not to pay attention to the words of the ignorant *'ulama'* among the commoners (*jahala 'ulama' al-'amma*).[57] The jokes about these ignorant *'ulama'* expressed the views of the classes who deplored the emergence of an alternative intellectual hierarchy that may have been less well versed in academic or scholarly matters: "I have a copy of the Quran in the author's hand-writing," said one of these ignorant *fuqaha*; another one, addressing some of the *'ulama'* of the Azhar, said to them, "I need a summary of the Quran because the original is too difficult for my students to read."

Likewise, those who were educated and intellectual without being scholarly articulated the same concern from a different angle. Muhammad Ibn Hasan Abu Dhakir, one such person of great sophistication, wrote, not without irony and humor, that when he was in the Azhar, everyone there, students as well as professors, came to hear about his own ignorance as a student (*jahli sha'a wa dha'a wa taraqa jami' al-asma' mi mashayikhi wal talaba*).[58] But his reader can clearly tell that this was an "ignorance" that related to a certain kind of knowledge, notably that linked to institutionalized, scholarly knowledge. In other kinds of knowledge, he surpassed many of his contemporaries who were more famous.

In conclusion, if we consider education to be only that process which takes place within the walls of a school or college, we reach one result; if we understand it to be part of a social context and a lived reality—if the transmission of learning taking place outside such institutions is understood as playing an important role in molding and directing the education of a person—we reach a different result. The diverse factors that the present chapter has identified as helping to shape education do not claim to be exhaustive or definitive. They are primarily suggestions to broaden the way we study Islamic education. Moreover, they go some way along the road to explaining how we can distinguish between an educated middle-class culture—erudite, well-read—and *'ulama'* or establishment culture, to explain how this educated middle-class culture could emerge in a context that was to a large degree dominated by institutions of education that had their own rules, their methodologies, their classics, and their curriculum.

These factors can also help explain how various cultural dimensions, religious and nonreligious, developed and coexisted. One of the aims of this chapter is in fact to show that the educational system in general and the *madrasa* in particular, which we often tend to consider to be rigid and static, could in fact produce a range of options. In other words, the by-products of the system of religious education were not homogeneous. We can make a distinction between, on the one hand, education in an institution like the Azhar, highly specialized, requiring years of training with a professor and extensive reading of certain works, guided by the rules of scholarship that had developed over the centuries, and on the other hand a more general education that had broader and more varied concerns, that was not necessarily scholarly, and that was influenced by a variety of factors. The potential that the system provided was dependent upon the historical conditions of given moments.

4

Books and the Middle Class

THE CONDITIONS that allowed access to education and to a multiplication of the forms and channels for the transmission of knowledge in some form or other coincided, roughly chronologically, with a phenomenon of an entirely different nature that encouraged the transmission of knowledge through another channel, notably that of the book. This was a phenomenon of a material nature, affecting urban dwellers of Cairo as well as of other cities in the region by making the book more accessible to them. The filtering down of the book from the upper to the middle class also roughly coincided with a similar trend occurring in Europe at a somewhat earlier date and on a different scale. In Europe the spread of the book was linked to the printing press. But in the Middle East the printing press emerged much later, in the nineteenth century as far as Egypt was concerned. And yet important developments took place in Egypt's early modern period that allowed a greater access to the book among people belonging to the urban middle ranks. This fact means that we need to identify the conditions allowing the spread of the book to occur independently of the printing press.

These considerations entail questioning the standard way of separating the eighteenth and nineteenth centuries into the period before and the period after the printing press. As a matter of fact, the French cultural historian Roger Chartier has cast doubt on the idea that the introduction of the printing press, so important in the European chronology, had the same importance for the diffusion of the book everywhere, suggesting that in other cultures the written culture was spread by various other means.[1] The data we have for the book in the eighteenth century requires us to reconsider some issues and to find explanations other than the introduction of the printing press for the expansion in book production—in other words, to dissociate the spread of books from the introduction of printing. One cannot minimize the importance of the printing press as an agent in the diffusion of the book, but one nevertheless need not ignore major developments that took place before its introduction. One can therefore suggest that there was an intermediary stage, before the introduction of the printing press and of commercial printing, during which a significant spread of the book occurred.

Material Conditions

A voluminous literature on the spread of literacy and of the book in various countries like France, Italy, Germany, and England has in recent years brought to light the access of urban dwellers to the book and their impact on what was written. This phenomenon was linked to the growth of cities in Europe and to the introduction of the printing press.

It is important to try to understand the way that these trends developed beyond the political borders of Europe and to identify cross-border factors behind their spread. Peter Burke considered the commercialization of books to be in part a consequence of the spread of commercial capitalism, a factor that would have had a bearing on conditions in Cairo.[2] The issue, however, is a complex one and requires us to consider a number of factors.

The development of a book culture among a Cairene urban class that was neither part of the ruling class for whom books of an artistic quality were produced, nor of the religious establishment for whom books were linked to religious education, is a significant cultural phenomenon. Such a development had the potential to affect the actual production of the book as well as its content. The present chapter explores this trend and the consequences that it had for the book market and for the readers.

The development of a book culture was in fact the result of a combination of different factors. In the first place, ownership of books was obviously linked to economic means and to the ability to purchase them. Consequently, we cannot separate the involvement of many sectors of the urban middle class in commercial capitalism from their ability to spend money on nonessential commodities like books. In the second place, their level of literacy provided them with access to books. In the third place, and most importantly, there are indications that the price of books decreased significantly and that cheap books became easily available as of the latter part of the seventeenth century.

As mentioned above, the availability of books on a broad scale is generally associated with the printing press. Many works have studied the impact of the press, the voluminous output of the printed word that allowed for an unprecedented spread of the book because of its cheaper cost. But was the demand for the book the consequence or a reason for the invention of the printing press? The dominant view among historians of Egypt is that the press, a state initiative established under Muhammad 'Ali, was behind the increase in the demand for books in the nineteenth century. For the early modern period, this explanation will not do.

To understand why the book became a commodity that numerous members of the middle class could afford in the seventeenth and eighteenth centuries, other factors must be elaborated. One of these had to do with demand. Demand was a result of an urban middle class that had, over a certain period, enjoyed material comfort, literacy, and education. To fully understand how this demand was satisfied, one needs to consider some of the material factors that brought down the price of the book to a level that made it more accessible to a large number of people.

This interpretation has a number of advantages, because it sheds light on certain phenomena, occurring in the seventeenth and eighteenth centuries in Cairo and presumably in other cities like Aleppo, Damascus, and Istanbul, for which so far we have no satisfactory explanations: first, the large number of books copied; second, the number of oral texts that passed into writing; third, the language used in many of these texts; and fourth, the popular (nonscholarly) character of many texts written during the seventeenth and eighteenth centuries. Finally, it provides an explanation for another trend that historians working on court archives in the Ottoman world are familiar with, notably the fact that paper, in the form of written documents, has a special importance in this context. It is a well-known fact that for a deed or a document to be valid, Islamic law does not require it to be put down on paper and that oral testimony had legal weight as evidence in a court case. The oral contract, for instance, if it were witnessed by impartial witnesses, had sufficient legal weight. In case of a dispute, witnesses could be called to testify in favor of one or the other of the parties. Yet during the seventeenth century, a significant modification occurred in court procedures: the written document was frequently used as evidence that the court recognized. This fact provides one more piece of evidence that paper was becoming more widespread.

Time after time, court records show that not only were contracts and deeds recorded by court employees in their voluminous court books, but that the interested parties, often ordinary urban dwellers, had a copy of the document that they presented for evidence in case of a dispute. When, for instance, in 1141/1728 a Coptic woman named Mariam b. Yuhanna brought a case in the court of Bab 'Ali against her former husband, Shihada b. Sulayman, on an issue related to maintenance while she was still his wife, and their stories did not conform to each other, she brought out a court deed recently drawn up in the court of Qusun and it was read out loud, after which he showed a deed issued from the court of Al-Salih to prove his statements.[3] In other words, the written deed kept by the parties concerned was being used as evidence, not instead of oral witnesses but in addition to them. This meant that, whether or not people like Mariam b. Yuhanna could read, they were keeping documents liable to come in useful to them in their homes, documents related to their marriage, deeds of property, deeds related to loans—those documents that could be used to protect their rights in a law court. This not only tells us something about the way the legal system was being adapted to new conditions, but that the use of paper in the form of deeds and contracts was also widespread.

The study of the spread of books provides a good example of how a scholarly examination entirely concentrated on a small scale such as one locality or one community can be misleading, and how important it is for such studies to go beyond the local to the regional, especially insofar as cultural trends are concerned. Recently, a number of articles were published around the theme of literacy and books in the Ottoman Empire. Colette Establet and Jean-Paul Pascual, for instance, in an article entitled, "Les livres des gens à Damas vers 1700," showed that a certain number of "ordinary" people in Damascus left books in their legacies.[4] Their findings are confirmed by the work of Bernard Heyberger on the Christians in Syria and Lebanon in the seventeenth and eighteenth centuries.[5]

These individual studies, each of which concentrated on a particular town or locality, suggest the need to find a common explanation for a trend that cut across political or administrative borders. Otherwise one may reach misleading results. If, for instance, a study considers one particular community, one may be led to conclude that literacy and books were a feature of members of this particular community, such as the Christians in Syria and Lebanon for instance. It is only by seeing the larger picture that such a study can be understood in its proper context.

There is also a regional dimension to this issue. There has been a recent interest in the study of books and reading. Work about literacy and on private and public libraries has been done for Istanbul, Salonica, Damascus, Lebanon, and Albania, among other places. There has, however, not been any attempt to study this phenomenon beyond specific cities or towns, or beyond regional borders. Yet the fact that in several cities of the Ottoman Empire there was a significant expansion in the private ownership of books suggests that the trend cannot be explained by local conditions in Cairo, Damascus, or Istanbul, nor understood within limited spatial borders. One has to turn to broader explanations to understand the phenomenon as a whole.

The expansion in the number of manuscripts written during the period is easily apparent from a perusal of catalogues of manuscripts in collections in Cairo and elsewhere. The catalogues of collections of Arabic manuscripts in the Arab world, Turkey, Europe, and the United States list hundreds of thousands of Arabic manuscripts, many of which were written or copied in the early modern period, attesting to the importance of the book culture during that time. The perusal of these catalogues of manuscripts dispersed in many parts of the world would in itself constitute an interesting study to show periods of activity and changing tastes with regard to what was written. The major catalogues of manuscript collections illustrate the preponderance of manuscripts copied in the eighteenth century, regardless of when they were actually composed, their numbers by far exceeding those of any other period. The manuscripts cover many fields of learning: scientific works, literary works, histories and chronicles, and so on. One example is the Mamluk chronicles; most of those that have reached us are not datable to the Mamluk period but were copied during the Ottoman period. Likewise the majority of scientific manuscripts bearing the dates when they were copied are also from the seventeenth and eighteenth centuries, including many that were actually composed centuries earlier, a fact that David King's *A Catalogue of the Scientific Manuscripts in the Egyptian National Library* easily confirms.[6] There are more manuscripts in this catalogue dating from the eighteenth century, in the fields of astronomy and mathematics among others, than from all other periods put together.

The catalogue of the Bibiothèque Nationale in Paris, *Fonds arabe*, shows a similar pattern, with a predominance of manuscripts from the seventeenth and eighteenth centuries, in literary works, tales and anecdotes, histories and chronicles, thus confirming this to be a general pattern. A few examples taken from the voluminous catalogue of Arabic manuscripts can illustrate this trend. The catalogue, for instance, contains one hundred catalogue entries (numbered from 1465 to 1565) of its holdings in universal histories. Of these, more than a third (thirty-seven out of one hundred) were copied in the seventeenth and eighteenth centuries (eighteen manuscripts in the seventeenth century, nineteen manuscripts in the eighteenth century). This pattern is repeated in other subjects. The catalogue lists twenty-three erotic manuscripts (nos. 3051 to 3074), of which twenty-two are dated or datable. The dates are distributed as follows: two from the fifteenth century, four from the sixteenth century, four from the seventeenth century, eleven from the eighteenth century, and one from the nineteenth century. Thus half of them were written or copied in the eighteenth century. Likewise, the catalogue's holdings in poetry (nos. 3075–3272) repeat the same pattern: 102 of 197 manuscripts (more than half) were copied in the seventeenth and eighteenth centuries.[7] These figures are indicative of a trend.

A parallel intensification in the copying of books can be observed with regard to the Christian manuscripts of the Coptic community in Cairo. Magdi Girgis's work suggests that there was a proliferation of Coptic and other Christian manuscripts that were ordered and financed by the Coptic civilian elite (rather than by the religious establishment of the Coptic Church), who had become very wealthy during this period. His research in Coptic manuscript catalogues showed that about 50 percent of all manuscripts were copied during the eighteenth century, and that this trend could be found not only in Cairo but in Upper Egypt as well. Thus Magdi Girgis, using different sources than those I used, came to similar conclusions. Notably, he has shown that a great movement in manuscript copying and in the translation of Ethiopian and Assyrian works was taking place in the eighteenth century. Presumably the same underlying factors were behind the multiplication of manuscripts copied during this period.[8]

The findings of Magdi Girgis in the Coptic archives are confirmed by a recent publication of illustrations from the Coptic manuscripts in the libraries of the Coptic Patriarchate, the Coptic Museum, and various churches and monasteries. This publication shows that many of these illustrations date from the period we are talking about: the seventeenth and to a larger extent the eighteenth centuries. It thus confirms that this period stands out with regard to the extent of written production. It also shows various levels of quality, from simple black-and-white drawings to high-quality illustrations with a lot of gold.[9]

The same impressions can be drawn from probate records. These deeds mention books, described in some detail with regard to titles, numbers, and prices, so we get an idea of the frequency of private libraries, the value of the books, and their sizes. Because these court records are so numerous over a long period, we can also observe the directions in which book ownership develops between early seventeenth and late eighteenth centuries. Here again, the number and the frequency of these libraries lead us to reach the same conclusion: that by around mid-seventeenth century the book was becoming more readily available to a larger number of people.

The repercussions of this trend can be observed at many levels. Figures from probate records indicate a clear increase in the number of people who owned private libraries between the beginning of the seventeenth century and the middle of the eighteenth century. A perusal of probate records for the ten-year period 1600–1610 in the courts of Qisma 'Askariyya, where the division of inheritances of the military was undertaken, and in the court of Qisma 'Arabiyya, which undertook the same function for civilians, revealed 73 private libraries. In the eighteenth century, this figure increased drastically: from 1703 to 1714 the records showed 102 private libraries (an increase of one-third in about a century); from 1730 to 1740 the records show another dramatic increase: 190 private libraries. Toward mid-century, as the economic crisis started to be felt, a decrease in private libraries became apparent, and the ten-year period of 1749–59 showed a reduction to 102 libraries.

TABLE I

Number of Private Libraries and the Books They Contain

Date	No. of libraries	No. of books[a]
1600–1610	73	2,427
1703–1714	102	3,535
1730–1740	190	5,991
1749–1759	102	2,077

[a] The number of books is not always indicated; in some cases, the only indication given is that books were included in the property of the deceased. Consequently, these figures are considerably lower than the reality.

The figures are significant, especially if we keep in mind that inheritance cases were taken to court only when disputes arose among heirs or if the heirs were minors. Individuals who owned books could bequeath them to a *waqf*; thus books would not be mentioned in their inheritance. Consequently the true number of books in people's homes must have been much larger.

Likewise, the total amounts of money that these books in private ownership were valued at (taking into consideration only those where the price was indicated) also added up to large sums of money.

TABLE 2
Total Value of Books in Given Years

Years	Total value of books (in *nisfs*)
1600–1610	365,964
1703–1714	332,220
1730–1740	797,703
1749–1759	600,706

Reasons for the Expansion of Books and Libraries

To explain such an expansion, we must make some inferences. With regard to paper, for instance, we must infer not only that it was readily available, but also that its price was relatively accessible. These points are best understood in relation to paper production and paper trade.

Little or no research exists about the paper used in the Arab lands in the seventeenth and eighteenth centuries. We know that paper was produced in Egypt in the Middle Ages. Papermaking was subsequently introduced into Europe, and Italian paper was first imported to the Middle East in the mid-thirteenth century. It is generally thought that local production of paper declined sometime in the fourteenth century and that paper was subsequently imported from Venice. Between the fourteenth and the fifteenth centuries, locally manufactured paper was therefore replaced, in most Arabic-speaking lands, by Italian paper.[10]

When paper was first introduced into Europe, production was limited. Following the introduction of the printing press, however, a great increase in demand for paper resulted in a spread of this industry to regions that had had no papermaking before, and eventually in technological developments in the seventeenth century.[11] These developments not only increased the production of paper but also decreased its price. Book production could benefit precisely because of this trend in Cairo and other cultural centers in regions where the printing press was established at a later date.

To understand the reasons behind the voluminous number of manuscripts of the seventeenth and especially of the eighteenth centuries, which today fill the major collections of Arabic manuscripts, we need to consider the availability of quantities of cheap paper. This period is poorly researched in relation to the trade and production of paper. It is evident, however, that different qualities, and presumably different prices, of paper were available. Some paper was of high quality. The paper used in the registers of court records is thick and solid; it has survived well over the centuries and probably represented an expensive paper. Yet a look at the descriptions furnished in catalogues of Arabic manuscripts suggests this quality was not always the case. Once in a while, such descriptions mention the poor quality of paper of a particular manuscript.

In the seventeenth and eighteenth centuries, Egypt was importing paper from Europe, Italy (both Venice and Genoa), and then France.[12] It was consequently benefiting from the relatively cheap production costs evolving because of the developments in paper production taking place in Italy and Holland and the expansion of paper production. As a matter of fact, paper became cheaper in Europe in the seventeenth century as a consequence of new production techniques following the invention and spread of the printing press and the increased demand for books. The cheap paper produced in Europe was, by the end of the seventeenth and the beginning of the eighteenth centuries, finding its way to Egypt, and it most likely found its way to other cities that had trading relations with Europeans. Thus, even though the printing press was only introduced in Cairo at a relatively late date, imported paper was cheaper than it had been in the fifteenth century.

There were other sources for paper, both local and imported, with which we are not yet familiar. A recent study by Nasir 'Uthman on paper and writing guilds in Cairo identified, on the basis of the seventeenth-century court records, some sixteen different categories of paper in use. Some were identified by their provenance (Venice, Genoa, Rumi, and local). Other qualifications (*waraq laff, waraq laff baladi, waraq Rumi abu ibriq*) we are not yet in a position to identify.[13] Yet it is significant, for our purposes, to realize that multiple sources of paper, and presumably various levels of paper quality, were available. Although the study of paper trading patterns with India does not seem to have aroused any scholarly interest, archival sources suggest that some Indian paper was used in Cairo.[14] Paper was in principle imported, but certain references suggest that part of the processing was done locally. Little research has been done on this prolongation of paper production beyond the fifteenth century. Some local paper was identified in the Geniza collections of the second quarter of the sixteenth century, but the majority of the Geniza documents of this period were on European paper.[15] Local production in the seventeenth and eighteenth centuries is attested to by the individual cases brought to the *qadi*. The documents indicate that a guild for smoothers of papers (*saqqalin waraq*) existed and that its members used both local paper (*waraq baladi*) and what they called *rumi* paper, presumably imported from somewhere in the Ottoman lands. André Raymond's list of guilds in 1801 confirms the existence of a guild for *lisseurs de papier* (paper polishers).[16]

What is described as the decline of local paper production should not be considered its final disappearance. There may have been a decline in the quality of the paper or in the quantities produced without necessarily entailing a total disappearance of the local industry. This local industry, which still needs to be researched, may have provided the market with paper of lesser quality, which would have considerably reduced its export markets but which continued to be demanded locally. The existence of this local industry is supported by references in contemporary sources, such as a reference, in 1144/1731, to a *matbakh waraq* (paper factory) located in Khatt Jami' al-Azhar, Suwayqat al-Shaykh Hamuda,[17] and to many references to *waraq baladi* (local paper). Frequent references in catalogues of collections of Arabic manuscripts of this period as to the poor quality of the paper used may have referred to a local paper. The indications of a local industry are clear, but no information exists about the volume of local production.

The fact that book ownership was spreading in Cairo can be understood in the context of the extensive paper production in Europe that followed the founding of the printing press. This spread was not limited to Cairo. As a matter of fact, Colette Establet and Jean-Paul Pascual found evidence for the spread of books with regard to Damascus. Their research in inheritance records in Damascus shows that a significant number of merchants (textile merchants and soap merchants mainly) as well as artisans (textile craftsmen such as cloth-dyers and tailors) owned books. Establet and Pascual estimated that one house in five in Damascus around 1700 had books.[18] For such a trend to occur, one can surmise that the production of books was not entirely a luxury production, and that at least some books could be cheaply produced. Likewise, Alexander Russell's comments on eighteenth-century Aleppo are indicative. A careful observer, Russell, who spent a long time in Aleppo in the mid-eighteenth century, noted that in his time a large number of wealthy merchants had taken up collecting books, so much so that the price of manuscripts had gone up.[19] This trend can probably be explained, at least in part, by the same reasons that applied to Cairo. The book was unlikely to have reached tailors, cloth-dyers, and other middle-ranking artisans and tradesmen without the spread of cheap paper. The seventeenth century witnessed another related phenomenon in Istanbul, notably the emergence of a large number of public libraries, initiated by the grand vizir Mehmed Pasha Koprulu (1656–61) and continued by several other grand personages.[20] The existence of these libraries too points to the realization that more books were available to a larger public.

Another aspect of the production of inexpensive books was the fact that there was a large number of copyists who could benefit from the conditions examined above in relation to paper. The organization of these copyists into a guild is suggested by al-Jabarti, but no such guild is mentioned in the list of guilds that the members of the French administration prepared in 1801.[21] However, the repeated references to copying and copyists suggest that even if such a guild existed, much copying was undertaken by people who were not part of the guild—teachers, students, tradesmen, or shopkeepers trying to make ends meet, especially at times when demand for books was on the high side. For some, copying was a secondary source of income, an additional activity they undertook together with their main activity. At other times, those who could not obtain a salary from a pious foundation, or who faced a job shortage, were attracted to the profession of copyist on a temporary or part-time level.

The large volume of seventeenth- and eighteenth-century manuscripts that have survived in numerous collections suggests that many people were involved in writing and copying these manuscripts. We can follow some of the more prominent copyists like Shaykh Muhammad b. Salim al-Hifnawi al-Shafi'i al-Khalwati, who in time of dire need resorted to copying books in order to survive, or Shaykh Husayn al-Mahalli al-Shafi'i (d. 1170/1756), a learned jurist who also had great expertise in arithmetic and the division of inheritance and who authored many works in the religious sciences, including a compendious work on the branches of law in the Shafi'i school of law. To enhance his income, he copied and sold books in a bookshop he owned near the Azhar.[22]

Another factor to be included in the equation is in relation to copying and copyists. The historian al-Jabarti indicates that some copyists were making use of writing techniques intended to increase the speed of production. Shaykh Ramadan al-Khawaniki (d. 1158/1745) used a technique of making multiple copies of his works, presumably for sale; to make several copies of a book at the same time, he copied the same page several times over so that he finished four or five copies. It is clear that the objective of the copier was speed and efficiency rather than aesthetic quality. It is also clear that these copyists made a distinction between quality work and commercial work. Shaykh Mustafa al-Khayyat (d. 1203/1788), a tailor by profession, copied almanacs that included festivals, feasts, new moons, and the Coptic calendar; he made some high-quality copies for elites (*khassa*) and ordinary copies for commoners (*'amma*), a clear suggestion that he was using a commercial technique for copying.[23]

Ultimately the result of this trend was that a relatively limited number of books was produced for quality, using high-quality paper and calligraphy, while a large number of books was intended for the kind of commerce that did not look for artistic quality. The combination of these factors had two consequences. First, it meant the production of a book that was, in relative terms, cheap. Second, it meant that the book could become the object of trade, rather than of patronage or of religious instruction only. The available prices of books confirm this trend. No wonder that the quality of the manuscripts produced declined. Catalogues of Arabic manuscripts often comment on the poor quality of writing: "The writing is a coarse and ugly Egyptian hand," or "Negligent Egyptian Naskhi."[24] This "decline" may be the result of the fact that these books were commercially produced and were intended for larger numbers of people rather than for the few. It probably also indicates that much of the copying was not supervised by the guild and perhaps was not undertaken by guild members who had undergone the necessary training and had learned the various forms of calligraphy. Rather, it was the work of persons who did not attempt to follow the "proper" rules of writing and calligraphy.

This "decline" did not affect all levels of writing or of book production. High-quality calligraphy continued to be in demand, especially in the eighteenth century when the Mamluks were accumulating large fortunes and creating a demand for luxurious and high-quality books. The new feature in the scene was therefore not so much the disappearance of high-quality books as it was the appearance of lesser-quality ones.

Book Prices

The price of a book was a major factor in its accessibility. Book prices seem to have decreased significantly during the latter part of the seventeenth century. At the end of the sixteenth century, for instance, a Syrian *qadi* employed in Egyptian courts complained about the price that books fetched in Cairo. "Books in Cairo cost three times as much as they do in Damascus," wrote Muhibb al-Din al-Muhibbi in a letter to his friend Shaykh Isma'il in 1580, a difference that might be linked to the price of paper.[25] Price was an issue then more than it was later.

One can discern the evolution of book prices between then and the later period through the probate records, a rich source for the price of books. At the death of a person, his or her books were often sold or auctioned in the book market and the proceeds were divided among the heirs. The prices that this source provides are thus the sale price for used books.

TABLE 3
Book Prices by Date from Probate Records[a]

Price Ranges in *Nisfs*	1600–1610	1703–1714	1730–1740	1749–1759	Total
1–30	723	1459	2322	898	5402
31–100	616	991	1692	504	3803
101–300	391	527	882	286	2086
301–500	98	130	197	61	486
501–1000	45	62	155	58	320
1001–10,000	37	45	105	51	238
over 10,000	0	0	1	0	1

[a] No. of probate records consulted: 1600–1610: 25; 1703–1714: 53; 1730–1740: 103; 1749–1759: 46; total: 227.

These prices indicate, in the first place, that the range of prices was very wide: the cheapest books sold at thirty *nisfs* or less; what were probably short treatises were often sold as cheaply as five to ten *nisfs*; the most expensive, several hundred times more (some eleven thousand *nisfs*), was in the possession of one of the *'ulama'*. The prices also show that the majority of books were in the lower price ranges. Only a few books (238 of a total of 12,562 books for which the price was available, or just under 2 percent) were in the range of 1,000 to

10,000 *nisfs*, a price that suggests luxury production, in terms of the quality of the paper and the calligraphy as well as the inclusion of illuminations. But the largest number of books were those in the price category of up to thirty *nisfs* (5,402 of the 12,562, or about 43 percent). These figures are telling, because they provide further confirmation of the fact that a cheap book had been made available, that there was a large price difference between the luxurious book intended for a certain class and the ordinary book that used inexpensive paper and was written in a plain way.

The price differences could be a consequence of the condition of the book, the quality of the paper, the quality of the calligraphy, the presence of illuminations, or the size of the book, all of which we cannot ascertain from court records. The wide range of prices, however, does indicate that not all of them were luxury manuscripts. Art historians, as a matter of fact, note that the great tradition of illustrated manuscripts had declined tremendously by this time.

In the second place, the same titles appear in a wide variety of prices. This variety could be an indication of the condition or appearance of the book, a fact that we cannot ascertain. But we also know that the books produced were aimed at a particular class of readership, that is, for those who either could or could not afford luxuriously produced texts. The private libraries mentioned in probate records show that certain books, like the works of al-Sha'rani or *Dala'il al-Khairat*, a Sufi prayer book, were to be found in a large number of these libraries, those of the ruling groups as well as those of tradesmen and craftsmen. These records also show that *Dala'il* existed in cheap copies, in medium-priced copies, and in expensive copies. The lower-priced copies were sold for as little as ten or fifteen *nisfs* and the better-quality ones, presumably copies that were illuminated in expensive materials, for several hundred *nisfs*. The same situation prevailed for the works of 'Abd al-Wahab al-Sha'rani (d. 1565), the Sufi leader and founder of a *tariqa* (Sufi brotherhood), whose great popularity continued well into the eighteenth century. Copies of Sha'rani's work were available in a wide range of prices, and it was found in the libraries of diverse social groups.

Prior to this development, books had been produced either for patronage or for scholars and students, or had been ordered by persons of means. In both cases, someone who wanted a book had to have it specially copied. In one of the letters that Qadi Muhibb al-Din al-Muhibbi addressed to Shaykh 'Ali al-Maliki in 1572, he wrote, "Shaykh Isma'il has repeatedly asked for a copy of Ibn Habib's history and he keeps sending reminders insisting that we have a copy of this book ordered and sent to him. I have commissioned a copyist to go ahead, but in the meantime, please contact Sidi 'Ali al-Qudsi and ask him to give you volume one."[26] It could have been a long wait and taken various contacts here and there before Shaykh Isma'il eventually got his book.

This little incident occurred toward the latter part of the sixteenth century, at a time when this was one of the few ways to get a new book, but ordering copies of books nevertheless remained a common practice until much later. By and large, many of the books produced (composed or copied) were intended for use by *'ulama'* and their students and did not per se form part of the book market. Many more books were produced *sur commande* by members of the ruling class. As the Mamluk ruling class rose to positions of wealth, with the consolidation of their households many of them came to own private libraries containing large numbers of books. Probate records confirm that their books sometimes were worth considerable sums of money, some 82,000 *nisfs* worth of books in 'Uthman Katkhuda's (d. 1736) library, for instance.[27] The luxury production of books, which required the use of expensive material—gold for illuminations, the use of precious or semiprecious stones to decorate the binding, the time and effort of high-quality calligraphy—all these required financing that the copyists alone could not undertake. Therefore patronage for such works remained a dominant incentive for book production through the eighteenth century.

The level of activity of the book trade, which had its center near the Azhar, may be estimated on the basis of those who undertook it. A deed dated 1155/1742 in the court register of Bab 'Ali gives an idea of the level of activity in the book trade. The deed refers to the selection of the head of the guild of book merchants, a selection that the guild members approved. Their names are given. The head of the guild was referred to as *min a'yan al-tujjar fil kutub*, an honorific title typically reserved for long-distance trade merchants that consequently reflected the importance of this person and of his wealth. That a book merchant should have such a title can be taken as a reflection on the book trade itself during this period. In addition to the guild head, sixteen other book merchants centered their activities in Suq al-Kutub; thus a total of seventeen book merchants functioned in one place, an indication of the level of activity in this domain.[28] They were the ones that the *qadi* consulted in case he needed to have the private library of a deceased person sold.

The Consequences of the Spread of Reading

Nevertheless book production for the market, even if it remained a limited portion of the total books produced, added a new element to the picture. Although texts intended for the scholarly community, teachers, and students by far dominated book production, the fact that so many people who were not in the scholarly world owned books suggests that a portion of book production was intended for commercial purposes.

How such a situation could have a bearing on what was produced, in terms of content or subject matter, in terms of quality, and in terms of volume or number, is a subject of importance to the historian. I have suggested elsewhere that the appearance of a "popular" kind of historical chronicle during this period, distinct from the standard chronicles in its style, its language, and in part its context, may have been a consequence of the spread of reading to circles outside that of *'ulama'*.[29] The matter is well worth pursuing, not only for the history of the book and book production before the introduction of the printing press, but also, and this is more important in relation to the present study, for what it tells us of the people or the society for whom this production was intended or of those who produced the books.

One can detect trends in terms of who owned which books. Occasionally the books were directly linked to a person's profession. A physician named 'Abdul-Rahman al-Shami al-Hakim owned eighteen small medical books priced at fifty *nisfs*, while a spice and herb trader who had a shop in Khatt al-Fahamin had two medical books that might be of help in his professional activity.[30] A more frequent trend was for certain books to be found in many libraries: for instance, small cheap books of prayers—a fifteen-*nisf* book of prayer that Shaykh Muhammad *al-qabbani* (weigher of goods) left at his death in 1151/1738—or a Quran priced at 120 *nisfs*—like the copy that was the only book in the inheritance of 'Abdul-Fattah b. Yusuf (*battati*), a weaver of a special kind of textile. Heyworth-Dunne noted that the most popular books among merchants, shopkeepers, and artisans were Sufi tracts and Sufi literary works. He considered that the multitude of Sufi orders that had emerged in the eighteenth century had played a role in shaping literary tastes.[31] This popularity of Sufi books is a significant dimension of the history of eighteenth-century Sufism, and one that should be taken into consideration in studies of its development.

Dala'il al-Khairat, a Best Seller

The popularity of Sufi works such as the prayer almanacs that indicated the times for prayer and that were sold in large numbers is confirmed by other sources. One work in particular comes close to what we can call a best seller in the language of today, notably the book that everyone had, that could be found in many libraries at a great range of prices, from very cheap to very expensive. The work was entitled *Dala'il al-Khairat*, a short Sufi book of prayers.[32] Private libraries in the eighteenth century indicate that it was copied again and again, perhaps more than any other book in the eighteenth century, and was found in a large number of these libraries. Al-Jabarti provides notices for at least three scribes who specialized in making copies of *Dala'il*, proof of its enormous popularity and of its commercial viability: people made a living from copying out *Dala'il*. Al-Jabarti's necrology of 1187/1773 refers to a scribe, Isma'il b. 'Abdul-Rahman, who specialized in *Dala'il al-Khairat*, of which he made innumerable copies. Al-Jabarti also includes the necrology of Shaykh Ahmad 'Abdalla al-Rumi al-Misri (d. 1195/1780), who was also a copier of *Dala'il*; Isma'il Afandi (d. 1211/1796) earned his living by selling coffee beans in a shop near Khan al-Khalili and by copying the Quran and *Dala'il al-Khairat*.[33] Clearly these instances indicate the presence of a commercialized kind of production, one in which the producer knew beforehand that his commodity had a buyer so that he would not be left with unsold goods on his hands. They also indicate that the spread of the book brought about a certain cultural leveling: members of different social classes read the same texts.

Inheritance records confirm that by the mid-eighteenth century *Dala'il* could be found more than any other work in private libraries. One in every five libraries, whether small or large, had a copy of *Dala'il al-Khairat*. Wealthy Mamluks had one or several copies; shaykhs and *'ulama'* had copies; artisans and craftsmen had copies. Thus among the social class who could afford books, *Dala'il* was prominent. Among people who had very few books, *Dala'il* was likely to be among them. Its use in eighteenth-century Aleppo is attested by the *waqfiyya* of Hajj Musa Al-Amiri: the deed indicates that a salary was paid to a man who would be reading it daily in the founder's mosque, an indication of the way that tastes and fashions traveled between Egypt and Syria.[34] One could find the same popularity with other types of books that emerged with some popularity during the period; lives of saints, books of magical figures, and prayer almanacs appeared in numbers.

It does not follow that everyone who owned a copy of *Dala'il al-Khairat* actually read it. Some owners might have done so, while others could have used it for reading out loud in a home or family context; others owned it as a blessing to the house, perhaps without reading it, especially if it were the only book that they owned; some might have memorized and recited parts of it.

Thus, for this popular book, the way the owners used it might have varied as widely as their social and educational background. Yet the very fact that this particular book was so widely read is in itself of some significance.

Reading Habits

People who owned books were not the only ones to know what was in them; books reached many more people because of the habit of reading books out loud.[35] If there were one literate person in the house, he could read out loud to the other family members. The English traveler Edward Brown, who came to Egypt in 1673–74, mentioned reading out loud as being commonplace, with people listening in their leisure time.[36] This habit, if it were as widespread as he suggests, could have played a role in the spoken word's penetrating the written word. Collective reading dates from an earlier period. Boaz Shoshan notes that in fifteenth-century Cairo, popular literature was recited publicly rather than read privately, mainly because few people could read.[37]

Moreover, the figures for private libraries suggest a clear progression in ownership of books among members of low- or middle-ranking religious positions, among tradesmen and artisans, among people whose profession is not indicated and who consequently were very unlikely to belong to the ruling establishment.

As ownership of books became more widespread and reached a larger readership, as books entered the homes of many people, other forms of reading were adopted. The material ease with which certain books could be obtained and the spread of the private ownership of books brought about a change in attitudes toward reading and in the way that a book was read. Traditionally, books were read with a teacher or out loud. The shaykh was central to the transmission of knowledge, because students normally read texts with their shaykhs. Students boasted of the shaykhs they had studied with, and the biography of a learned person was based on the teachers he had studied with and—if he were lucky enough—the students to whom he transmitted his knowledge, thus forming a chain.

Reading could also be a collective exercise under the supervision of a shaykh in a more or less formal setting. This student-teacher relationship could develop within the educational institutions or in an informal way. Al-Jabarti tells us about students who were the disciples of his father, Shaykh Hasan al-Jabarti, coming to live in the house for years so that they could be in constant touch with him. Implicit in this form of transmission was that the shaykh guided the student's readings, directing him toward a fuller understanding of a text but within the shaykh's guidelines. Once the book became an article of trade, a commodity available at a price that not only the ruling class but also the merchant, tradesman, shaykh of a guild, and so on could afford to buy, a new element was introduced to this relationship. Books could be read, enjoyed, and understood by an individual without any particular guidance. Private reading can thus be linked to a greater access of the book. This does not mean that private reading was nonexistent prior to this time, but that it was not as well regarded or as widespread. Elizabeth Sartain notes in her study of Jalal al Din al-Suyuti that private reading at the end of the fifteenth century was still considered to be negative; one of al-Suyuti's critics, Ibn al-Karaki, hurled criticism at him to the effect that "we study under shaykhs while you read books alone."[38] Suyuti's extensive reading was sneered at by al-Sakhawi and Ibn al-Karaki because of the belief that books could be misunderstood unless a qualified teacher explained them.

That these eighteenth-century conditions continued to raise concern among the community of scholars is evident. Such concern arises from advice to students written in 1155/1742: "[D]o not hesitate to read the Maqamat of al-Hariri but do so on under the guidance of a shaykh who will explain its meanings. This work will be the dessert of the meal."[39]

Yet the development of a book market and the accessibility of books to a broad readership seem to have affected attitudes toward books and to have brought about a more reconciliatory attitude toward the changing realities. Toward the latter part of the eighteenth century, with the changes in production of books that brought about cheaper and more accessible versions, attitudes toward the book and toward private reading seem to have undergone a change. A couple of literary sources praise individual reading very highly. One of them is an anonymous compilation of stories and anecdotes entitled *Anis al-Jalis* (dated 1187/1773) in which a person finds consolation from the ills of the world when he turns to books: "Better are books than people, they keep you from being lonely." One *hakim* (wise man or scholar) went to visit another and said to him, "You must be very lonely." The wise man answered, "I am not lonely because I have a thousand scholars and poets to talk to: Galinos, Socrates, Plato, the Bible. Some of these books I study, some I converse with, and with some I argue." He was talking of a very personal relationship with books: his reading was a private affair.[40]

This attitude was also expressed by certain very prominent religious figures whom we would not necessarily expect to be receptive to such ideas. Among them was Muhammad al-Mahdi, shaykh of Azhar at the end of the eighteenth century and author of a book of anecdotes. One of his tales talks about a certain young Abdul-Rahman al-Iskandar, who has lost both parents and who in spite of the fortune he inherited was despondent and lost. Not knowing what to do with himself, he took the advice of a shaykh who had been his father's friend. The advice given to him was to go to the book market and buy books on history and literature, because they would help him structure his life (another indication as to the existence of a market for books). The book was thus a remedy for certain ills, a cure for this man's grief. J. J. Marcel, who translated this work into French (there is no evidence of the original manuscript), did not bother to translate the list of books that Abdul-Rahman actually bought because it was too long.[41]

Thus the transformations brought about by material conditions had resulted in a new relationship between the individual and the book. One could conclude that there was a link between these new mental attitudes and the spread of cheap paper.

Consequences for the Middle Class

What clearly emerges from the rich source of probate records is that book ownership was far from being a prerogative of the *'ulama'* or scholarly class.

A few members of the middle class owned books at the start of the seventeenth century. During the first decade of the century (1600–1610) around 12 percent of the libraries found in probate records belonged to members of the middle class, those in religious professions as well as tradesmen and artisans. This percentage was to increase in the course of the following century. Of 102 libraries in 1703–14, 10 belong to merchants and 17 to artisans (spice traders, weighers of goods, jewelers), meaning that 27 of 92, or about a third, belonged to an economically active population; 14 belonged to *afandis* or bureaucrats. By contrast, this sample includes 15 persons in religious professions such as *'ulama'*, *imam* of a mosque, employee in the court, and so forth. This is far from being an overwhelming presence of the religious classes. The same is true for the ten-year period 1730–40: of 190 libraries, 36 belonged to merchants and artisans; of these 12 were owned by *tujjar*, 24 by artisans (weighers of goods, spice traders, silk makers and other textile workers), 45 by *amirs*, 12 by *'ulama'*, 23 by other religious professionals, and 18 by *afandis* or bureaucrats. For the ten-year period 1749–59, out of 102 libraries, 15 were owned by *tujjar*, 14 by artisans (weighers of goods, coffee traders, sugar traders, millers); 17 by *amirs*, 7 by *'ulama'*, 12 by *afandis*, and 12 by other religious professionals such as *qadis*. (These figures relate to the people who left books when they died but does not take into consideration the size of the library or the number of books it contained.)

TABLE 4
Professions of People Who Owned Libraries

Date	1600–1610	1700–1714	1730–1740	1749–1759	Total
Military	14	10	45	18	87
Afandi	8	14	19	12	53
Merchant	9	10	12	15	46
'Ulama	33	6	13	7	59
Middle-rank *'ulama*	2	9	23	12	46
Craftsman	5	17	24	14	60
Woman	1	0	5	0	6
No profession[a]	1	36	47	24	108
Total	73	102	188	102	465

[a] People with no profession—addressed simply as *hajj*, *shaykh*, or *muhtaram*, meaning "respected"—were certainly ordinary urban dwellers rather than military or religious dignitaries, because these were always addressed with their full titles. Thus the numerous people with no profession (108) almost certainly belonged to the middle ranks.

In Europe, the printing press had had the same consequences, with books reaching the ordinary person, the trader, the artisan as never before. In France, where extensive scholarship has been done on this subject, a growing number of private libraries are evident from the fifteenth century. On the basis of inheritance records, Pierre Aquilon found that for the period 1480–1530, artisans and merchants were becoming book owners in Avignon, in Rouen, in Aix-en-Provence, although the number of books they owned was small; sometimes their libraries contained only three or four books. Libraries had moved from monasteries and cathedrals to colleges and universities, from the ownership of princes and notables to that of more ordinary people who were not linked to the establishment.⁴² In other words, for different reasons and with a different chronology, the same trend had spread over a large region.

In social terms, these figures can be read in different ways. In all cases, the picture we get from these records is a complex one. The number of people constituting part of the urban middle class who had books in their houses is significant, whether they were merchants, tradesmen, or artisans practicing a variety of activities. The picture challenges the dominant views that books were rare before the printing press, that only scholars and princes could own or read them, and that the middle class could afford them only as of the nineteenth century. Moreover, when there were books in a house, it was not only the owner who had access to them. Other family members were likely to use them too, either by reading them or by listening to them, since reading out loud seems to have been a common practice.

Probate records include among book owners merchants and the members of the more prosperous crafts. Many of the trades mentioned in the period 1749–59, for instance, were directly or indirectly linked to international commerce: the sugar producers (*sukkari*), the coffee trader (rather than coffee merchant) (*bannan*), the spice trader (*'attar*), the weigher of goods (*qabbani*). Many other book owners practiced trades that were not directly linked to the world of international commerce. Hajj Ahmad b. Sulayman al-Sharshuhi was a miller (*mudawlab fil tawahin*); the books he owned, which included among other works the *Khitat* of al-Maqrizi, the *Mizan* of al-Sha'rani, and al-Suyuti's *Husn al-Muhadara*, added up to 3,500 *nisfs*. Producers of luxury goods often made good revenues by catering to the demands of the wealthy aristocracy, which was, in the eighteenth century, expanding its fortunes. Shaykh 'Abdul-Rahman al-'Inani, for instance, a jeweler in Khan Hamzawi, left a little library that included copies of *Dala'il al-Khairat* and *Maqamat al-Hariri*, another very popular work.⁴³ In other words, a variety of people engaged in economic activities were being incorporated into a reading public.

Court cases indicate that the middle ranks of the religious establishment—that is, shaykhs who were not *'ulama'*—also had some access to book ownership. Court employees such as the scribes who recorded in the court registers the cases that appeared in front of the *qadi* had, because of the nature of their work, a great familiarity with the law and legal practice, but were by no means either persons of great wealth or among the top layers of the establishment. They often figured among book owners. Shaykh Daud b. Shaykh Makram Allah, the chief scribe of the court of Bab al-Sa'da wal Kharq (*rayyis al-kuttab bi mahkama babi al-Sa'da wal Kharq*), had in his inheritance forty books that were priced at 500 *nisfs*. Another court scribe, this time in the court of Bab 'Ali, Shaykh Muhammad al-Maqdisi b. Ya'qub al-Hanbali, also owned a little library among which could be found the classic *Dala'il al-Khairat*.[44] Men who practiced other modest religious professions, such as *wa'iz* or *miqati*, also occasionally left a few books in their inheritances.

From a broader perspective, the fact that so many people in the middle ranks had books does not allow us to conclude that all or even the majority of the middle class owned or read books. Book owners might have constituted the more prosperous members of this class and the more educated among them, those who could both read and whose means allowed them to spend money on nonessentials. Yet because of their weight in numbers by comparison to the ruling class—military or religious—the middle ranks were potentially of some significance in terms of a market. In good times, when the coffee trade was flourishing, for instance, and cheap paper had become widespread, the value of books owned by members of middle ranks—craftsmen, shaykhs, *'ulama'* in middle-ranking positions, or even people whose professions were not indicated—could represent a significant portion of the total value of books in the probate records of a given period. For the period 1730–40, of a total book value of 797,703 *nisfs* in the legacies of deceased persons, 172,503 *nisfs* formed the share of members in the middle ranks; that share is between one-fifth and one-quarter of the whole. This proportion had decreased by 1749–59, as economic conditions became less favorable, to less than one-sixth: 95,393 *nisfs* out of a total of 600,706 *nisfs*. Thus the influence of these people in terms of a market was not negligible, a factor that could have had an impact on the content of books.

The Changing Equation

The introduction of the printing press under Muhammad 'Ali had important social and cultural consequences. It brought about a greater diffusion of books than had ever been possible before, especially as commercial presses emerged. Books became much cheaper and were thus made available to many more people, a situation intensified by the reforms in the school system and the consequent spread of literacy among large numbers of people.

Yet these facts should not blind us to some very important changes that occurred before the printing press, nor should it blind us to diverse and complex consequences that the changes brought about. There were social consequences, for example. With the spread of books and the emergence of new ways of reading them, a new element was introduced into the balance between the educated middle class and the religious educational establishment. To the professor and his student reading a book together, and to the emir enjoying a beautifully illuminated literary work, one can add a growing sphere of people who were neither establishment scholars nor princes; who read different kinds of books; who read them in a different way; and who might be able to choose the books they wanted to read without the guidance of the institutional setup and the professors who supervised students' readings. Together with the various cultural forums that were available, the book provided one additional channel for the transmission of learning that could be reached both inside institutions and independently of them. Books may, as a result, have been a factor in developing an "educated" middle class distinct from the scholarly class.

The diffusion of the book introduced certain complexities into the picture, adding new dimensions to the relationships between the different social groups. At one level, the fact that members of different classes, of different levels of wealth, and with vast differences in education read the same books brought about a kind of social and cultural leveling among groups that were otherwise diverse. At another level, the written word became a sphere where different interests, different cultural trends, and different trends of thought could emerge. Prevailing conditions at any given time would determine the space that the middle class could have in this arena. Moreover, what the spread of books meant was that a greater diffusion of power could take place, that groups other than scholars could use the written word as a vehicle of expression. The degree to which this diffusion of power actually occurred will be discussed in the following chapters.

Furthermore, these developments signaled a greater possibility for the middle class to develop its intellectual potential while becoming autonomous to a certain degree from the religious establishment. The greater availability of books opened a channel that they could potentially use as a form of expression. A certain number of people whose culture had been essentially an oral one could thus be integrated into a written culture.

On the other hand, the production of inexpensive books brought about adaptations of subject matter to the new readership. That the book should become more accessible in terms of language, style, or subject matter was a normal outcome of prevailing conditions. The spread of literacy and of reading, of a book culture in milieus that were neither part of scholarly circles nor of a courtly culture, and the various new ways of using or reading books all had an impact on the content and style of the written word. In France, the *bibliothèque bleu*, for instance, were cheap books that popularized courtly and heroic literary forms and were widely diffused in the mid-seventeenth century.[45] Elsewhere in Europe the spread of the book was also accompanied by a popularization of its contents.

One can go a step further. On a broader level, emerging at a time when the culture of the urban middle class was consolidated by commercial conditions and by a loose type of power structure, we need to ask how the spread of a book culture helped shape this middle-class culture and how it allowed it to reach people in the establishment. Much more research is required for these questions to be answered, but the following chapters will nevertheless address them and suggest some possible answers.

5

Shaping a Culture of the Middle Class

THE PERIOD of relative economic well-being of the middle class coincided with local and regional transformations that proved to be significant factors in the consolidation of their culture and its legitimacy in the social arena. At the regional level, the weakening of power at the center in Istanbul and of the tensions between local power structures and the central state resulted in a shift toward the provinces. The shift was not a simple process, because important fluctuations were occurring for most of the seventeenth and part of the eighteenth centuries. These fluctuations and tensions between central authorities and local power groups were true of Egypt as they were true of other provinces. For most of the eighteenth century, for instance, the governors of Damascus belonged to a single local notable family, the 'Azm family.

Ottoman state policy following the conquest of 1517 was to keep conditions much as they had found them, making sure that the tax revenues reached the Imperial Treasury, setting up an administration that guaranteed their continued control. Around 1600, profound changes were emerging, notably political and geopolitical changes affecting the region as a whole, which pushed the balance in favor of the local power structure. With greater political and economic autonomy in the latter part of the eighteenth century, as Mamluk households came to control tax revenues and to expand their political weight in relation to Istanbul, more manifestations of local culture and local dialect appeared. As far as the middle class was concerned, the consequences proved to be both an advantage and a disadvantage. The shift in balance between the central state and the provinces was a factor in the legitimization of a local culture that was theirs and with which they were consequently familiar. This shift coincided with a period when the middle class was prospering, and consequently the shift in power combined with prosperity brought them greater opportunity for expression through a familiar culture.

The potential problem that the changing situation created for the middle class was that the local military rulers, at first the members of the militias and subsequently the Mamluk households, could have a freer hand in exploiting the taxation system to their advantage and to the consequent disadvantage of the urban classes. For a while these classes were protected by the constant infighting among the military rulers, but by the latter part of the eighteenth century, their exploitation of the taxation system was an important element in the impoverishment of the middle class and the resulting reduction of its cultural space.

However, in the seventeenth century another factor worked to the advantage of middle-class culture: its relations with the religious establishment and with the level of control that the religious elites had over the culture and education of the rest of the population. The *'ulama'* carried on the teachings of Islam, upheld its laws, promoted good, and condemned evil. Yet the extent to which *'ulama'* had a hegemonic control on society and culture is a matter of debate. One standard view took it for granted that the religious establishment controlled society to a large extent, that it was able to prescribe behavior on a large scale, and that consequently the culture as a whole could be defined through its religious teachings. This view did not sufficiently take time and place into consideration or study the *'ulama'* in the context of the broader social, economic, and political structure. The relationship between the culture of the religious establishment and that of ordinary urban dwellers could be one of more or less domination, of more or less rigid or static barriers separating them. A study of historical context is in fact indispensable to understanding the level and the kind of control the religious establishment had. The study of specific historical contexts can show the extent to which the learned establishment defined the whole culture, and the extent to which other voices in society could be heard.

A major factor in the equation concerns the structure of the religious establishment. As a rule, the culture of the establishment was stronger, was better able to impose itself, during periods of greater centralization. The middle-class culture had a better chance of development and of expression during periods of lesser centralization, when the religious establishment was less able to impose its cultural models, on the one hand, and to exploit the population economically through abusive taxation, on the other. Middle-class culture was, for obvious reasons, weaker at times when rulers exploited it more. The absence of rigid models increased the possibility for the culture from below to penetrate the culture of the establishment if other factors were favorable. A more flexibly structured social setup left more room for diversity of views, for difference, and for dissent than did a well-structured establishment. This approach can partly help to explain some of the phenomena that this study explores, such as the spread of the colloquial as a medium of written expression or the fact that scholars were influenced by modes of expression that came from below.

There were significant regional differences between Cairo, Syrian cities, and Istanbul in this respect. In Cairo, the Azhar, to which many of the most famous scholars were attached, was the most prominent institution in the seventeenth and eighteenth centuries. Yet it was in no way comparable to the bureaucratized structure of learning in Istanbul at about the same time, either in terms of hierarchies, the way to reach the top, the leadership, or the way leadership was chosen. If the bureaucratization policies under Mehmet the Conqueror and Sulayman the Magnificent had organized scholarly pursuits in a clearly hierarchical structure in Istanbul, this was certainly not the case in Cairo.[1] During the early Ottoman period, the position of Shaykh al-Azhar (rector of the Azhar) became the preeminent position in the religious hierarchy in Cairo. Nevertheless, a significant degree of informality and absence of state intervention characterized the Cairene institution until the early nineteenth century, when the policies of Muhammad 'Ali changed the situation by making the Shaykh al-Azhar a state appointee, thereby seriously curtailing the flexibility of the institution. Until then, the way that the Shaykh al-Azhar was chosen by the other shaykhs, for instance, was characterized by informality. There were no evident steps for promotion to this post, except for the personal qualities of the candidate, his scholarship, and his ability to make political alliances both with colleagues and with outsiders.

Another important regional difference can be observed between Egypt and Syria in the domination of scholarly families. In Bilad al-Sham in the same period, many of the prominent *'ulama'* belonged to families that had been in the scholarly tradition for generations. The Ramlis, the Kawikibis, the Muhibbis, for example, dominated the scholarly scene for one generation after another in the seventeenth and eighteenth centuries in Syria, filling the important positions in teaching institutions and the judiciary. This domination of the *'ulama'* circles by a few families in Bilad al Sham was almost nonexistent in Cairo. Possibly such dominance was linked to a strong family and tribal element in the Syrian social structure. The religious hierarchy of Syria thus had more homogeneity and more structure, but less social mobility, than the *'ulama'* in Cairo, where the Azhar was open to students of very diverse social origins.

In Cairo, by contrast, during the seventeenth and eighteenth centuries, many of the prominent *'ulama'* were from rural or provincial origins and either from peasant, craftsman, or trading families; the educational institution was a door to their upward social mobility. Rural families were religiously motivated to send one of their sons to the Azhar. Once there, religious education was a way for anyone to reach the top class, including people from rural and provincial origins. This rapid upward social mobility of the *'ulama'*, even in the second half of the eighteenth century when there was less flexibility at many other levels, can be illustrated by a shaykh al-Azhar such as Ahmad al-Damanhuri (d. 1192/1778)) or 'Abdalla al-Shabrawi (d. 1171/1758), who had started their lives in provincial and rural areas and were from modest or poor origins. Because *'ulama'* were of very different social and geographic origins, and because they were socially very mobile, many of them who joined the scholarly community brought their own cultural baggage with them.

The changing relationship between religious authorities and civilian populations can also be observed among Copts, especially as of the late seventeenth and throughout the eighteenth centuries. One significant factor affecting Coptic culture was the rise to a position of great influence of a wealthy class of Coptic notables with close links to the ruling Mamluks. The confluence of a number of factors led to a parallel result, notably a less powerful control of the religious hierarchy over the civilian populations and a greater prominence of a civilian leadership. The head of the Coptic community was a patriarch who also led the religious hierarchy. His leadership of the community was both religious and political because he was the person that the Ottoman authorities recognized. Copts had for a long time served in important administrative and financial positions, in the Imperial Treasury, for instance, as well as worked in the private service of the ruling class, doing accounting and auditing and investment of their fortunes. These services brought them in close contact with those in power. With the growth of Mamluk households and the expansion of their wealth and of their financial activities, the Copts working in their services came to benefit from their links to Mamluks, both in terms of their enrichment and of their closeness to those in power. Those among them who reached the greatest social and economic prominence in their generation took the title of "the head of the Coptic notables" (*kabir al-arakhina, al-arkhan al-ra'is,* or *sultan al-Qibt*). One of these, *mu'allim* (another title given to these notables) Lutfalla b. Yusuf (d. 1720), working in the employment of amir Muhammad Kadak Katkhuda Mustahfazan, was said to have been unequalled in his wealth.

The enormous fortunes that some of these notables accumulated from running the finances of Mamluks and from their closeness to those in power enabled them to control the Coptic religious hierarchy. As of the mid-seventeenth century, they came to control the appointment of the Coptic patriarch, to the exclusion of bishops and other religious functionaries. The community was in fact led by a civilian rather than by a religious authority. As these notables came more and more to finance Church activities such as the construction and repairs of churches, monasteries, and schools, their control over the Church hierarchy increased tremendously, so much so that by the eighteenth century it was they rather than the Church hierarchy that had become the main decision-making body on all religious as well as nonreligious matters, such as the elaboration or the implementation of Church laws. Thus a civilian rather than a religious hierarchy was running Church affairs and providing leadership to the community, especially in view of its close relation to those in power and its ability to intercede in behalf of the members of the community or of the priests, bishops, or patriarch.[2] Thus emerged the structural basis for the development of a nonreligious dimension to culture. The manifestations of this nonreligious culture still need to be fully understood.

Culture through the Written Text

These historical conditions had consequences for the culture of the urban middle class that are not easy to analyze because of the problem of sources. To explore these consequences we need to use traditional sources like chronicles and biographies in a different way than they are used for the study of the Mamluks or of the *'ulama'*. Such exploration also necessitates using other kinds of sources that can shed light on this matter, such as literary sources so far unexploited by historians of Ottoman Egypt. This chapter explores the culture of the middle class through texts written by, for, or about them. These written texts will also explore its relationship to other cultures to see how middle-class culture influenced or was influenced by the culture of the ruling circles and the establishment. Ultimately such an analysis helps put this culture in the larger social context and the transformations that the society as a whole was undergoing. In other words, the study of cultural transformations enlightens us on certain social aspects that other sources do not usually offer.

The issues at hand are complex. One of the complexities that we face is in the way that literary sources can be used for social history. The historian has to decide on the degree to which one can associate a piece of writing with a specific social class. One is treading delicate ground in trying to look for an attitude that was specific to the middle class, or that distinguished it from the establishment in the written texts of the period. The historian also has to see the extent to which written texts can be considered as vehicles of expression for a social group. We know, for instance, that the *'ulama'* used the genre of biographical dictionaries not only to record the life and the deeds of prominent scholars, but also as a vehicle to express their own values, or as a way to project an image of this class. The question is: can one identify texts that did the same for the middle class?

To identify the culture of the middle class through these writings meant that a number of points had to be considered, such as the identity of the writer, his concerns (especially social concerns), the style and language used, and the subject matter. But even presuming that a tradesman or merchant wrote a book, was this enough to associate it with a particular class? In other words, did a writer who owned a shop or ran a business write in a different way or say different things from a member of the religious establishment?

Part of the difficulty in answering such questions is the fact that the terrain is still virgin and consequently the possibility of comparison minimal. Thus whatever answers are provided are exploratory and do not claim to be conclusive. Yet the subject is important enough, not only for cultural history but also for social history as well, to try to open up channels for further exploration.

For this purpose, I consulted a large number of texts, mostly in manuscript form. Most of them are nonreligious in nature. They belong to different genres such as historical chronicles, dictionaries, books of tales and anecdotes, books of conduct and proverbs—in other words, a variety of texts including some that were academic in nature, such as the chronicles and dictionaries; some that were more popular, such as the stories and anecdotes; and some that were literary texts or belles-lettres. These texts yielded information that proved to be relevant to social analysis in terms of their content, their style, and their language.

A Greater Middle-Class Presence in the Written Culture

In the seventeenth and eighteenth centuries, the culture of academic scholarship, intended primarily for *'ulama'* and for students, dominated the intellectual scene and written production. It is the culture that chroniclers like al-Jabarti, upon whom modern historians rely heavily, knew best and wrote about most. It is consequently the culture that modern scholarship has explored the most. Voluminous works in the religious sciences, jurisprudence, traditions, and commentaries were produced and copied for or by these people. Such works constituted the bulk of written production. Learning associated with establishment education, in Cairo as in other major centers of religious instruction, enjoyed the recognition and respect of the ruling classes and of the population. One could refer to this as establishment culture or as scholarly culture, which because of its very nature, requiring a high level of training and of specialized knowledge, was created by and for a few people. It was at the same time a culture with religious and ethical dimensions, which aimed at creating models of conduct for a broad social body. It also aimed at transmitting its views on issues related to this world and the next and at maintaining the elevated status of *'ulama'* as such, enabling them to continue playing a religious and social role.

Another trend also came to the fore, less dominant but of considerable significance for our understanding of culture and society during the period and of subsequent developments in the nineteenth century. The favorable economic conditions of the middle class and the widening of its channels for the transmission of knowledge, especially but not uniquely through books, had led to an expanded sphere of middle-class culture and to a greater presence of this class in the written word. The expanding sphere manifested itself in several directions and took many forms. It involved both the members of this class and establishment scholars. On the one hand, the culture of the middle class was imposing its mark on certain kinds of writing; on the other hand, the middle class constituted an audience, a readership, a market that others aimed at and adapted their writings to. The middle class was thus both subject and object.

The conditions that brought about new vehicles of expression through the written word also brought about possibilities of control or guidance. Both made the written word, by various mechanisms, less exclusive and more accessible to a larger number of people.

The Impact of the Middle Class on the Written Word

While the basic objectives of the culture of *'ulama'* remained the same, we can detect in the writings of some high *'ulama'* a space for the middle class, inherently recognizing its expanding sphere. This recognition was an acknowledgement of a new readership and an attempt to reach them. It was a recognition of the social prominence of this class and of its cultural weight. It is evident that we have to exclude the voluminous output of religious scholarship, the studies in *fiqh* (jurisprudence), *tafsir*, and *hadith* (traditions), which followed their own methodologies and approaches and were unlikely to be influenced by the impact of middle-class culture. Yet in other kinds of scholarly or academic writing, such as dictionaries and chronicles, which were not essentially religious, this expansion was more evident.

At the level of methodology, this trend incites some comment. That *'ulama'* could be part of the democratization of written culture in seventeenth-century Cairo has implications for the way that these scholars are usually seen. This picture of scholars does not fully conform to the standard view. Nevertheless, it can help us to understand some of the complexities of the *'ulama'* class and to overcome a major problem in the study of *'ulama'*, notably that of ahistoricity. The *'ulama'* are sometimes seen as an ahistorical social category that did not change over time. One problem in some scholarship is the suggestion that scholars of ninth-century Baghdad were essentially the same as scholars of eighteenth-century Cairo or Istanbul, and that it was consequently permissible to study them with the same methodologies and the same classifications. By considering them in the context of significant transformations taking place and their reaction to these changes, we not only historicize them but also understand some of the complexities of this group. This approach can also shed light on a related issue, notably the relationship between the learned culture of *'ulama'* and popular culture, sometimes perceived as confrontational, at other times as two unlinked categories. This relationship can instead be put in a historical context to see how it changed in time and place.

First, there was a reaction by the members of the *'ulama'* class to the changes taking place; second, they did not all react in the same way; and third, those who chose to react had several different objectives for doing so. For some *'ulama'*, the objective in adapting their writing was to reach a larger readership. A more popularized form of writing that carried their teaching could reach many more people who were literate or educated but not necessarily linked to religious educational institutions. The spread of a book culture had in fact provided scholars with a wider audience than the circle of professors and students and thus with a new channel to spread their ideas, a channel by which to reach, to guide, and to direct the new readership. The spread of a book culture among people who were not primarily scholars and the active involvement of some of these people in writing or passively being read to had an impact on works of religious teaching.

From the spread of a book culture developed a body of texts written by scholars but apparently aimed at the nonacademic reader. There is nothing very new in this. Historians have drawn attention to the way that establishment writers and thinkers used the simple language of ordinary people to communicate what they wanted. A recent study by Adam Fox on sixteenth- and seventeenth-century England shows how the Church used proverbs and sayings from the popular tradition as a way of disseminating its ideas. Fox also noted the way that Erasmus made ample use of proverbs to diffuse his thoughts among ordinary people in a language and style that they could understand, enjoining them to accept their poverty with patience, and so on.[3]

An early example of someone who adapted his writings to the level of the middle-class reader was 'Abd al-Wahab al-Sha'rani, one of the most prominent Sufi leaders and writers of the sixteenth century, who was also an *'alim*. 'Abd al-Wahab al-Sha'rani specifically addressed tradesmen, craftsmen, workers, and simple people. His works, as he himself tells us, aimed at reaching the artisans and craftsmen who addressed questions to him because they wanted to understand in a comprehensible language their duties as Muslims.[4] They were unable to follow what the *'ulama'* said because it was too complicated and too academic. He therefore wanted to explain to them in a style and language within their reach the basics of how a good Muslim should conduct himself. His numerous writings were consequently easy to read in spite of their sophisticated content. Often referring to himself or to some of the shaykhs that he personally knew, his style was concrete, simple, and illustrated with examples from his own experience, in other words a style that was relatively easily accessible. Sha'rani's work was significant at several levels. The source that inspired him to write in the way that he did was his potential reader. Moreover, he represented a prominent person addressing his writing to that specific audience by adapting his style accordingly. As an early example of a trend to adapt style and content to a nonscholarly readership, al-Sha'rani was followed by later *'ulama'*.

Some *'ulama'* writing in the seventeenth century also adapted subject matter and style to this public. *'Ulama'* were well aware that the growing Sufi movement had an increasing number of followers and disciples. Some of those within this movement developed a mystical approach that stood well within the framework of orthodox beliefs, but there were also others moving away from orthodox practice, a potential threat to the authority of scholars. Thus certain *'ulama'* may have attempted to counteract this trend through easy writings aimed at the ordinary believer.

In other words, we observe a self-conscious attempt to popularize religious teachings. Texts were aimed at nonscholars with the objective of providing moral guidance and diffusing religious teachings, and perhaps also with the objective of selling books, perhaps to counteract the great influence that the works of al-Sha'rani had had. Najm al-Din al-Ghayti wrote texts on how a good Muslim should conduct himself in his religious duties, such as during the pilgrimage or in performing his ablutions, and this in a simple way, in a few pages, so as to be comprehensible to a person who looked up to the *'ulama'* for guidance. 'Abdul-Ra'uf al-Munawi (d. 1031/1621), one of the most prominent and prolific scholars of his time, also wanted to reach a broader readership than that of institutions of higher learning.[5] In one of his books, he says as much: "What I indicate is for the *khassa* [elites] and for the *'amma* [commoners]." In fact he was not really writing to the *'amma;* his work is not "popular" in any sense, but made relatively easy reading that could potentially reach an educated but not necessarily scholarly public. Al-Munawi was in fact adapting *adab* literature, originally a courtly form of writing addressed to rulers and princes advising them on how to conduct themselves, to another purpose, notably one aiming at daily concerns. His book advised people on how to behave in a public bath, an institution used by different social groups among which the ordinary urban dweller was present.[6]

During the first half of the seventeenth century, people like Yusuf al-Maghribi, 'Abdul-Mu'ti al-Ishaqi, and Ahmad al-Khafaji reflected, each in his own way, certain significant dimensions of the expansion of middle-class culture into the territory of the scholarly work. Therefore, by exploring some of the works they wrote, we can on the one hand see how scholarly works integrated middle-class culture and on the other hand trace and explore the expansion of middle-class culture into the social surroundings. This exploration means posing the question in a different way than is usually done; rather than elaborating on the influence coming from above, we can, through a consideration of some scholarly works, explore the influence coming from below. The influence of *'ulama'* and Sufi shaykhs on populations is well known, while the influence that impacted on them has, by and large, been overlooked.

Prevailing conditions worked in favor of such an influence. The expansion of the sphere of middle-class culture was taking place at a time when the power structure was diffuse rather than centralized, when the military class was not yet in full control of local resources and had some shared interests with the middle class. These conditions were providing the members of this class with a certain economic stability. As a result of this situation, one can observe some flexibility in the borders between the cultures of above and below, some overlapping and interpenetration between them. A number of scholarly texts in fact show that the expansion of the middle-class cultural sphere was influencing the culture of above.

This impact could take a variety of forms. For many scholars who came from rural or provincial areas, or whose families were involved in trades and crafts, the flexibility of the learned structure meant that upon entering the establishment they did not have to fully forgo the cultural baggage that they came with. The structure of the learned hierarchy, as well as the impact of middle-class culture on the global scene, had given a level of legitimacy to the culture from below. We have an interesting but not unique example in Yusuf al-Maghribi (d. 1019/1610) because this person gives his personal testimony of the way he started his life as an artisan, then moved to the scholarly world, but did not, in doing so, relinquish his cultural baggage. Coming from a family of craftsmen, he learned in his youth the profession of maker of swordholders (*hamayil sayf*), a product mainly destined for Bilad al-Sudan, and worked at it for many years until he thoroughly mastered it. Yet what he really wanted to do was scholarly work. When his reading kept him awake far into the night and stopped him from performing in the daytime, his uncles (his father was dead by then) at first tried to stop him, but he persisted. He had a chance to fulfill his wishes when one year the Sudan caravan did not come as expected, and the uncles had to take their products there themselves, leaving him the responsibility of the shop in Cairo and of taking care of their wives and families. He bought books and read them, then went to the Azhar, eventually dropping his craft entirely.[7]

This kind of personal trajectory was a fairly common one, because many of the Azhar *'ulama'* were either of rural origin or of trade or artisan origin. However, the significant feature with regard to Yusuf al-Maghribi was in the way that he integrated the culture of the ordinary urban dweller into his learned writings; in other words he brought into the field of learned writings some of the features of his culture. He wrote a dictionary of the colloquial dialect of Cairo, thus combining a scholarly form with a nonscholarly content. His dictionary used the techniques and methodologies of scholarship and yet in its content it was not using the language of scholars. As a dictionary that followed the format of other similar works in this genre, it was nevertheless the first of its kind in the Arabic language to concern itself with the dialect of Cairo as an object of scientific study. The reasons why such a significant innovation should appear in Cairo earlier than it did in Syria and Anatolia is partly linked to the power structure and the structure of the religious establishment, which was at that period clearly more flexible and consequently more receptive to this kind of innovation.

Even more significant were the reasons he gave for writing this work. Notably, he found reasons to justify his use of the colloquial: he was in fact undertaking a scientific study, based on observation of what he heard, of the spoken language used in Cairo during his lifetime. In other words, the writer was using the format of a dictionary, much like the classical dictionaries with which he was familiar, for a content that integrated and gave legitimacy to a written form of the spoken word. Thus at a time when serious and important language studies were taking place in the institutions of learning, another level of language, which did not follow the rules of proper usage but instead remained close to the spoken word, emerged in written texts of many kinds. The colloquial represented a culture from below making its way up, becoming incorporated into literary and scholarly texts, entering a domain that had previously been that of classical language.

The expansion of middle-class culture into the domain of scholarly genres took an entirely different form in the work of another early seventeenth-century scholar, 'Abdul-Mu'ti al-Ishaqi (died c. 1650), a *qadi*, an *'alim*, a historian, and a poet according to his biographer, al-Muhibbi.[8] Al-Ishaqi's chronicle, generally considered mediocre in terms of historical achievement, can be considered an encyclopedia of local cultural practices and beliefs. His text puts down in written form some of the accepted beliefs, tales, and practices of his society, the popular culture of his time. His use of the chronicle as a genre suggests that he considered it a format into which he could fit the material that he was concerned with. In fact, the actual chronological narrative that he provided has little that is new; he covered the well-known periods—

Umayyads, Abbasids, Tulunids—with little of his own to add. The real interest of his work, however, consists in the comments and stories he interspersed into the chronology that have nothing to do with his historical narrative. In a somewhat clumsy way, al-Ishaqi's text included cultural beliefs and practices, often written in an entertaining and amusing fashion, within the structure of the narrative. Al-Ishaqi incorporates into his chronicle subjects so diverse as to defy classification. These subjects included medical recipes for various ills and ailments, such as eating chicken to increase sperm. They also included odd pieces of useful information. Among these were a magical formula that could be used against evil persons;[9] the diverse uses of cobwebs, such as making a wound coagulate and cleaning silver;[10] advice on how to decrease the power of a domineering woman, notably by feeding her the tongue of a gazelle dried in the shade; and a number of amusing sexual or pornographic stories.[11]

Nevertheless, what is worthy of our concern is that al-Ishaqi made use of the chronicle, a well-known genre of historical writing, to record popular local practices and beliefs that were current in his time. By including them in that format he was in fact "elevating" the knowledge and the beliefs of a local culture into an academic or scholarly form: They were worthy of notice and of being recorded in writing. His chronicle can therefore be considered a further manifestation of the broad trend that involved giving the local culture of the ordinary urban dweller a level of legitimacy among the scholarly community.

Over twenty manuscript copies of al-Ishaqi's history are extant. We can infer a certain level of popularity, otherwise it would not have been copied many times over. To say that the market factor could have been an incentive to write certain kinds of books need not be farfetched. In fact, al-Shirbini, author of *Hazz al-Quhuf*, explicitly suggested that he had his eyes on the market and that he wrote a work that he thought would sell. Those who write in an eloquent style go hungry, he tells us, while those writing in a licentious style had an easier time making a living. Al-Shirbini said that people prefer licentiousness (*khala'a*) to eloquent writing (*balagha*) because they need to relieve their anxiety.[12] Licentiousness brought about restfulness to a worried or depressed person and was a remedy for inner tensions. In spite of the relative size of his book, which indicates it was not meant for the casual reader, many of the amusing stories and anecdotes it contains could provide entertainment for both those who could read and those to whom the stories were read.

In short, whether scholars looked for a middle-class market or allowed themselves to express their cultural origins in a written scholarly genre, they were not alone, and the expansion of middle-class culture into the written word was not undertaken solely by *'ulama'*. As a matter of fact, one of the more important dimensions of this trend was developed by members of the middle class themselves. Because historical studies have focused on scholars and *'ulama'*, little is known about writers who stood lower in the hierarchy. They are more difficult to identify because they do not regularly appear in biographical dictionaries. Their works are less well known for obvious reasons. The volume of written works produced by the middle class is of course not comparable to the written production of the higher *'ulama'*, which was enormous. Yet one cannot measure its importance only by the number of works produced. To neglect the output of those who were not at the top of the hierarchy, thereby missing the total picture, may lead to a distorted view of the culture as a whole. Whether or not this trend was a new one is difficult to ascertain in view of the absence of parallel studies for other periods. The whole domain of the class background of writers, thinkers, and intellectuals, in the Ottoman Empire in general and in the Arab-speaking lands in particular, is waiting for further exploration. Literary production is often studied independent of its class, and few studies have gone into this issue at any length.

The written production of the period encompasses a noticeable presence by middle-class writers such as craftsmen and tradesmen, ordinary people whose exact identity is not always known because they were not important enough to be written about by their contemporaries in chronicles, histories, or biographies. There are a few exceptions. Shaykh Shihab al-Din Al-Khafaji (d. 1069/1650), a prominent scholar who spent some time in Istanbul and while there was appointed Qadi al-Qudat of Egypt, included a number of craftsmen and artisans in his biographical dictionary of poets, *Rihana al-Al-ibba*. This work mentions, for instance, a poet called Muhammad Badr al-Din al-Zayyat who started his life producing and selling oil and butter before becoming a poet. The poet Hamidi was head of the paper seller's guild of Cairo (*shaykh ahl al-warraqa bi misr*). Al-Khafaji's biographies also include two weighers of goods (*qabbani*), a merchant, and a jeweler (*sayigh*) who composed poems.[13] There are two issues to consider here, first that these tradesmen should be prolific writers, and second that their literary production should attract the attention of those who were firmly part of the establishment, a sign of the acceptance beyond their own circles of what they had to say.

Often, however, the identity of writers remains more or less blurry. What we know about them is restricted to bits of information here and there. Sometimes a writer wrote a little about himself or provided the reader with some autobiographical data interspersed in his text. A particularly interesting example is the eighteenth-century Damascene chronicler Ahmad al-Budayri al-Hallaq, who according to his own testimony was a barber by profession.[14] He was obviously also a person of some learning, familiar with the way that chronicles were written in a format that followed the chronology of rulers and that included events and obituaries. He was attached to an important shaykh, Shaykh Abdul Ghani al-Nabulsi, calling him his shaykh and teacher on the occasion of the obituary of his shaykh's son Isma'il.[15] Yet his own identity as a practicing barber emerges in different ways in his book. Al-Budayri al-Hallaq includes the obituaries of artisans like himself, barbers, for instance, and tanners as well as the obituaries of important personages in Damascene society. One example of these obituaries is that of Hajj Ahmad Hashish, the barber who taught him his craft and who shaved prominent shaykhs such as 'Abdul-Ghani al-Nabulsi and Murad Afandi al-Naqshabandi.[16] Significantly, it was in the exercise of his daily profession that he gathered part of the data that went into his book, chatting with the people he was shaving about the daily occurrences of his time, then recording what they said in his chronicle of events. The sources for this chronicle and the way that these were used were thus a function of al-Budayri's position.

Al-Budayri was Syrian, but examples of writers from circles other than that of students and scholars can also be found in Cairo, evidence of an active participation in cultural production by those in the middle ranks. Like al-Budayri, the anonymous author of *Kitab al-Dhakha'ir* seems to have been a craftsman, judging from his familiarity with guild practice, perhaps a barber or a doctor practicing popular rather than academic medicine.[17] Another example at hand is that of Ibn al-Siddiq, a person with some familiarity with the writing of chronicles, but who apparently had not undergone a college education. Ibn al-Siddiq, author of a work entitled *Ghara'ib al-Bada"i*, narrates the events of Muhammad Abul-Dhahab's expedition to Syria in the late eighteenth century. He wrote in a language in which the basic grammar was faulty, an indication that his education was incomplete; perhaps he had had an elementary education and no more. His spelling of words showed a confusion of the verb ending in *waw alif* for a plural ending, and the ending *huh* to indicate the word *katabahu*. He misspelled a name as common as 'Uthman (which he spelled with a *sad* as 'Usman).

Consequences for the Written Word

The conditions of the middle class during this period had a number of consequences for the written word. Without being exhaustive or definitive, I suggest some of them below. Among them, one can observe features of oral literature emerging in the written word as more people became literate and thus entered the world of books. A concern for the ordinary person, presumably also the result of the spread of books, can also be detected. Furthermore, one can observe an interest in features of local culture, a trend related to the geopolitical situation.

Influence of Oral Tradition

As of the seventeenth century, when we can detect the early stages of a book culture among the middle class, we find evidence that oral culture was penetrating written culture. People were, it seems, bringing their oral traditions with them as they penetrated the world of reading and writing.

The transposition of the oral to the written had several dimensions, in terms of the forms of expression as well as of the content. In terms of content, a literature that for centuries had been essentially part of the oral tradition now appeared in writing. One of the many examples one could cite, the Juha jokes, have been part of the oral tradition for centuries. Stories of Juha were in the realm of popular culture, using "everyman" as characters rather than elites, based on bawdy humor with frequent sexual overtones. Juha's acts were in the domain of everyday acts of daily life, such as Juha's being sent to the market to buy a grilled head of lamb or Juha spending the night at a friend's house.[18] In the seventeenth and eighteenth centuries, they appear as compilations of stories, as, for instance, in a manuscript of humorous and obscene Juha stories, in colloquial style, written about 1650 and described as "thirteen absurd and often obscene" stories.[19] Or, as is often the case, Juha stories were interspersed in books of anecdotes or in various other literary genres, as in the anonymous compilation of *Anis al-Jalis* and in al-Shirbini's *Hazz al-Quhuf*.[20] Thus the people who were entering the world of books during this period were bringing with them the culture with which they were familiar. In doing so, they were making books more accessible.

Madiha Doss, a historical linguist who has done extensive work on the language of seventeenth-century chronicles, detected strong evidence for the ways the oral tradition came to penetrate a well-established genre, the chronicle. She also noted the trend by chroniclers toward using the technique of the *rawi* storyteller. These techniques, well known in the oral tradition, were common among the numerous storytellers that frequented the coffeehouses of Cairo and other cities, some of them moving from one location to another, others attached to a particular coffeehouse. Similar comments can be applied to the use of another technique, notably the *sajʿ* (rhymed prose), which was commonly used in the period in general and in chronicles in particular.[21] *Sajʿ* has a long history in Arabic literature. It became very popular in the seventeenth century, probably for the same reasons: the influence of oral literature on the written word and the relative ease with which it could be memorized. The tradition of storytelling had received an impetus from the development of the coffeehouse, which provided a fixed place for the performance of this art and an audience that had expectations for performers to fulfill.

Another influence of the oral tradition on the written word emerged during this period. As of the seventeenth century, proverbs (*mathal*, pl. *amthal*) became extensively used in writing, sometimes in the form of compilations of books of proverbs but more often interspersed in texts on different subjects to support a statement or to illustrate an idea. The popular proverbs represent a long tradition of an orally transmitted body of sayings. These *amthal* represent a popular wisdom based on a long collective history, to which one can turn in order to find explanations or models of human conduct. They are used in texts as a guide to people's conduct, as indications of how to behave in given circumstances. As such, their proliferation in written texts has a special significance. The guidance that these proverbs provided, based on a collective experience, was significantly different in approach and method from the guidance based on authority that *ʿulama'* used. Scholarly methodology made extensive use of precedent and of authority to support views or statements. The use of the proverb as a way of supporting what one wrote was to turn to a popular form, easily accessible to everyone and giving the weight of authority. Many writers used the concrete language of everyday life, taken from the world that the ordinary person was familiar with. They used the proverb in different kinds of texts to make what they wanted to say concrete. The proverb could be a guideline for the way people should behave or an analysis of a situation they were describing. Use of proverbs is a significant trend because it brought into the written word a content that ordinary people were familiar with, that they could identify with, and that was an expression of their view of the world.

Proverbs proliferated in the writings of the period. Al-Maghribi's dictionary, for instance, contains some fifty of them.[22] Writers such as Muhammad Abu Dhakir or Yusuf al-Shirbini used this wisdom as a regular source of knowledge, using proverbs as advice on how to confront the daily difficulties of life. If one could not get what one wanted, one had to accept what was possible or available, an idea expressed in metaphorical terms related to a dish of meat: "If you cannot attain the meat, dip your bread in the gravy" (*illi mayuhassil al-lahm ya fitt fil maraq*). Another piece of wisdom was related to discretion: "Walls have ears" (*al-ha'it lahu adhan*). Age was an asset, bringing with it fullness (*al-dihn fil 'ataqi*); "Crunch dry bread rather than be hungry" (*qarqash wa la al-ju'*); "Marriage is happiness for a month, disgust for the rest of time and back-breaking" (*al-tazawwuj farah shahr wa ghamm dahr wa kasr dhahr*).[23]

Muhammad Abu Dhakir's work includes proverbs on every other page, interspersed within the text. Whatever the subject he was dealing with, he found a way to support it with evidence from one of these popular proverbs. His work contains tens of these proverbs at appropriate points to support his statement or elaborate on an idea. The extensive use of proverbs in many kinds of writings incites us to look at them as source material to explore attitudes and views that are often not explicitly expressed. In fact, in some domains the worldview expressed in proverbs was often at odds with dominant views.

Emergence of the "Ordinary" Person

The combination of a complex set of conditions brought about another significant impact on the content of books—on their subject matter, their language, their points of view and perspectives. This impact was the emergence of the "ordinary" person and of "ordinary" life as subject matter and as a focus of interest in literary texts.

This phenomenon constitutes an important historical development. Charles Taylor considers it to be a major aspect of the modern identity, rooted in production and reproduction—in work, marriage, and the family, in the promotion of ordinary life. It contrasted with the aristocratic search for glory, leveling culture because its concerns were broad or even universal, not only those of the leisured few.[24] The interest in the ordinary person implicitly suggested that the study, observation, or recording of his acts or thoughts were as valid a subject matter as those of important people or people in power. Writing about an ordinary person and about his everyday life stood in stark contrast to the style and approach of the voluminous biographies of prominent persons, religious or political, who either performed great deeds or were saintly and virtuous. The biographical dictionaries preferred to bring out the exceptional—deeds and acts out of reach of the ordinary person that could serve as a social ideal.

The biography of a shaykh, for instance, not only conformed to a certain style and provided standard information such as the shaykh's students, his teachers, and the books he wrote, but also often projected an idealized image of a person in particular or of the *'ulama'* class in general. Biographies of shaykhs often idealized virtues such as learning, saintliness, generosity, or charity, for instance, as did the biographies of Sufi saints.

The concern with the ordinary person may therefore be seen as adding an important dimension to seventeenth-century culture that has long been either overlooked or misunderstood. It also shows the important influence of the middle class in shaping this development, a consequence of both their greater social prominence and their greater presence in the world of writing.

The focus of interest on the ordinary person and on ordinary life can be observed in different literary genres, such as in compilations of stories, in anecdotes and jokes, in dictionaries, in belles-lettres, and in chronicles. It was manifested in the focus on work, on the home and family, on food and drink; it was also manifested in its style, in a type of language that was close to the spoken word, and in the extensive use of proverbs.

Thus, at the same time as the literary tradition of heroic personages such as Baybars and Genghis Khan was developed and became part of the coffeehouse repertory, other works were written or compiled in which the ordinary person was the "hero"; what happened to him could happen to anybody. One example, the anonymous compilation of stories and anecdotes *Nuzhat al-Qulub*, has stories of a prosperous schoolteacher whose wife is about to deliver, and of a housewife who received a letter from her absent husband but cannot read it because she is illiterate.[25] Any of these events could happen to one's next-door neighbor.

Use of the "ordinary" person means that the famous book written toward the end of the seventeenth century by Yusuf al-Shirbini, *Hazz al-Quhuf*, generally considered to be a unique book because it dealt with the society of peasants in the Egyptian Delta and because it was written in colloquial Arabic, can be put in context. The book remains unique insofar as it was entirely devoted to peasants. This is in fact unique not only in the context of contemporary

Egypt but anywhere. In the seventeenth century, in the Middle East, the Ottoman world, or Europe, books were not devoted to peasants. But at another level, this work was part of a trend in its interest in social groups that were at a distance from the ruling class, from the establishment, and from the power structure.

The Work Context

Court records have provided us with data on many aspects in the life of traders and craftsmen: their business dealings, their marriages, and their houses, in other words, the material conditions in which they lived. It is significant that a few literary texts of the seventeenth and eighteenth centuries should also concern themselves with writing about work and workers. A good example can be found in the anonymous book *Kitab al-Dhakha'ir wal-Tuhaf fi Bir al-Sanayi' wal-Hiraf*. As its title indicates, it is a book about craftsmen and guilds.[26] The person who wrote this work was familiar with the traditions upheld in guilds, and seems to have been personally close to, if not part of, the guild system. A similar concern with artisans and craftsmen is evident in a poem that has a large section on craftsmen, written by Shaykh Muhammad al-Azhari, shaykh al-Qabbaniyya (head of the guild for weighers of goods) in *Anis al-Jalis*, an anonymous compilation of stories, anecdotes, poems.[27] Such writings on the ordinary artisan or craftsman are indicative of a certain social setting. Likewise, Yusuf al-Maghribi noted the vocabulary of the various crafts, mentioning the words that were used by builders, spice sellers, carpenters, textile workers, and tailors. Thus, unlike the legal language that scribes used in court registers, what we have here are the terms that they coined based on their work traditions: *'ilba*, the container that spice merchants used to weigh their spices, *da'ak*, to smoothen a textile, *silk* for thread, and many more.[28] His interest in the vocabulary used by craftsmen is both rich and significant because al-Maghribi was familiar with the marketplace, he himself, as he says in his own words, having spent the early part of his life working and selling his products. He consequently had a firsthand knowledge of this vocabulary and close connections to the tradesmen and craftsmen who used them. As a result, the vocabulary related to crafts and production that we find in his dictionary opens up a new dimension of our understanding of the lives of craftsmen.

The Home, the Family, and Women

Attention to such day-to-day affairs as the home, family relations, women, and children constitutes an important facet of ordinary life to which the texts of the period paid attention. Thus the absence of women in the chronicles of the Ottoman—in al-Jabarti, for instance, who wrote a male-dominated chronicle in which women like Sitt Nafisa, wife of Murad Bey, were the exception—constitutes one particular approach rather than a generalized cultural feature as is sometimes suggested. It is not in the elite-oriented works that the family and the home emerge, but in other, less famous texts.

Family relations, the home, and women are, for instance, very present in some of the books written during this period, such as al-Maghribi's dictionary. His very choice of words to define is indicative. He defines words like *hamati*, for instance, meaning "mother-in-law" in local dialect, and words like *hamila*, meaning "a pregnant woman."[29] Terms relating to household duties are included in his dictionary, notably those denoting the sweeping of floors, the cleaning of houses, and the dusting of ceilings.[30] He also occasionally defined terms that were used specifically by women and children. When women said *"Al-raha tawrith al-milaha,"* they meant that rest engenders beauty, and when they talked of a *"mustantafa,"* they meant a woman who plucked facial hair with a twisted double thread (the hair being caught between the two strands and pulled out as the thread was passed over the face) and removed her body hair with a sticky paste.[31] Al-Maghribi also included baby language in his dictionary, such as the words *tata* (walking), a word of Pharaonic origin still used today in baby talk; *baba* to mean father;[32] and *zaqzaqa*, playing with a child to make him laugh.[33] Yusuf al-Shirbini tells us that when a child was thirsty, he said *anbuh*, and when he tried to touch something dirty, he was told *kukh*, to keep his hands off.[34] All these words are still used today in baby talk.

Family relationships and women often appeared in the proverbs that are frequently used in the literature of the period. A large body of these proverbs was linked to the feminine world, to the home and the family, suggesting not only that they had their source in the home, but also that collective wisdom was often passed down orally from generation to generation by the women of the house. As a matter of fact, Shirbini was explicit in his statement, repeated more than once, that he had heard a piece of wisdom from his mother or a proverb that he could remember from the time he was young.[35]

Through the proverbs from the feminine domain feminine voices could be heard. Their subject matter, focused on food, drink, and the kitchen, was based on feminine experience rather than on authority and prescription. Moreover, this source was given a validity that applied not only to women but to everyone. We can trace a level at which women are a source of knowledge of a particular kind: practical, concrete, and born of experience.

We thus see an additional dimension of urban women's lives. It confirms what we already know: that contrary to the impression we get from chronicles like al-Jabarti's where women were for the most part not visible and not actively involved in the creation and transmission of culture, they were visible and they had a significant social and cultural role. The picture we get is not that of the isolated, exploited, and submissive wife so popular among modern feminists who write in the modernization paradigm. Instead the picture shows women who had an influence that went beyond their own circle of women and children, even if their time was mostly spent inside the home, much as that of their contemporaries in other Mediterranean societies.

It also shows the practical aspect that we so often find in the court records of the period. Women's practical wisdom and common sense, as applied in their daily lives, is illustrated by the practicality we find among the women who appear in court records. According to court records, among women of the merchant class, this practical and commonsense approach could mean running their business and investing their money from their own houses, as in the case of 'Atiyat al-Rahman, wife of the head of the merchant guild, Isma'il Abu Taqiyya, in the early decades of the seventeenth century. 'Atiya al-Rahman supervised a *waqf* foundation and attended to her property, either right in her own house or through occasional visits to the court.[36] Women of more modest substance occasionally helped their husband in his work, especially those who wove textiles, especially in making the yarn, often a woman's job. The practical side of life that women had to confront daily occasionally appeared in court records because, even if they were wives, they expected payment for their work. Court records show a fair number of cases in which a woman takes her husband or ex-husband to court to demand her wages for yarn she has made for him.[37] Thus the literature is not very far from the reality these records show.

The feminine world appeared in a variety of other forms in the literature of the period. A particularly interesting one can be found in the writings of Abu Dhakir in which he narrated how he assumed a female role when particular conditions pushed him to do so. On two occasions in his manuscript, he consciously assumed this role. One occasion occurred when he was stranded in the town of Qina in Upper Egypt, with no boat to take him home to Cairo and having run out of money. The conditions that he was facing forced him to cope with an unusual situation, that of cooking and taking care of the house, a female role that he had never done before. He narrates with good humor his abilities in the kitchen; he describes a recipe he invented made with meat and a vegetable, which he called *al-warqana* because of the green leaf that he rolled the meat in, to rhyme with al-'Arqana, a prison in Cairo. On another occasion, he tells us what he learned as a child from the womenfolk in the house, in particular what midwives did. Much later in life, he could boast that he knew all the steps to be undertaken in order to deliver a woman in labor. He was proud of his knowledge, even though he did not put it into practice, and was confident that in an emergency if a midwife could not come in time, he would be able to do the job. Both males and females assumed multiple roles, or roles that could be changed or modified according to circumstances in time and space. This approach to women and the feminine world constitutes a significant break from the views we often read in the works of some members of the academic community. Through it a different view of society emerges, one seen from other than the dominant ideology.

An alternative to the dominant paradigms also emerges in relation to polygamy. Abu Dhakir, with his habitual openness about his personal life, narrates his experiences in relation to polygamy. In his mature years, long after he had formed his own family, his mother tried to convince him to marry a friend of hers, a proposition he strongly objected to on the grounds that he could not afford to have two wives. In parentheses, we are informed that the prospective bride did not make his heart tremble or excite him in any way (*lam bi qalbi raghba wa la tahyij*). To his mother, he said that he could barely meet his expenses with one wife so how could he afford to have two. In spite of the mother's promise of financial aid ("which I knew she would not keep," he tells us), he rejects the offer.[38] The text thus shows us an aspect of polygamy and of the issues it raised within the family that we rarely find in other texts in the early modern period.

Therefore the picture that these literary texts provide is closer to the one that we are familiar with in court records than it is to the one that al-Jabarti provides in his chronicle. The comparison can shed light both on our understanding of women during this period and of al-Jabarti. Rather than take al-Jabarti as the norm, one can try to place his work in context. Some writers, as he did, implicitly excluded the feminine presence from their work. Others were more explicit, expressing negative views of women that were probably commonplace in certain sectors. One of these is a work entitled *Kitab al-'Unwan fi Makayid al-Nisa* by an *'alim* called 'Ali b. Umar al-Batanuni al-Abusiri. The objective of this book of anecdotes was to show that women were ignorant of the *shari'a*, that they had excessive sexual appetites without knowledge of what was sinful, that their intellect was lacking, and that they could lead a man to sin and to adultery.[39] To prove his point, he included anecdotes showing that it was a woman who was behind the death of the caliph 'Ali, and another woman behind the killing of al-Hasan, 'Ali's son.[40] Sexual categories were clearly defined in these writings: The male was to restrain, the female to be restrained. Works of this kind must certainly have had a certain popularity among the reading public: the Bibliothèque Nationale (Paris) alone has four copies.[41]

Recent scholarship on gender has sometimes tended to focus on works that express attitudes such as these toward women and to consider them as representative not only of a particular society but of all Islamic societies regardless of time and space. This approach is partial insofar as it concentrates on one trend and treats it as if it applied to the totality of society and insofar as it fails to take historical change into consideration. Rather than see such views as being "traditional" or "Islamic," or as being representative of the position of women and the views toward women before the modern period, they can be put in perspective within the broader picture of society. This perspective means that we have to take into consideration the fact that at any one time there were different views and different expectations, and that these were often determined by class differences. Simple descriptions only serve to blur complex realities.

The emergence of the "ordinary" person evidently went beyond the confines of Cairo, although it is difficult to draw any precise geographical boundaries. One can, however, easily trace a focus on the "ordinary person" in parts of Syria, indicating that the patterns we can identify in Cairo had their parallels in other towns and cities, possibly for the same reasons. The ordinary person is, for example, very present in a chronicle of the Syrian city of Hums, written by Muhammad al-Makki Ibn Khanqah (d. 1135/1722). This historian records some public events in his chronicle, but much of the data is on very local and everyday issues regarding local Humsi families: their marriages and births, the circumcision of their children, their divorces, and their deaths, including those of their womenfolk. We are told, for example, of the death of a shaykh *suq* (shaykh or head of a market) called 'Umar b. 'Abdullah;[42] or the marriage of the son of another shaykh *suq*;[43] or the birth of a son to a shaykh *suq*;[44] or of circumcisions.[45] This chronicle is not unique in Syria, but serves as an example to show that concern with ordinary people and ordinary events was part of large social and political transformations. It was thus part of a wider regional framework. The conditions observed in Cairo had their parallels elsewhere, and to fully understand these conditions, much more exploration is needed.

Spread of the Colloquial

The spread of a form of writing that was close to the spoken word may also be considered as a manifestation of the concerns and the language of the ordinary person. The impact of middle-class culture is one of a multitude of factors behind another very important trend in the written culture of the seventeenth century, notably the spread of the vernacular language in written texts through certain forms of the colloquial or semicolloquial that linguists call "middle Arabic." Thus, at about the time that an academic interest in the colloquial appeared, as manifested in dictionaries of the colloquial like those of al-Maghribi and al-Muhibbi, a parallel trend was also making its appearance in texts, literary or otherwise, that were actually using written vernacular language.

The extensive use of a vernacular language close to the spoken word became prevalent in written texts at the beginning of the seventeenth century. As a result, the written word became more accessible, more inclusive, potentially even more marketable, as the language used was modified and made simpler. The process actually meant a number of things. It meant the emergence of a written culture more meaningful and more accessible to many people. They could understand it, identify with it, and use it to express themselves. It also meant that a strong dose of local culture, as opposed to a regional "Ottoman" culture or a universal "Islamic" culture, had gained some ground. A local culture among an educated class of people was, as this use of the colloquial clearly indicates, not the result of the construction of a modern nation state but part of a long and complex historical process with roots going back earlier than the modern state. This is a significant trend that had important repercussions in the nineteenth century. Thus it is important for our understanding of middle-class culture around 1600, but it is also important because of subsequent developments.

This development is highly complex and cannot be understood either as an abstract linguistic development or solely through contemporary social conditions. The spread of the colloquial in the seventeenth century was a consequence both of a long historical process and of contemporary social conditions. The fact that nonestablishment Arabic, or colloquial Arabic, became a growing medium of written communication among the literate was in and of itself a significant trend for which social factors can be evoked. Thus the expanding use of some form of colloquial as a medium of written communication raises many questions as to why it occurred at that moment in time. The reasons why it proliferated and the consequences of such a development must be studied in a broader framework than that of linguistic studies because of its social and political implications.

Al-Maghribi's dictionary has illustrated another significant dimension. The world of Islamic scholarship, of the religious sciences such as jurisprudence and traditions, and of the auxiliary sciences such as language, had a universal dimension insofar as scholars and scholarship traveled, because the books written in one center of learning were read and used in another. By its very nature, Islamic scholarship was not bound by political borders but aimed to reach scholars and students in Islamic communities everywhere. The dimension that al-Maghribi's work added to a genre that was well known in Islamic scholarship was a local one. He emphasized a local rather than a universal culture because he was concerned with the colloquial of Cairo (*lughat ahl misr*), with the way that the Arabic language was used in a specific community. Al-Maghribi, who was quite conscious of the fact that the spoken language of Cairo differed from that in other places, was giving the colloquial his attention as an object of scientific study, a language worth listening to, recording, and compiling; he was the first to devote an entire dictionary to the spoken language. As such, al-Maghribi's work constitutes a landmark in the history of the written colloquial. By writing this work, using the format of older dictionaries by putting the words in alphabetical order, he raised the colloquial to the level of academic work, worthy of study.

His methodology was also quite new, because he reached his definitions of words by using methods unlike those of his predecessors. In the tradition of Arabic dictionaries, the origin of the word was provided with a lot of *isnads*, or authorities, on the way that previous important writers had used it, sometimes going back centuries, often providing a large number of examples. Thus the word was defined in relation to past use. Here again the dictionary of Yusuf al-Maghribi constitutes an important landmark. A comparison with a classical dictionary like the fourteenth-century Firuzabadi dictionary shows how innovative he is. Firuzabadi, following the tradition of dictionary writing, indicated how previous scholars and classical religious texts had used a word; he provided the different meanings that were defined by these texts. Al-Maghribi was different. Because he was essentially writing about the colloquial of Misr, his source was what he heard and the way that people around him used a particular word.

It was by paying attention to what he heard and by listening that he reached his conclusions. Therefore, the method he used was essentially different because his material was different. Al-Maghribi defined a word by the way it was used by people; in other words, he defined it by its context rather than by reference to authoritative texts. In Egypt, he wrote, a *makhala* was a container for *kohl* (black eye makeup); but he heard some people use it to mean *bunduqiyya* (gun).[46] He was aware that the meanings of words change in time. The way a word is used and described in a dictionary of a previous period does not necessarily correspond to its use in his day. Thus al-Maghribi was less concerned with correctness than he was with context, notably the context of the ordinary urban dweller rather than the scholar, in the context of a lived reality rather than the authority of books.[47]

Language constituted one of those fields in which conflict was played out between those who were receptive to nonacademic influences and those who were not, or between those who stood to uphold what was classical, universal, and those who stood for what would reach a larger number of people, for what was a local culture. As such, through language, a larger battle was fought between the local and the universal; between those who maintained a strictly scholarly approach to culture and learning and those who were willing to expand their borders; between purists and innovators. One can see parallels between conditions in the seventeenth century and those in the late nineteenth century. As Amira El-Azhary Sonbol has shown in a recent publication, language was likewise an arena where various tensions were played out between those, representing the upper classes, who used French both in private and in public. The viceroy of Egypt, Khedive Abbas the second (1892–1914), once addressed the public in French during a ceremony in Alexandria in 1894. Arabic had become by that time, the language of the others, those who were not part of the ruling class and were not educated.[48]

Therefore, one cannot presume that there was a consensus among scholars as to the developments that they were witnessing. Representing a more purist line was the Syrian scholar Muhammad al-Muhibbi (d. 1111/1699), the author of the famous biographical work *Khulasat al-Athar*. Al-Muhibbi, in reaction to and in disapproval of what was happening, composed a dictionary of non-Arabic words that had entered the Arabic language, *Qasd al-Sabil fima fillugha al-'arabiyya min al-dakhil*. One of his aims was to pinpoint colloquial words that were used by the *'amma*. He distinguished them from imported words (*dakhil*) with the aim of showing them to be distortions (*tahrif*), or Arabic words that the *'amma* distorted.[49] He considered the use of the colloquial to be a negative development and one he disapproved of. His work nevertheless indicates that the question had by his lifetime become one of open debate, a significant phenomenon in itself.

The upsurge in the use of and interest in the colloquial at that particular moment in time can be put in context with social conditions. The presence of a middle-class culture in the written word is one of the factors that can explain this development. As of the early seventeenth century, the members of this class were using the book, were writing, were being addressed, and were being written about. Moreover, the status of this class—its social and cultural weight—is another factor to consider. The spread of the colloquial and the consolidation of the middle class coincide roughly chronologically, giving additional support to the argument that a link existed between the two. Other factors are linked to the spread of literacy and of Arabization, to the adaptation of the colloquial to certain kinds of informal or humorous writing.

The use of written colloquial predates the seventeenth century by a long time. From the first centuries of Islam, colloquial language can be traced in some of the written texts that have come down to us. In this early period, it had links to the process of Arabization in the centuries following the Arab conquest. The way that Arabic was used in the extant documentation of the early Arabic presence shows that the spoken language permeated these early texts. The papyri that Adolf Grohman studied, the earliest documents written in Arabic in Egypt, some of them dating from the eighth and ninth centuries some decades after the Arab conquest of Egypt, show that colloquial language appeared very early. Official documents, according to Grohman, used *fusha*, while other economic or private documents were written in an Arabic that did not distinguish between *sad* and *seen* or between *dad* and *dal*, and did not make use of the dual (*muthana*) endings. Misspellings were frequent in the private letters.[50] That they are examples of early written colloquial is clear. They might suggest that writing was broadly used. They might be the result of scribes who had not, at this early date, mastered the Arabic language; familiarity with the "classical" language remained limited except for rites of religious observance.

Historians have not yet determined the dating or the processes by which the Coptic language, in the period that followed the Arab conquest, was discarded in favor of Arabic. What is clear is that it was a slow process that took many centuries to complete. In the first period following the Arab conquest of Egypt, Arabic was spoken by a few people associated with the Arabs, and to a large extent in the centers where the Arab armies were situated. People were likely to be bilingual when they lived in proximity to the centers or converted to Islam. In the last stage, the population was totally Arabic-speaking. However, for most people, the only Arabic language they knew was that form of Arabic which they spoke. It was a localized form, influenced by the Coptic and Pharaonic languages. Its vocabulary continued to make use of words from these languages. The colloquial appeared in written texts as people were introduced to the written word.[51]

Thus the local dialect permeated the written word at an early date. It was a dialect that transposed, more or less closely, the spoken word, thus neglecting the grammatical rules of classical Arabic. For a long time, learned Arabic and literacy remained confined to the administration and the religious establishment, while the rest of the population used the spoken dialect they were familiar with.

One can make a link between the spread of the written colloquial and the spread of literacy. As large numbers of the urban population became literate without getting a thorough education or joining an institution for religious scholarship, they brought into the world of writing the language that they knew best: the local, or colloquial, form of Arabic. And as the number of literate people grew—those with a limited familiarity with the rules of proper language—the vernacular found a fertile ground in which to develop. As more people became integrated into the world of writing, the language of the written word became closer to the colloquial spoken word. Thus when large numbers of people received a basic education and learned to write, a thinning down of correct language was likely to emerge.

In France, where extensive work has been done on the history of books and the history of reading, a change in the language used emerges when books spread to those outside the religious and learned establishments. In the sixteenth century, for instance, the popular books were written in vulgar language rather than in Latin and, as noted by Guy Demerson, in a language that was intended to be clear and simple, Latin being the language of religion and learning.[52] Consequently, the popularization of knowledge was a function of broader literacy. Thus broader literacy is a partial explanation for the spread of the written dialect in Egypt, as it may well be in other societies with the same conditions, whether in other parts of the Ottoman Empire or of the Mediterranean region.

Although colloquial or semicolloquial language appeared in a few Mamluk texts (1250–1517), these were few and far between. Ibn Danyal (d. 711/1311) in the fourteenth century and Ibn Sudun (d. 868/1464) in the fifteenth century used Egyptian dialect or "substandard" Arabic as a medium of communication, according to Arnoud Vrolijk in a work full of humor and irony.[53] The fifteenth-century historian Ibn Iyas resorted to the colloquial when he reported direct speech. However, colloquial writing never spread very far during this period, remaining restricted within a small number of writers.

The number of works dating from the early decades of the seventeenth century suggests that we are in the forefront of something new, that this period was in fact a significant turning point in the history of colloquial writing. It became a means of expression by those who were well trained in language skills and had a great familiarity with the language as it was taught in institutes of higher learning. Even more significant, colloquial writing became a subject of academic concern: observed, studied, and written about in a scholarly fashion, as the dictionary of Yusuf al-Maghribi suggests.

This aspect in the development of colloquial writing is of great importance in the social context because it raises a number of questions as to why at that point in time it was extensively used in different kinds of writing—in literary texts, chronicles, and dictionaries. It also raises the question of why it was used both by people who may not have known the rules of grammar and by those who, like al-Shirbini, knew the rules of Arabic very well and had an excellent command of the language, as his other texts prove.

Starting roughly around 1600, we can observe two trends. First, a proliferation of texts on different subjects and written in some form of colloquial by people of varying levels of education. Second, we see different levels of colloquial writing. The categories that linguists use, *colloquial* and *middle Arabic*, do not fully show the great diversity within this category. The term *middle Arabic* does not distinguish, for instance, between the writings of a semi-educated person who misspelled commonly used words and names, combining the spoken word with elements of *fusha*, and the colloquial of a highly educated person who used colloquial words because it suited his purpose. Seen from this angle, *Hazz al-Quhuf*, which is by far the most, if not the only, famous work among those mentioned here, can be seen to be part of a context or trend that touched various kinds of writings in different ways.

Colloquial language used prior to this period was at times the result of limited linguistic skills, as in the early papyrus, or it was a colloquial by choice, used by people like Ibn Sudun or Ibn Iyas. Both were well familiar with the rules of grammar but chose to move between the classical and the vernacular, which was more informal or more suited to a particular text. Both these trends continued in the seventeenth century. Educated people who had a perfect knowledge of the Arabic language chose to use colloquial either because it was more informal, or for direct speech, or in a particular context such as funny or bawdy stories. They moved between the two with equal ease. Yusuf al-Shirbini, for instance, knew *fusha* very well, but he also knew that colloquial language had its own rules and he did not confuse the two. He wrote his famous *Hazz al-Quhuf* in a type of colloquial language while in his other works he used proper language perfectly. Others as well used both colloquial and classical, in different texts and sometimes in the same text, thus moving between two languages with ease. In a single text, for example, Muhamad Abu Dhakir used colloquial (mainly in direct speech), semicolloquial, and *fusha*.

The concern with colloquial language as of the seventeenth century had other dimensions. One of the most interesting developments was that people were listening to the various ways that different social groups were using language. In other words, language was being linked to context and to society, with distinctions between the ways that different words were used by Turks, by Syrians, or by Maghribis, including Arabic words that Turks mispronounced.[54] Abu Dhakir paid attention to the dialect of Syrians and the words used by Turks, for instance.[55]

An even more interesting seventeenth-century development was that these writers were listening to and recording in writing the language of subordinate groups. The dictionary even includes words like *haha* that donkey owners addressed to their donkeys.[56] The language of the *'amma*, or commoners, and the words used by *awlad al-balad* also attracted the attention of Muhammad Abu Dhakir.[57] The language of these less dominant groups was given the same scholarly attention as that of others, a significant social statement. This ability to listen to the differences in accent or in dialect between various social groups, and to consider it worthwhile to note the richness and diversity of the way they spoke, is in part a social phenomenon, part of a larger social picture, worthy of our consideration. The language of the ordinary person was being scrutinized, listened to, interpreted, and recorded. In part, this was a cultural reflection of the shifting social structures.

The innovations in the way that language was used constitute one dimension of much larger changes that affected society. They can be put in the context of the regional transformations taking place on a geopolitical level as the center of power in Istanbul was becoming more diffuse and as the accumulation of power in the various provinces was changing the balance. These transformations were not only political, but could also be linked to certain cultural changes emerging during the period, such as those affecting language, as the power shifts may have brought with them a greater emphasis on what was local, including local culture, local usage, and local dialect. Local culture, in other words, was gaining in importance and being given a growing legitimacy. The ruling class that was attempting to gain control over provincial government would not have been adverse to such a development.

This development of local culture had other manifestations. One of them can be seen in legal works that showed a similar emphasis on the local as opposed to the universal. The work of scholar Ibn Nujaym (d. 970/1562) contains important observations on local practice. He was greatly concerned with the legal weight that local practice (*'urf*) had as a source of law. For him, in fact, practice had the weight of the *shari'a*. The emphasis on local custom was justified juridically on the basis of social need. Certainly he was not the first to believe this. Johansen mentions an earlier jurist like al-Bazzazi (d. 817/1414) who was concerned with the issue of *'urf*. However, no one before Ibn Nujaym had, to the same extent, elaborated and developed the idea of local practice as a legal source for jurisprudence.[58] Muhammad Siraj finds his work on this subject to be pioneering insofar as it elaborated a theory on *'urf* and provided guidelines as to this theory.[59] His work thus adds one more link to the larger picture.

Thus a number of factors coincided to bring the local culture and the middle-class culture to the fore. At that level, the developments that can be observed during this period have a special significance as far as the modern period is concerned. The emphasis on what was local rather than on the universal became more widespread by the end of the nineteenth century and can be considered an important source for the identity being forged then.

This trend had a certain longevity that went beyond the period during which the middle-class culture was expanding. The fact that it survived in some form during the later eighteenth century when the cultural sphere of the middle class was being reduced is attributable to another set of factors.

As the middle class became burdened with overtaxation, its revenues were reduced as a result of the commercial transformations; it lost its former prominence, and its relation to the written word underwent transformation. Yet the middle-class influence on the written word, popularized text with its reliance on proverbs, and the literary texts that used colloquial language in some form or other all survived in the literature, the belles-lettres, of the latter half of the eighteenth century. But this survival was not a simple continuation of the trend. New factors had in fact intervened.

The New Demands of the Ruling Class

In the course of the late seventeenth and the eighteenth centuries, the Mamluks emerged as a force in the social and political scene, leading at the end of the eighteenth century to a culmination of their control. The whole issue of the educational and cultural contours of the Mamluks of eighteenth-century Egypt is still virgin terrain. We know little about their education or about the language or languages in which they communicated. One important cultural distinction emerging in the eighteenth century was the one between newly imported Mamluks and local Mamluks whom sources refer to as *misirli*, or Egyptian: those whose identity and interests were more closely associated with the local scene. Here again the elements of local culture and local interests play a role in shaping the picture. Unlike the Mamluks of the fourteenth and fifteenth centuries, the Mamluks of the later period were not as exclusive in terms of admitting non-Mamluks to their circles. Those born in Cairo had a much greater exposure to Arabic and to various facets of the local culture, and they were culturally closer to their environment, taking Arabic names like Muhammad, Ahmad, or 'Ali rather than the Turkish names of the earlier Mamluks, which were more difficult for the Arab population to pronounce. Moreover, a certain number among them, born in Egypt and sons of Mamluks, had some knowledge of Arabic. For many, this knowledge remained superficial. They might know how to speak some Arabic or how to use basic writing, because a Mamluk ordinarily underwent some religious education as a child. Some of them were much more familiar with Arabic, which they could read, and some, as probate records show, owned important private libraries.

Another distinction can be made in terms of education, a few Mamluks being known for their love of learning, for their enthusiasm for poetry and literature, or for their large private libraries. For many of those who had acquired some education but who had no scholarly inclinations, the easier vernacular language was more accessible. If they knew Arabic it was very possibly limited to the spoken language. Al-Jabarti's account of the evenings in Ridwan Katkhuda al-Jalfi's house, where poets and prose writers gathered to recite verses and poetry, certainly indicates that Arabic was the language in use, and that to appreciate poetry and literature a certain level of familiarity with the language can be presumed.

Among some of the Mamluks, a familiarity with the written word must have also existed, as suggested by the many libraries that they owned.[60] Yet among those who were familiar with the written word, most might have had a preference for easy language. It is of some significance, for example, that the letters of Murad Bey (d. 1801) that have survived were written in dialect. The Mamluks were consequently potential readers or audiences for works in colloquial language. As a market for works written in an easy language, the Mamluks may have created an incentive for such texts. This incentive is one of the explanations for the longevity of the tradition of writing in dialect.

It was perhaps in part to address the Mamluks that a number of literary works were written by the most prominent late eighteenth-century *'ulama'*. Among these, we find scholars who held the position of Shaykh al-Azhar, the highest religious position in Cairo: 'Abdalla al-Shabrawi, Ahmad al-Damanhuri, and Muhammad al-Mahdi. In their writings all three of them showed themselves to be open to cultural influences from below. Al-Shabrawi's work, for instance, was a combination of different genres: a compilation of poetry, wise sayings, and advice on conduct embellished by numerous stories and anecdotes. Written in an easy style, sometimes conversational, sometimes more classical, incorporating direct speech, these texts had nonreligious concerns such as miserliness and generosity; for example, "a person who cannot keep a secret is like a container that cannot keep what is in it."[61]

Likewise, a compilation of proverbs from the end of the eighteenth century may well have been addressed to this audience, with the supposition that people with various levels of education easily understood proverbs. Ahmad al-Damanhuri (d. 1192/1778) compiled in an alphabetical arrangement proverbs and sayings in his *Sabil al-Rashad ila Naf' al-'Ibad*.[62] This work is interesting because it contains the inherent contradictions of the last decades of the eighteenth century. Al-Damanhuri continued the tradition of using local proverbs and bits of wisdom that had become popular in the seventeenth century (*amthal, hikam*). Such an undertaking on the part of a person known as one of the greatest and most prolific and respected scholars of his time, bringing together a significant number of proverbs and useful bits of wisdom (*fawa'id*) intended to guide people in their daily lives, is significant for two reasons. He continued the trend of bringing the local and the popular into an academic form, because the method used was that of arranging entries in alphabetical order as was utilized in dictionaries. Light and amusing, his choice of proverbs is nevertheless significant: many of them aimed at showing difference, at emphasizing the dominant view of *'ulama'* and of the state. He used this cultural form that was popular among ordinary people as a way to control populations. Among his compiled sayings were pieces of wisdom such as "*idha arad Allah bil nas khayr, ja'ala al-'ilm fi mulukihim wal mulk fi 'ulama' 'ihim*" (if God wants his people to prosper, he gives their kings religious knowledge and he gives the rule to their *'ulama'*);[63] "*khayr al-umara' man ahabb al-'ulama' wa sharr al-'ulama' man ahabb al-umara*'" (the best emirs are those who love religious scholars, and the worst religious scholars are those who love emirs).[64]

Thus, even though we know this last period before the Napoleonic invasion to have been one of great exploitation of the population, both urban and rural, conditions had developed in such a way as to forge a level of common culture between otherwise very different social groups. In fact, the form of expression through which the urban middle class had entered into the world of writing and books survived after this class stopped being as articulate as it had been earlier. The survival of this form of expression rested upon another group with different demands.

6

Radical Intellectuals

A Culture of Crisis

THE RELATIONSHIP between the middle class and the ruling class underwent important changes between the end of the seventeenth and the end of the eighteenth centuries. The social conditions that emerged, intermittently at first, then more continuously as the eighteenth century developed, drastically changed the power structure. By the eighteenth century, as power was becoming more and more concentrated among a few emirs like 'Ali Bey al-Kabir and his successors, the urban population began to suffer the economic consequences of their abusive taxation. The recurrent crises that hit the population and the exploitative taxation on urban dwellers suggest an end to the partnership between the middle and the ruling class, now much concerned with rural wealth and an erosion of the fortunes of the middle class. A process of centralization of power in a few hands was started, and it continued, with ups and downs, throughout the eighteenth century.

As power became more concentrated in their hands, the members of the ruling class expanded taxation on the urban population in two ways. First, they gained more and more control over the state tax farms, which meant that they could increase taxation rates without much state intervention. Second, the eighteenth century was characterized by the emergence of a multitude of new tax farms created by powerful individuals over which the state had no control at all. Taxation was therefore increased in terms of both the number of taxes that were payable and the amounts that had to be paid. The members of the ruling class who controlled these tax farms greatly increased their private fortunes at the expense of the taxpayers. The net result was a reduction in the economic level of the urban middle class, well illustrated in probate records that show impoverishment for many of them.[1]

This trend had direct consequences for the cultural scene. The flexible lines between the ruling-class culture and middle-class culture and their interpenetration were replaced with more rigid frontiers and a less easy flow between them. Although there had always been significant barriers between the culture of the ruling class and that of the middle class, overlapping of cultures had made the lines that defined them more fluid and more flexible. With changing conditions, this flexibility was being replaced by a greater cultural polarization. Greater social, even political, concerns were becoming discernible among the middle class. The class seems to have developed a more discrete cultural and political identity as time proceeded (and even, perhaps, in terms of chronology, as their numbers dwindled and circumstances worked more against them). The importance of trade and commercial capitalism had granted them space, resources, and opportunities. These opportunities were linked to the shared interests that they had had with the ruling class that had protected them for a number of decades. It was only when these conditions started to erode, when an impoverishment started to emerge, that the spokesmen for the middle class voiced their differences and their dissociation from the ruling classes in their writings: "The luxury of their clothes and their food, the shiny decorations worn by their horses goes beyond that of the Abbasid caliphs and their successors," wrote a contemporary.[2]

In other words, the victims of these abuses were becoming articulate and their views about their social context were becoming distinct at a time when the economic opportunities for merchants, tradesmen, and craftsmen were being reduced. It was then that a political dimension emerged in their culture.

Ruling-Class Culture in the Eighteenth Century

The culture of the ruling class has not been sufficiently explored; it remains for the most part poorly understood at best and misunderstood at worst. We have to accept as a given the fact that it was a complex and multifaceted culture and that we cannot fit it into a simple model. The elite culture of the ruling class in Cairo seems a far cry from the courtly culture of Istanbul that Cornell Fleischer described in relation to Mustafa Ali. Those who attended *majalis* could boast of their knowledge of Persian poetry and of Arabic scholarship.[3] The *majlis* that al-Jabarti described sometimes tended toward vulgarity and licentiousness, devoid of the polish and refinement of the poetic sessions that Mustafa Ali attended. Therefore, even though we refer to Mustafa Ali's sessions and Ridwan al-Jalfi's sessions as a *majlis*, they were very different with regard to their mood and their content. The whole issue of Mamluk culture is in need of further consideration. Ruling-class culture fulfilled several functions at the same time. It consolidated its members' own social position, giving them legitimacy, providing them with the leisure that their money could afford them, and fulfilling their religious obligations. At the present stage of research on this subject, what can be done is to make sense of what we do know about its development in the eighteenth century and attempt to understand its relation to the culture of the middle class.

In the course of this period, the Mamluks developed a culture that was linked to their newfound wealth. As they consolidated their power and became more exploitative, they needed to reenforce their legitimacy in various ways. The eighteenth century was in fact the period when the Mamluks were founding important charitable and religious buildings like schools and mosques. The most important builders of public monuments of the Ottoman period in Egypt, for instance, lived during the eighteenth century, such as 'Abdul-Rahman Katkhuda, known for the many mosques, elementary schools, public fountains, and other structures he constructed in Cairo, and Muhammad Bey Abul Dhahab (d. 1191/1777), who built the religious complex next to the Azhar.

They also did so by encouraging various writings that consolidated the social ideology, supporting those at the center of the power structure and enjoining obedience to them. The authority was the person of the Ottoman sultan or the *'ulama'*, whose support of the military class was necessary. In his introduction to *'Aja'ib al-Athar*, al-Jabarti's placement of *'ulama'* in the social structure is close to the view held by Ibn Jawziyya and Ibn Taymiyya five centuries earlier. Al-Jabarti classified the *'ulama'* immediately after prophets, at the top of the social hierarchy, followed by kings and princes (*muluk, umara*).[4] The idea that the legitimacy of the state was based on its support for the *shari'a* and for the *'ulama'* was said and repeated in the eighteenth century by many *'ulama'*. At the end of the eighteenth century, for instance, Ahmad al-Damanhuri (d. 1192/1778) found the Ottoman state to be the closest to the early caliphal state on account of the mutual need for and support of the *shari'a* and for *'ulama'*.[5] An anonymous work, "Raha al-Rawh wa Salwa al-Qalb al-Majruh," tells us the importance of the Ottoman sultan at the top of the structure to hold it together: "[T]he *ra'aya* without the sultan is like a body without a soul"; it continues by saying that *'ulama'* were put by God above everyone else.[6]

This traditional view of the ideal social structure was repeated in learned works and in works of literature and ethics. This idealized social structure that gave religious scholars a special place should not be understood as a description of a social reality. It is some time now since the French scholar Gilbert Delanoue very convincingly argued such a structure to be a theoretical model that corresponded to the image that *'ulama'* wished to project rather than a description of a social reality.[7] It not only supported the status quo, but more importantly it represented order, harmony, and social cohesiveness versus disorder, disruption, and conflict. Respect for those in authority was an important part of this social harmony. As a rule, large segments of the population, especially in times of calm and prosperity, gave their support to this ideal. But whether in troubled times they accepted it at face value is another issue, one that the following pages address.

Another dimension of Mamluk culture was its greater patronage of artistic activities that combined leisure and pleasure with an attempt to enhance their public image. As the Mamluk ruling class accumulated great fortunes, it patronized and financed literary production. A certain type of cultural life developed around some of these Mamluks, often taking place inside their houses in the form of literary sessions. The household of Ridwan Katkhuda al-Jalfi (d. 1168/1754) in the first half of the eighteenth century engendered a new center for the patronization of artists. Ridwan Katkhuda was in fact famous for the numerous literary figures with whom he surrounded himself. When he and Ibrahim ruled, Egypt was in a state of prosperity and public security. In his gatherings music, dance, and licentious poetry amused the guests and brought them leisure and pleasure. Luxurious living was an important dimension of the newfound wealth of this class.

A further dimension was development of a public image that corresponded to the position of this class in the social structure. Ridwan Katkhuda attracted many poets to his sessions. Al-Jabarti tells us that poets sought his favor and praised him in odes, rhymed prose, and stanzas. He rewarded them with valuable gifts.[8] Some artists could only survive through patronage, seeking amirs to finance them, such as Shaykh 'Abdalla al-Idkawi (d. 1184/1770), a poet who reached great fame in his lifetime. Patronage provided artists and poets, especially those whose qualities in artistic creation were recognized, with an entrance into a social group to which they did not belong and among whom they were likely to be maintained in modest conditions. At the same time, it opened the possibility of gain, of fame, and perhaps of some security that others of their rank and status probably did not have, while at other times it forced them to move from one patron to another and to travel to places where they could ensure a living. Al-Muhibbi narrates that the poet Muhammad b. Ahmad al-Raqabawi was born in Imbaba, a village to the west of Cairo, and was brought up in Cairo, where he earned his fame as a poet. He subsequently travelled to Mecca and to Yemen, where patrons provided him with a generous yearly revenue in addition to many gifts and prizes for the poetry he composed in praise of patrons.[9] This was not an unusual trajectory for people like al-Raqabawi.

Typically, this patronage led to certain types of production that were intended to enhance the image of the ruling class and to show, often in lofty or stylized language, the idealized world that they lived in, far removed from day-to-day realities. Panegyrics are a good example of the type of writing that this relationship could bring about because they allowed the artist to shower praise on his benefactor. One of the most famous panegyrics of the eighteenth century was al-Idkawi's *Al-Fawa'ih al-Jinaniyya fi Mada'ih al-Ridwaniyya*, a work he wrote in praise of amir Ridwan Katkhuda al-Jalfi. Of this kind of verse, several examples are recorded by al-Jabarti, who gives us a taste of their content. One poet that al-Jabarti called "highly gifted in poetry and prose" wrote in praise of his master words to the effect that "My eyes and ears yearn to see you, / Not even the sun in the morning when it becomes visible to us in its best apparel . . . bestows such precious exhalations."[10] This kind of flowery verse full of embellishments and ornaments flourished under the social conditions and the relationships of patronage that developed in the eighteenth century; the one provided here is typical.

Variations on poetical "jugglery," whereby every word in a verse started with the same letter, or every other letter was dotted, for instance, were highly esteemed in these circles.[11] Likewise, occasional verse was quite popular and could be recited during the *majalis* (literary sessions) that were frequently held. Shaykh 'Abdalla al-Shabrawi (d. 1171/1757), for instance, wrote with a strong strain of lyricism in his many occasional verses, as for instance verses he composed on the occasion of an important personage's finishing a construction project in 1146/1733; on the occasion of Shaykh Ahmad al-Khulayfi's death in 1127/1715; on the occasion of the end of Ramadan; on missing Egypt during a voyage.[12]

The shifting social structure and the greater polarization emerging in the eighteenth century had another significant impact on culture: dissociation of the emerging ruling-class culture from the urban population. This dissociation was expressed in different ways. One of them was in their residences and in the way they lived. As the eighteenth century progressed, the palaces of the ruling class tended more and more to become self-sufficient entities incorporating the facilities that guaranteed the inhabitants would not need recourse to public facilities. Palaces of the eighteenth century increasingly had their private baths, their private mills, even their private prisons, so that many of them became more autonomous and their inhabitants did not have to make use of public amenities.[13] When Shaykh Muhammad Abul Anwar (d. 1228/1813), head of the wealthy Sufi order of al-Sadat al-Wafa'iyya, rebuilt his palace along Birkat al-Fil, he added a mosque, complete with pulpit, where he could make his Friday prayer without going to a public mosque, because, as al-Jabarti said, he did not like mingling with the "common people."[14] On the part of the military and religious ruling class, social polarization was thus accompanied by a greater desire for isolation from the populace.

The culture of the court was an extension, a reflection of the social and economic conditions of the ruling class. It had its patrons and its followers; it had its rules and its objectives. It also had its limitations and its restrictions, was never fully open to those outside certain circles. It was a culture that legitimized the ruling class and that reflected its interests. The people who created this culture could, regardless of their own background, reap direct or indirect benefits from their involvement in it. The poets who praised Mamluks, for instance, often themselves of modest origins, were paid generously, and their association with those in power gave them prestige among their own kind.

Culture Outside the Courtly Circles

Outside these ruling-class circles were many other educated and articulate people who were forming another circle, developing another cultural sphere. The development in the eighteenth century of a courtly culture and language around the Mamluk households had repercussions on the culture of those outside Mamluk circles. Thus, at the same time as this courtly culture was taking shape, it was influencing another culture being developed in another direction.

From the social, economic, and educational contexts of the period there emerged an educated elite amidst the middle class, more and more excluded from the religious hierarchy as polarization developed, notably a few articulate and educated men who saw things from a particular angle and who observed and recorded the realities around them. Thus, although they may have had links to the institutions of religious education, the views they were expressing were diverging from those of elite *'ulama'*. In fact, what we can detect in their writings are the reactions and the views of a social group or groups other than those that we read about in writers like al-Jabarti, who was elite-oriented. We need to consider the extent to which these texts were representative of the writer's own personal views or of the views and attitudes of the middle class or of the ordinary urban dweller. The answers can help us to identify the way that the ordinary urban dweller lived through these important changes in economy and politics, answers that we find through the writings of others.

In fact, the analysis of some literary texts detects a reaction to the changing conditions, more specifically a reaction from those whose voices were not usually heard, notably those outside the power structure. This analysis entails reading these texts in a way that emphasizes the social dimension without regard for inherent literary qualities. It therefore entails a consideration of texts that may have little literary value but that can shed light on the social dimension or can tell us where a writer places himself on the social scene. Finally, it entails placing these texts in the context of the process of a middle class developing its social and cultural identity. In other words, rather than use them as cultural production, the texts can be used as themselves being part of the social change and of the historical process. Such an approach to cultural production follows in the steps of those cultural historians, like Walter Benjamin and Raymond Williams, who saw cultural productions—literary works, for instance—not as having their own history that could be studied or understood independently of social or political conditions but instead as part and parcel of a larger picture of the social tensions of a particular period.[15]

As a matter of fact, the writers in question can best be understood in the context of the socioeconomic conditions through which their generations lived, as "organic intellectuals" emerging as a result of these conditions rather than as intellectuals working closely with the establishment or with the authorities. The more or less acute economic crises that befell ordinary urban dwellers were expressed in street demonstrations of variable scope in 1678, 1687, 1696, 1715, 1724, and 1733, sometimes by the closure of shops as a sign of protest at the injustice of the authorities, at other times by more violent acts like pillage and destruction of property. Often the participants were the "populace," that is, an unidentified popular group, notably the poor of the city who suffered the most from these crises, but at other times joined by Azhar students and occasionally by artisans and tradesmen.[16]

These writers were raising questions of an intellectual nature that the ordinary person would probably not express in writing: questions on, for instance, some of the givens of society or of the social or intellectual order. They were expressing a discomfort and dissatisfaction felt by many others living in the same conditions who were less articulate, and their expressions suggest their dissociation from ruling groups and the establishment. This dissociation is particularly evident in writers who were in the lower-ranking religious positions, whose loyalty or identity was divided between their position in the religious hierarchy and their belonging to a middle class.

The texts show a latent dissent expressed directly or indirectly at the social order and a concern with economic issues. For example, some of them challenged aspects of the dominant ideology in relation to social structure. Others challenged the existing intellectual leadership, the definitions of knowledge, and the ways to reach knowledge. They sometimes questioned, implicitly or explicitly, the authority, conduct, and methods of *'ulama'*. These attitudes toward the establishment had a bearing on the subject matter that they dealt with, notably their concern with money and with impoverishment. They also had a bearing on the way they expressed themselves, using realism, personal observation, and personal narrative, another way of distancing themselves from the lyrical and panegyric establishment literature.

Contemporary texts show that what some educated people outside the establishment thought or wrote did not always correspond with the views of those within the establishment. Consequently the views and attitudes of the "great" writers and thinkers, with which we are more familiar, cannot always be taken as representative of their age, but should be seen as those who were more listened to and more visible. Thus the ideas that subordinate groups always blindly accepted their situation without any kind of questioning, for religious or other reasons, that the only kind of dissent against authority was the street riots and demonstrations that occurred as a result of food crises and the resulting famine, that dissent was not rational or thought out but was simply a cry of hunger, are in need of serious reconsideration. These views fall well within the framework of the passive East versus the dynamic West that the Orientalist framework has used to understand Arab societies before the penetration of the West. The reality is, as the texts show, much more nuanced. Such texts can therefore be used as a framework for the analysis of society and social ideologies.

To a large extent, the trend that was distinct from establishment culture was closely linked to, or even an offshoot of, the expansion of the cultural sphere of the middle class and the greater presence it had in the written text, discussed in the previous chapter; members of the middle class were part of a reading public and they were authoring books, and the contents of books, whether they wrote them or they were addressed by others, reflected these realities. However, even though these writers were influenced by the use of expressions linked to everyday speech and by, in a general way, the growing sphere of the culture of the middle class, they nevertheless developed in a different direction, first because of a sophisticated educational level and second because of the changing economic climate. They were clearly more intellectual, more educated than the bulk of the middle class. Consequently the texts they wrote were beyond the reach of many because their proponents or spokesmen belonged to the "educated" sector of the middle class, presumably people who had been exposed to different forms of learning and to the prevalent cultural forums. At that level, they were not representative of the middle class, but rather of its educational elite. Yet at the same time, the views and attitudes they expressed, the social and economic concerns they developed, were those of the larger group. Thus their expression and language, as well as their critical attitude and their social realism, make them significant precursors of the nineteenth century.

This little recognized but important and innovative trend sheds new light on our understanding of the period and on the nineteenth century. In fact, the late seventeenth and eighteenth centuries witnessed the emergence of a social cultural dimension that historians have guessed at but not fully explored, probably because the answers cannot be found in traditional sources. The nineteenth century built upon some of the features of this culture, a fact that gives nineteenth-century culture more historical depth than is usually attributed to it by scholars who only consider it in the context of the formation of the modern state and of Western influences. These people writing in the seventeenth and eighteenth centuries thus provide a significant level of original thought and innovation, in their approach to social realities and in their point of view regarding authority and the establishment. They expressed an attitude toward the establishment reminiscent of the more famous late nineteenth-century writers like Ya'qub Sannu' (1839–1912) and 'Abdalla Nadim (1845–96). Their use of a form of colloquial language that was accessible to larger numbers of people and more adapted to the content of their writings than formal language was likewise influential in the nineteenth century. They, in other words, provide a foundation for some of the later developments.

That innovative forms should emerge from people who were marginal to the establishment or to the power structure should not be surprising. A number of scholars have debated the issue of how much change comes from within or from outside institutions, of whether innovation in culture was linked to institutions of learning or took place outside these institutions. This debate has been going on for some time in relation to universities in Europe at roughly the same time, the sixteenth to eighteenth centuries. Questions have been asked about the role of English universities like Cambridge in the big changes that were taking place in the seventeenth century, for instance; one scholar, John Gascoigne, has described Cambridge as an intellectual wasteland, the scholarly work issuing therefrom of little or no value in scientific developments.[17] Universities used a restricted curriculum that was not often changed in response to changing conditions. Because European, like Islamic, universities had their origins in religious study, until the eighteenth century in Europe and the nineteenth in Egypt, questions can be asked about the extent to which they influenced or played an active role in a dynamic nonreligious context. In France, for example, the educational institutions with the strongest influence on scientific and philosophical thought were the state-initiated academies rather than universities. Opinions around this issue are divided, and for some historians the role of universities is considered to have been vital to the intellectual movements of eighteenth-century Europe.[18]

The same debate is applicable to the Ottoman world. Historical research on Egypt, Syria, and Turkey has tended to emphasize the role of the state in bringing about a nonreligious culture by reforming the educational system in the nineteenth century. The importance of these reforms cannot be questioned, either in their scope or in the consequences that they had for modern culture. And yet it is misleading to ignore certain similarities that may have had a bearing on such developments. Structural and geopolitical factors emerging prior to the nineteenth century also require some consideration.

Identities

Who are these writers and what is their background? Because they are not prominent scholars or part of the establishment, the little we know about some of them is usually confined to what they tell us themselves. Of these a most interesting literary autobiography is that of Muhammad Hasan Abu Dhakir. His untitled work is interspersed with extensive autobiographical information. The sophistication of his views on the world around him, the analysis he provides of his surroundings, and the level and relevance of the details he includes by far surpass those of the others, although his position was in all likelihood representative of many others. He never became rich or famous. He did not receive great consideration from his contemporaries as a thinker or writer. He was educated and well read, thought independently, and was articulate in his views. Yet he remained throughout his life in the middle echelons; this position neither fulfilled his aspirations nor provided him with the material security he wanted.

The autobiographical data is of particular interest because it does not dwell on great achievements but, on the contrary, on the ordinary aspects that any average student might face. Abu Dhakir, like many others, only attended the Azhar for a limited period and did not continue his studies for financial reasons: he had to support his family. Unlike what we usually read in the biographical dictionaries about successful scholars who reached important positions or wrote great works, Abu Dhakir was a student who did not make it, whose stay in the Azhar was not greatly successful, who did not do brilliantly in his studies—in other words, his was the experience of many students. The difference is that Abu Dhakir did not hesitate to articulate this experience clearly for his reader. He wrote a short piece that explained why he distanced himself from the Azhar. In part, he attributed his dissociation to his doubts about the knowledge and the morals of some of the scholars that he knew and to the fact that many of the scholars and students looked down on those who were less fortunate. "They made fun of him, they pointed their fingers at him, because he occasionally had to work to earn his living," at a time when it was necessary for him to find funds in order to support his family.[19]

Subsequently, with the help of his stepfather, he got a position as scribe (*katib*) in a *waqf*, notably that of Sultan Muhammad, a middle-ranking position that he seems to have kept all his life. The job gave him a certain stability and he remained forever grateful to his stepfather for having helped him through his relationships to obtain it. Yet there is a sense of frustration at this situation because the salary he received from his job always kept him needy for more. His frustration was deepened by the realization that those who materially succeeded in life did not necessarily have any intellectual merit. In many ways, Abu Dhakir's life story was typical of the many people with some exposure to higher education that could last for a shorter or a longer time, whose subsequent professional activity did not lead them to the higher ranks and whose attempts to increase their revenues by various means more often than not were unsuccessful.

The same kind of detailed information is not equally available for others who wrote in the same vein. Even in the absence of comparable life-story information, however, it is still possible to see common attitudes. For example, the writings of Hasan al-Badri, Yusuf al-Shirbini, and Shaykh 'Amir al-'Anbuti are also the expression of those outside of the power structure who see a discrepancy between themselves and those in power, or who do not associate themselves totally with the dominant ideology. Part of it they accepted and other parts they did not. All of them observed society and had social concerns. The sophistication of these writers can be measured by the many ways they found to express their views, by talking about social groups, about food, about language; by the way that they observed social behavior and interpreted its motives; and by the many levels of language that they used, moving from colloquial to semicolloquial and to establishment Arabic. Their life spans extend roughly from the end of the seventeenth century, when a new power structure was emerging, to the latter part of the eighteenth century when this power structure came not only to dominate economic resources, but also to shrink the cultural sphere that the middle class had enjoyed for some time.

Among a few writers, most of whom were not well known, a type of writing emerged with social and economic concerns, with an intellectual content, and occasionally with a political content. Their influence on their contemporaries is more difficult to determine because only a few are mentioned in chronicles or biographical dictionaries. Perhaps they were not prominent enough to be talked or written about. Perhaps they did not pose a threat to the establishment worthy of bringing about a reaction, in the way that it reacted to public disorder, for instance. In other words, the political weight of these writings cannot be established. But their importance for modern historians is not so much in the influence they may have had on their contemporaries; it is more in the fact that a few people, whose writings are discussed here, seem to be expressing the concerns and attitudes of whole social sectors of the urban population. They put into words what many others, literate or illiterate, were perhaps not capable of articulating in writing. They consequently provide us with a picture of their society as seen from the bottom up. Among these writers, many of whose lives spanned the eighteenth century, is a class awareness of their difference from others, especially those in the power structure, and a tension linked to their economic conditions or at times to deprivation. Their style of writing distinguished them from the literature of the establishment: they were realistic, concerned with what they saw around them, rather than with being lyric or laudatory, giving their own observations great weight. This more realistic style becomes more and more evident in the eighteenth century, as taxation, usually abusive, befell the middle class. Their views on poverty and on issues related to money emerge as individual rather than as collective voices, expressions coming from a person rather than a class with common interests. In the long term, the impact of these writers remained limited, and the conditions of the latter part of the century seem to have reduced their sphere considerably.

The authors of these works have not received attention for a number of reasons. They were not part of the power structure nor were they prominent scholars. Because of their situation on the margins of the power structure, and because of the nature of the sources used by scholars, historians have not explored the role that these men played in expressing the thought of their time. It is important to widen our scope and to include them as a social and cultural force from about the mid-seventeenth century onward, playing a role that needs to be identified and explored.

At this point we can ask if these writers can be called intellectuals. Scholars have long debated the issue of the emergence of intellectuals. To a certain extent, the answer they gave was linked to the way "the intellectual" was defined. The French historian Elisabeth Badinter suggested that the intellectual emerged when a separation occurred between the religious scholar and the educated person who was not a religious scholar. She linked this phenomenon to the development of state academies in France, the first of which appeared in 1634.[20] In the Arab-speaking world, the emergence and rise of intellectuals has been associated with the late nineteenth and early twentieth centuries. Hisham Sharabi, for instance, considered that the rise of an educated elite separate and distinct from the religious elite (the *'ulama'*) was a result of education as well as of increasing contact with Europe.[21] His view falls well within the paradigm that sees changes in the nineteenth century as coming from two sources: state policies and European models.

What we see among these writers is in fact a kind of intellectual who was educated and articulate yet did not see himself nor was seen by others as a religious figure or a scholar. Moreover, those who gave intellectual expression to the concerns or to the crises of the urban middle class were not necessarily themselves shopkeepers, artisans, middle-scale merchants, or shaykhs. Their level of education, as suggested from the texts that some of them wrote, indicates a literary sophistication higher than the basic literacy many people obtained in the *kuttab* (elementary school); most of them had some exposure to college education, or to some other channels of learning, formal or informal. Some we know to have been Azhari. For instance, Hasan al-Badri and Muhammad Hasan Abu Dhakir added "al-Azhari" to their names in order to indicate their link to the Azhar. Yusuf al-Shirbini, about whose education we do not have a clue, nevertheless shows a high level of erudition. He was familiar, for instance, with the works of al-Ghazali, with the history of Ibn Khalikan, with the literature of Abul 'Ala' al-Ma'ari, with al-Hariri, with the geographical works of al-Masudi. He thus leaves no doubt about the breadth of his reading. Likewise, Abu Dhakir's work has references to al-Ghazali, al-Maqrizi, al-Suyuti, al-Munawi, Ibn al-Wardi, and Ibn Sudun, an indication of the breadth of his readings in literature, in history, and in the religious sciences, and of a familiarity with works from the twelfth century, from the Mamluk period, and from the sixteenth and seventeenth centuries.

Yet it is not in the capacity of learned men that they emerged; nor did they present themselves as scholars, even though their writing suggests a familiarity with religious sciences and with the classical heritage. Instead, they were intensely concerned with issues of nonreligious dimensions. The social concerns that they wrote about, the issues of money, of poverty, and so on, were precisely those of a broad urban middle class. Consequently these writers stood on the lower scale of the intellectual scholarly class in terms of the positions they had or their economic status, but they stood at the top of the educational hierarchy of the middle class, giving expression to the class's social concerns because they shared the same economic crises. As conditions in the eighteenth century became more critical, their association with the interests of the urban middle class and with its sense of class awareness was brought to the fore.

In structural terms these intellectuals were quite distinct from the academic intellectuals or scholars, the *'ulama'*, about whose hegemony historians have often debated. But, as Raymond Williams has remarked, the consideration of a singular and static hegemony (which in an Islamic society would be that of the *'ulama'*) does not sufficiently show the complexities of social formation. Hegemonies were challenged and continually had to be defended and even modified. Raymond Williams proposed a model that allowed for this kind of variation and contradiction and that could be part of a historical process.[22] Thus, by including these writers in our picture of eighteenth-century society, we can have a better understanding of the tensions among the different social and cultural identities and of the processes of social change in this period.

Through their writing we see the social and economic transformations that the society of Cairo experienced, not through the eyes of the establishment—of the winners—but through those of the losers. Thus the culture that they expressed was representative not only of these few observant and critical writers whose works are discussed, but in many ways of the numerous people who underwent similar experiences but who were less articulate. One can take this matter a little further and suggest a kind of social awareness on their part about the predicament of the urban middle class and of its culture.

Many of these writers, moreover, were influenced in their writings by the popularization of written texts that has been described in the previous chapter, by the level of the language used, by the content and subject matter. In the tradition of many others before them, they used a vernacular form; they often switched between proper and spoken Arabic, but clearly they used language in order to express specific thoughts or ideas rather than to be correct. Moreover, as mentioned earlier, they made profuse use of popular proverbs and jokes, thus bringing into their writing those forms and expressions of the culture with which the ordinary urban dweller was familiar. Thus they were influenced by, or were even products of, the trend toward democratization of the written word. Most significant, their work highlighted the condition of the ordinary urban dweller as his situation worsened. They were moving between two cultures or two identities. One of them was with people like themselves who had a significant exposure to education, regardless of how it was obtained, and familiarity with the Islamic heritage. The other was with the worries and concerns of the ordinary person having to face the problems of everyday living, of supporting a family, of confronting potential exploitation by those in power.

This double identity was at the root of a certain ambivalence, of an oscillation between being part of the religious hierarchy and being a victim of the greed of those at its top. This ambivalence, which on the personal level was a cause of suffering, may well have been an impetus for new thoughts and for new channels and styles by which to express them. Whereas at the individual level ambivalence may have been negative, it may also, on a general level, have produced the questioning that emerges in the written texts.

Abu Dhakir's experience and observations led him to conclusions that collided with various social and intellectual traditions of his time, yet the strength of the tradition that elevated *'ulama'* in society permeated him even as he was strongly critical of their acts. Another angle that crept into his writing occasionally was the reminder that his own training had been in the Azhar, that in some way he remained connected to, influenced by, some of its teachers and teachings. This ambivalence may have been the lot of many people linked to the *'ulama'* but dissociated from the establishment.

At another level, the questioning of or challenge to the dominant ideology or the establishment culture did not mean a rejection of this culture. The objections to it, explicit or implicit, were not a call for total change or for revolution. What they indicate is the ambiguity felt by intellectuals outside the power structure. People like Abu Dhakir and Hasan al-Badri al-Hijazi, a well-known poet who was also an Azharite, did not blindly accept the dominant ideology and did not speak of the social structure in the terms that those in power used. Thus some parts of society were acceptable and others were not. Regarding the *'ulama'*, for instance, they pointed out what they considered to be discrepancies between material success and intellectual capacities. The poet Hasan al-Badri, quoted by al-Jabarti, expressed these views thus: "The mighty Lord of creation has afflicted al-Azhar Mosque with many coarse and rude people . . . They make their turbans big and their sleeves broad in order to appear as masters . . . Under their arms they carry texts of traditions 90 fascicles or more. These they display wherever they go, for the purpose of hunting money." A little later he adds: "Do not ask about the *'ulama'* of your age, for their worth is very clear. The benefit you can receive from them is nil, whether for this world or the next . . . if you avoid them you will feel more comfortable." "Follow the lessons of *'ulama'* without looking at their deeds," wrote Abu Dhakir.[23] We can trace an ambivalence in these statements.

On the one hand, these statements show that Abu Dhakir did not totally reject the status quo. On the other hand, they implicitly point to a trend that his generation was starting to witness, notably the enrichment of high *'ulama'* to new levels of wealth. One of the earliest to amass a great fortune was Shaykh Muhammad Shanan al-Maliki, who died in 1133/1720–21. He was wealthy and prosperous, according to al-Jabarti one of the richest men of his time. He had black slaves, white slaves; one of his Mamluks was Ahmad Bey Shanan.[24]

His fortune and his level of consumption were comparable to those of the ruling emirs, a phenomenon that can be observed in the early decades of the eighteenth century and that develops to the end of the century with people like Shaykh 'Abdullah al-Sharqawi and Shaykh Muhammad al-Mahdi. Yet the status of *'ulama'* in society was deeply ingrained and neither Hasan al-Badri nor Muhammad Abu Dhakir, both of whom were quite critical, totally denied or rejected it.

The place that Abu Dhakir gave *'ulama'* in the hierarchy of people, in an abstract construction, was not much different from that of al-Jabarti because in the hierarchy the *'ulama'* came right after the prophet and his companions.[25] He saw a different picture when it came to real life. Al-Shirbini, who likewise aimed severe criticism at the *'ulama'*, distinguished between the high *'ulama'* who deserved respect and the other *'ulama'* whom he accused of being half-educated. Thus, this was not revolutionary thought that pushed for change of the status quo, but part of a critical appraisal of the dominant views, some of which were accepted while others were rejected.

Writers with social and economic concerns tended to be more realistic about their surroundings, to base themselves on observation of the realities around them. Their texts show a concern for what people ate, what they wore, and the material conditions of life. In stark contrast to the lyrics of the courtly circles, these writings showed a keen observation of an unembellished reality. Their dissociation from the academic approach, which put a heavy emphasis on precedence and authority as a source of knowledge, led instead to observation and individual experience as a source of knowledge. The attitude of these writers thus represented unofficial expressions from the culture below the elite, shunning literary canons and linguistic norms, displeased with the status quo, opposed to the more polished official culture that aimed at maintaining stability and social harmony. This conclusion is in some ways reminiscent of the approach of Mikhail Bakhtin, the great Russian literary critic and philosopher whose study of the sixteenth-century French writer Rabelais became a classic. Bakhtin considered that Rabelais' work incorporated the folk traditions of the carnival, of folk culture and folk humor. Through its use of the vernacular, its burlesque, its humor, its satire, it aimed at attacking authority and the established order in general. Through its use of the style and tone of the marketplace, it was a parody and a travesty of the medieval ecclesiastical method of persuasion, narrow-minded and intolerant.[26] For Mikhail Bakhtin, what had until then seemed to be the irrational and even immoral conduct that the illiterate masses displayed—in their festivals, their songs, their farces, their pornographic imagery—was a reaction to a power structure that had become distasteful.[27]

But people like Abu Dhakir cannot be identified with the "folk" culture that Bakhtin studied. They were too sophisticated and too well read. Their culture was not in any way a "carnival" culture, but a book culture. The spread of cheap paper had made writing accessible as a vehicle of expression and the book as an arena to air out differences; the written word, not the carnival, was their mode of expression.

The unofficial character of the educated middle-class culture and its approach to its social surroundings raise another question, this time in its relationship to the public sphere. This culture was not tightly bound by the restrictions that institutions of education imposed, by the methodology of academic study, or by the hierarchies of such institutions. The texts expressed more freely the individual views of the writer, founded on an intellectual or rational approach that neglected many of the accepted norms and went well beyond their boundaries. In these features the culture comes close to the "public sphere" of Jürgen Habermas, the space within which a rational as opposed to a traditional dialogue took place, in which what was said was of more significance than who said it. Newspapers and clubs where people met and exchanged views constituted the public spaces where the bourgeoisie could challenge authority and traditional norms.

But to consider this as a rational versus a traditional culture does not fully reflect the reality of the situation. This sphere was very much the reflection of a social situation rather than an abstract form of rationality. It reflected the views of contesting or conflicting partners, each of which used both the oral and the written to advance their views and further their interests.[28] As a result, it was largely shaped by the shifting social structures.

Emerging Cultural and Political Identity of the Middle Class

One of the most interesting dimensions that can be detected in the texts in question has to do with the emerging cultural and political identity that was expressed by some of the more educated and more articulate members of the middle class. The texts contain views and attitudes counter to establishment views or to the dominant ideology, expressed in either implicit or in explicit terms. These differences are evident in approach, in the way that social surroundings were understood or interpreted, in views of what constituted valid knowledge and the proper ways to reach it, in style and in language. An important manifestation of this middle-class identity was its concern with social and economic realities and its realistic rather than idealistic view of the world. At the level of style and language, writers expressed themselves in a realistic, empirical, and concrete style, and in straightforward language. The emergence of realism and empiricism in writing can be linked to groups outside the establishment, those that do not express the dominant view idealizing certain social structures.

Language can be considered as one of the manifestations of social change and of class tensions. The norms of the written word and the canons of correctness and polished writing, so important among a certain segment of the establishment, were broken intentionally by the use of a language that was used to express an authentic and intimate experience rather than for reasons of "correctness" or beautiful expression. The previous chapter discussed various factors that encouraged the spread of the colloquial in texts, notably the spread of literacy and a book culture, the emergence of writers and readers among the middle class, and the importance of having easily accessible texts. Writers made use of colloquial language in some form either because it was the only vehicle of expression that they knew, because it sold, or because it was more adapted to their subject matter. Abu Dhakir gave a new twist to the use of the colloquial or semicolloquial. By his time, some form of the colloquial was commonly used in various types of literary texts and chronicles, encouraged by the development of a book culture among people who were not primarily scholars.

A number of texts written in the eighteenth century suggest that the semi-educated were making use of the written word, that writers who had a rather limited exposure to education and for whom some form of colloquial was their habitual mode of expression were writing books and chronicles. Nevertheless Abu Dhakir's comments on the use of language are significant. They suggest a self-conscious form of dissociation both from the establishment language and from the literary tradition or literary canon. About a century earlier, al-Maghribi's justification for his interest in colloquial language was to show that it essentially followed the proper form; in other words, it was an important object of study because it was not too different from establishment language. Thus, although generations before him had been using the colloquial for a variety of reasons, Abu Dhakir was actually calling for its use because he saw its positive aspects. He defended, more than any of his predecessors, the use of a freer type of language that expressed what the writer wanted to say. Abu Dhakir considered that language should be flexible and made to reflect meaning rather than to follow rigid rules of correctness. For him, what really counted was the meaning that one wanted to express, rather than the correct use of proper forms. He therefore consciously advocated the use of freer expression and of language neither tied to the rigid rules of correctness associated with scholarly learning nor filled with the ornaments and embellishments of high literary canons. Abu Dhakir was explicit about his dissociation from the rhetorical literature to which many writers of his generation resorted and from the scholastic tradition practiced by those he called, with some sarcasm and with implications of pomposity, *ashab al-ta'alif wal tasanif* (the writers of books and tracts). He said that he was incapable of writing like them in academic language. In terms of form and expression, he advised his readers to follow him insofar as he used language in a way that expressed himself, even if it meant that the language was weak (*rakik*). He used colloquial language as an expression of difference, not only in language but also in attitude. Abu Dhakir's words indicate a support, a justification, for flexible expression that was independent of the more scholarly and literary use of language.[29]

His comments must be put in context with the importance that was given to language in scholarly circles. The Azhar was in fact particularly strong in language and linguistic studies and prided itself on this strength. Abu Dhakir's comments thus went against the prevailing scholarly attitude toward language. His words in fact constitute one of the most explicit and daring justifications for the use of dialect, for its usefulness as a means of written communication, and by implication for its greater relevance in comparison to standard use of language. More important, the comments he made had social connotations because he associated correctness with scholars and free expression with those outside of the scholarly community.

Another domain in which differences emerged was in the subject matter that was considered relevant. A particular dimension that suggested a middle-class identity, emerging with the economic crisis, was a view of society based on material concerns rather than on an abstract ideology. These concerns were subject to transformation as a result of broader conditions. Concerns with material life emerged in al-Shirbini's *Hazz al-Quhuf*, notably in his awareness of the difference between the haves and the have-nots. He expressed this sense of social difference in his section on food, comparing the food of the rich with the food of the poor: the rich cooked food in butter, while the poor cooked it in water, for instance. Abu Dhakir expressed concern with material life in his section on traveling. Travelers, he said, were of three kinds: the rich, the middle, and the poor. Each of the three had its level of comfort, and based on these differences he wrote a section of advice on how to travel, what to take in terms of luggage, the means of transport, and so on, each section clearly indicating the difference in wealth of the traveler.[30] Thus, although the writers were not always explicit, the social classifications that they were making or implying were in fact quite different from the social ideology that was current, an ideology that divided society into two groups, the *khassa* and the *'amma*. "I neither belong to the *khassa* nor to the *'amma*, but am lost somewhere in between the two," said Abu Dhakir more explicitly, because he considered himself to be in the class between the elites and commoners, meaning that he neither belonged to the one nor to the other, but to a class in the process of finding its self-awareness.[31]

A significant feature of these writings was their concern with money and work, typically middle-class concerns: how to make money, how to keep it, the deprivation that its absence brought about. In the context of a society that was witnessing significant social flux, punctuated by a number of crises caused by natural and man-made disasters, the awareness of the value of money came to the fore. More or less severe monetary crises kept recurring: André Raymond identified some thirteen of them between 1690 and 1736, resulting in a radical rise in the price of basic food commodities.[32]

By considering the concern with money and with poverty, we can trace transformations that were occurring between the seventeenth century and the mid-eighteenth century. Optimism linked to the greater material possibilities available in the earlier period was giving way to a sense of deprivation and anxiety about money. Toward the end of the seventeenth century, Yusuf al-Shirbini wrote a text entitled "Kitab Tarh al-Madad li-Hall al-'Ala' wal-Durar" that is of exceptional interest in the present context. If one overcomes his writing technique of composing a text made up entirely of undotted letters, one can find an illuminating attitude toward work and money. This is in a sense a book of conduct telling people how to behave under various conditions. One recurring theme has to do with al-Shirbini's advice not to be lazy. In one section addressed to fathers he advises them to bring up their sons to be virtuous, but also to teach them to make money. For that, they should stay up late at night and avoid laziness, because laziness will stop them from earning money; he enjoins fathers to teach their sons to work and earn a living, advice that can only have been intended for members of the middle class.[33] There is a note of optimism in al-Shirbini's work, a suggestion that under the right conditions and with sufficient effort, a person could attain a certain economic comfort. Work and money came together—the effort one put in work could bring larger earnings—views that fit with the ideals of commercial capitalism and advice that corresponded with middle-class concerns.

As the eighteenth century progressed and taxation weighed more heavily on the urban population, a darker mood and a sense of material deprivation emerged and came to the fore in some of the writings of the period. The poetry of Shaykh 'Amir al-Anbuti al-Shafi'i, who died about the middle of the eighteenth century, expressed the feelings of someone from the wrong side of the tracks. He talked of the different foods that people ate according to their place in the society. For those who had wealth, there was a platter of lamb and trays of rice—the foods he dreamt of when he had an empty stomach and was waiting for a meal. But what he got was the food of ordinary folks or of the poor, like lentils, *kishk* (a dish made with yogurt and flour), mashed beans, and onions. What concerned him most was the difference.[34] One can sense a social and political dimension in these words. The comment that they make is in fact about the social structure as seen by someone on the lower end of the scale.

This same political dimension came to the fore at different times of crisis in the eighteenth century. Famines due to a bad flood frequently brought the masses to the streets to proclaim their hunger, usually in a spontaneous way. But not all protest was the same. Among shop owners, one way to show disapproval or dissent with the policies announced or applied by the authorities and the ruling class was to close their shops or sometimes the whole market, a form of passive resistance to what was believed to be an injustice imposed by rulers.[35] Thus the writings on these social concerns were an intellectual expression of lived realities.

Issues related to money and social relationships also came to the fore. The poet Hasan al-Badri (d. 1131/1712) exclaimed in one of his poems that a true friend cannot be found in this age: the only friend that can protect one against difficulties is money; he who has money is sought after and called on. People find him faultless; whatever he says is right; they make way for him when he passes, even dogs wag their tails for him. Therefore, advised Hasan al-Badri, guard your money carefully, because if it goes, your luck will go with it.[36]

Abu Dhakir, more articulate than al-Shirbini on money matters, was consistently concerned with the value of money, the power that money gave, and the problems that its absence created. He often wrote about poverty, and yet it is not the poverty with which we are familiar from chronicle sources. We know very well what poverty meant in the eighteenth century. The chronicles of the eighteenth century, al-Jabarti's, for instance, or 'Abdul-Ghani Shalabi's, give us a clear picture of what these historians observed at times of economic crisis or famine, notably the influx of country people to the city, the lines at the bakers, the high price of basic foodstuffs like wheat, and most of all people eating from the garbage. Although Abu Dhakir wrote about poverty, it had nothing to do with these conditions that the chronicles described.

He in fact vacillated in the way that he classified himself. In a text he wrote in 1170/1756, he stated in clear terms that he belonged to the middle ranks. Following a long and eventful trip to Jirja in Upper Egypt, Abu Dhakir offered his readers his advice on how best to travel so as to avoid unnecessary dangers or discomfort. Throughout this piece, the advice depended on whether the traveler was rich, middle, or poor. He clearly distinguished between the wealthy traveler who could afford to have all kinds of facilities to make him comfortable, the poor traveler who had to do with very little comfort, and the middle traveler with whom he identified, who had means but whose means were limited. He compared the middle-class traveler to the wealthy traveler whose only concern was to avoid danger and discomfort regardless of cost, and to the poor traveler, devoid of financial means, who had to get from one place to another regardless of discomfort and danger.[37] As for himself, he clearly stood with those in the middle.

Yet it is with poignancy and with a close knowledge of his subject that he talks of his feeling of poverty and deprivation. His concern with poverty was neither an abstract notion nor one with religious or charitable connotations. In fact, the poverty he was talking about was not the poverty of those on the bottom of the hierarchy that we are familiar with from the chronicles of the period nor of the poor during times of famine, roaming the streets of Cairo in search of food, begging for their daily bread, eating the peel of watermelons thrown in rubbish heaps, or dying from hunger. He makes no mention of them or of their poverty. Rather the "impoverishment" he was concerned with was that of the middle class, of those among them who had known better days. In fact, the probate records of the last decades of the eighteenth century show that inheritances of the urban middle class had been reduced to nearly half of what they had been a century earlier.[38] "I have left aside good food and nice clothes and am locked up in my house for lack of money," Abu Dhakir wrote in 1174/1760, comparing his present state to the more prosperous times that he had known.[39]

More important than times of crisis due to natural causes was the overarching move toward impoverishment from the end of the seventeenth to the end of the eighteenth centuries. He makes no mention of the events linked to times of crisis. Yet his writings indicate an overriding concern with poverty. He does not miss an occasion to show what material deprivation meant to him. In fact, it touched on a number of aspects of life. First, as his many proverbs tell us, *"lathat al dunya la tuktasab illa bil amwal"* (without money there were no pleasures in life). Second, without money one's social image was negative. Poverty brought out one's defects (*saya'at*), wealth emphasized one's good qualities (*hasanat*).[40] Abu Dhakir was very aware of the way that money determined relationships between people. One piece of advice he offered his reader was not to hold a person in contempt on account of his ragged clothes or his hunger (*la tahtaqir insan wa law ji'an 'aryan*).[41] Bad times push him even further to say *"Man kana jawfahu jay'an yuqna' bi ay shay' kan,"* meaning that a person with hunger inside can be convinced to do anything; he goes on to say that he can be forced to eat the carcasses of dead animals.[42]

Consequently, although chroniclers of the period such as al-Jabarti did not fail to mention the periods of economic crisis, whether caused by floods, famine, or other causes, and the consequent poverty that appeared in the streets of the city, the approach to poverty by writers like Abu Dhakir was different. For them poverty was the cause of humiliation and social rejection. When Abu Dhakir wrote about it, he was doing so not as an observer or bystander watching it, but describing an experience he lived, a personal testimony. Moreover, the suffering that his poverty brought was less linked to a crisis or famine—an exceptional event, the result of a natural catastrophe to which one had to resign oneself—than a consequence of the social pressures brought to bear upon this class. He was also very aware of what it means not to have money in spite of how hard he tried. This awareness affected his overall view of his place in society.

Abu Dhakir's bitter conclusion of his experiences was expressed in the proverbs he repeatedly used: *"Al-ghina yu wari al 'uyub wa yikhfi al zunub"* and *"al-faqr ya'lin al-saya'at wa yuwari al hasanat"* (poverty highlights one's bad qualities, wealth highlights one's better qualities). Even if a man became impotent, his inability to perform sexually was less of a problem if he had money (*law kan la yaqdar 'ala al-jama' fa in al-mal yuwari 'uyubuh*)[43] Toward the end of the century, similar bitter remarks were made by another writer, 'Uthman Efendi ibn Ahmad al-Safa'i al-Misri (d. 1205/1790), for whom money was an issue even in love relationships. He yearned for his love, but both of them were penniless.[44] His words reflected the disenchantment and sense of deprivation that many people of his generation were feeling as the economic crisis became more acute.

Whether it was love, money, or food that they wrote about, a political message was implicit, even though it was never formulated as such, nor did the message either contain specific demands or suggest alternative structures.

Muhammad Abu Dhakir's Distancing Himself from the Dominant View of *'Ilm*

Another manifestation of the difference between the views of social classes took a more intellectual turn. It involved the issue of what constituted valid knowledge and what was the way to reach it, knowledge (*'ilm*) being considered a prerogative of the *'ulama'* class and its methodology developing along very sophisticated and academic lines that were beyond the reach of those outside their circles. Thus the dissenting voices were touching a fundamental issue when they took stands against the status quo.

In one of his more daring and aggressive comments, Abu Dhakir undermined one of the oldest and most commonly used mechanisms in the science of jurisprudence, the *fatwa*, a nonbinding legal opinion that scholars gave on a multitude of subjects. The fact that he himself had studied in al-Azhar and knew what he was talking about gave weight to his criticism.

In a piece dated 1173/1759, Abu Dhakir criticized in no uncertain terms one of the most important mechanisms of *fiqh* (jurisprudence), the *fatwa* (legal opinion) or, to be more accurate, the way that the *'ulama'* of his time made use of the *fatwa* to the exclusion of common sense. More explicitly, Abu Dhakir was critical of the theoretical knowledge of the *'ulama'* that was sometimes divorced from reality and from the needs of those around them. "'*Ulama*' write on abstract situations that could never take place in real life," he said, doubting not the truth but the usefulness of what they said. Because they put their effort into farfetched or impossible situations that we cannot rationally expect ever to happen, they were divorced from practical reality and consequently their usefulness was doubtful. For instance, he wrote, one of the *'ulama'* was asked if a man penetrates a woman, must he wash himself afterward? The answer that the scholar gave was, "If he has no pleasure, if he does not ejaculate profusely, he does not have to wash." More useful than such theoretical statements about situations that would never happen would be practical knowledge that could save a man in critical situations. Abu Dhakir advocated another approach, another type of knowledge, one more concrete, more realistic, more adapted to everyday conditions. It was much more useful, he wrote, than talking about abstractions, to know how to act in time of crisis. If, for instance, he were alone with his pregnant wife, in a place where it was not possible to call on a midwife, and the wife was in labor, he should know what to do. He must be able to act as the midwife would have done. The author then goes into great detail on how a man can help in the delivery of his wife. He must roll a towel and put it under her anus, then block the opening; the energy will be pushed to the front opening. He must stretch his feet under her legs and lift her slightly from the ground. Once the baby is born, he must put the newborn in a cloth. In the meantime, he holds the two sides of his wife's genitals until the placenta appears. These, he tells us, are the things he learned as a youth from the women of the house, by watching and by listening. He is not ashamed to put these observations and experiences, learned as a child from the women caring for him, on the same par as the theoretical abstractions of learned scholars.

What Abu Dhakir was saying here is that under these circumstances, practical knowledge, the experience he learned from his surroundings, from the women in his house, from the lived culture around him, was more useful than the abstract or theoretical knowledge that was required to issue a *fatwa*. He was in fact putting on the same plane as the knowledge of the *'ulama'* the knowledge of the midwife and what he himself had learned as a child from observing household matters. The essential complaint is not against the *fatwa* as such but against the distance that academicians had put between themselves and people's daily concerns, and against their concentration instead on abstract notions. His criticism constitutes a demystification of the *fatwa*. The implications are important. He is telling us that there are other forms of knowledge besides religious knowledge, and that these forms are important. Access to these forms of knowledge was, moreover, from other sources than the *'ulama'* and the educational system.

These comments are significant on many levels. The whole idea that the *'ulama'* have a monopoly on certain kinds of knowledge was put into question by his criticism of the *fatwa*, one of the important tools that was used in jurisprudence. He moreover questioned the traditional hierarchy of knowledge, which put religious knowledge above other kinds of knowledge. Common sense, for him, was better than abstractions, and consequently his way of doing things was just as good as that of the 'ulama'. Nonreligious knowledge was therefore in his view as valid as religious knowledge, a daring statement but one that nevertheless probably reflected the view of many people of his class and generation.

He was, moreover, making an implicit but daring comment that *isnad* (authority) relying on tradition, on what was passed down—a method so important in the scholarly world—was not the only kind of valid knowledge, that other sources and approaches had their own validity in various contexts. His challenge of establishment knowledge is apparent in his discussion of other issues. What use was it to be good at reading texts if one were incapable of acting wisely in a given situation, or to know all about books but nothing about life? Likewise, the search for knowledge, *'ilm*, was a positive thing, but only within certain limits. There were times when a little knowledge was enough and when too much of it could be harmful. That was why, for people who like himself were responsible for feeding a family, their time was more usefully spent in earning a living.[45] His seemingly innocent story on how to deliver a woman in labor was in fact an attack on both the dominant hierarchy of knowledge and on those scholars whose position in the social structure was dependent upon it. His comments about the *fatwa* imply a positioning of the writer in relation to a subject that was supposed to be a given, beyond any debate. They gave validity to forms of knowledge that were much more accessible to many more people. He thus raised doubts about major issues related to the dominant ideology and social structure.

Abu Dhakir's concern with the issue of knowledge was at the same time part of his own personal experience and part of a wider debate on what constituted knowledge. The debate was not confined to Islamic *'ulama'*, but had a wide framework in the early modern world. Peter Burke discussed this debate with regard to early modern Europe in his book *A Social History of Knowledge*, showing how it took the form of competition, conflict, and exchange between what he calls the intellectual systems of academic elites and other forms of knowledge, or alternative knowledge, such as everyday knowledge, local knowledge, the knowledge of peasants or of artisans as opposed to that of academicians. The debate touched on the validity of academic medicine as opposed to popular medicine.[46] This debate among Muslim scholars was between a restricted definition of what constituted knowledge versus a wider definition of knowledge and the hierarchy of religious knowledge versus the nonreligious hierarchy. Elite ideology concerning the *'ulama'* depended on a classification of knowledge that put the religious at the top of the hierarchy of different forms of knowledge. The social status of *'ulama'* was in part due to their access to *'ilm*, a status that they were loath to lose.

A few decades earlier, Mustafa b. 'Abdalla Hajji Khalifa's classification of knowledge was both eclectic, because it had room for various types of knowledge, and hierarchical, giving religious knowledge the top place. He found a place for both religious (*dini*) and nonreligious (*ghayr dini*) knowledge in his scheme, but gave religious knowledge a higher value. He then categorized nonreligious knowledge according to whether it is praiseworthy (*mahmud*), blameworthy (*mathmum*) (like the study of magic or of talismans), or permitted (*mubah*) (like history or poetry that is within the limits of decency (*la sakhaf fiha*). He concludes his passage with an eclectic statement to the effect that knowledge of any domain is better than ignorance.[47] Both Hajji Khalifa and Abu Dhakir leaned toward a broad definition of knowledge, but Abu Dhakir went further and was more explicit in expressing his position.

This broad definition of knowledge was evident in various texts. Books on how to do things, how to carry out the practical side of life, indicate a form of knowledge worth recording and passing on in written form, one in which anyone's experience could be worthy of attention. During his trip to Jirja, mentioned earlier, Abu Dhakir shows the importance of practical knowledge. He describes, with some pride and with much humor, how and what he learned to cook when forced to do so by conditions, including a recipe he made up. The items a traveler should take with him on a trip were based on personal knowledge: "[T]ake some cotton to block your ears and stop the fleas from trying to enter them; soap to wash your hands; ink pot and paper in case you need something to write with."[48] This kind of knowledge, based on personal experience, expressed in simple language, could be provided by anyone with common sense and observation, and it could be useful to many people, especially if they were literate. In other words, a form of knowledge of potential significance to many could be provided by an "ordinary" person with some education.

The context that has been described above also encouraged the development of the personal narrative: individual observations and comments were used as valid sources of knowledge. The trend to make the written word an expression of the inner self can also be linked to changes in book production discussed earlier, notably the fact that the book was no longer a luxury commodity limited to a few. By Muhammad Abu Dhakir's lifetime, the spread of the relatively inexpensive book, a result of cheaper production costs, had made reading and writing an individual rather than a collective experience. As books became more accessible and more people owned them privately, reading also became a more private experience, and the book a private companion. That companionship, in fact, was what one of the prominent '*ulama*' of the eighteenth century, 'Abdalla al-Shabrawi, experienced. In his work "Kitab 'Arus al-Adab," which contains a long section on his own private relationship to books, he tells us of their importance to his inner life. In a somewhat lyrical style he talks of books as the joy of one's thoughts, giving sight to the blind. There is sincerity in what he says about them. He could do without companions as long as he had a book with him. In a section of his work entitled "*fi madh al-kutub*" (in praise of books), he tells us that a person who has a book does not need another pastime.[49] 'Abdalla al-Shabrawi was expressing a very personal relationship between him and the book. From personal relationship, using the book as a way to express one's inner self was one step away. The result was an ease in narrating events of an intimate or personal kind that was rare before the book culture spread.

The personal narrative was often integrated into other genres. Al-Jabarti's biography of his father, the longest in his chronicle, combined traditional biography (a person's shaykhs, his teachers, his students, the books he read, and the books he wrote) with a personal family history telling his reader about the more intimate aspects of family life at home. Such personal narrative could be a smaller or larger part of the genre.

Even interspersed in a large work, we can reach, as in Abu Dhakir's book, some of the very personal aspects of his life, including his life with his mother, his relations with his wife, the friends he met with at different occasions, and less personal but nevertheless private facts such as his bodily conditions, the rheumatic pains in his knees. Finally we reach a level of intimacy that it is difficult to find even in works written as autobiographies, notably the pains of aging, of loneliness, and of the sexual impotence that came when he attained about seventy years of age. He describes such personal experiences as the circumstances that led to the divorce of his first wife, against his own wishes. Abu Dhakir had married soon after having reached puberty and had found happiness with his young wife, a happiness that was soon interrupted against his will by his forceful mother, who imposed the divorce because she had quarreled with the bride's mother and who would not hear his tearful pleas to the contrary.[50] He did not sleep for forty nights, he tells us, and the tears did not leave his eyes because of the grief he felt for his loss. Many years later, toward the end of his life, even though he had remarried and had children, he kept remembering her big glowing eyes and her breasts that were like marble; he wrote, when he reached old age, that she was still in his heart and that he had not forgotten her.[51]

One of the most intense personal crises that Abu Dhakir faced as he was aging was the agony caused by his sexual impotence. Preceding him was a centuries-old tradition of writing on sexuality and on pornographic works in the Arabic language: intellectual works, humorous works, pornographic texts written for the purpose of laughter and entertainment. Sexual writings were at times meant to be humorous, and were presumably popular in the *majalis* or literary salons where an atmosphere of relaxation sometimes reigned, inductive to laughter, in which case the more vulgar and explicit they were, the funnier and more amusing. At other times, pornographic writings aimed to excite the appetites of the sexually weak and to incite them, in which case they were part of medical science, according to Hajji Khalifa. His *Kashf al-Dhunun* classifies this purpose as *'ilm al-bah*, the science of exciting the sexual appetites among those with weak capacities, through the appropriate foods and herbs, by narrating appropriate stories, or by describing the different positions to be followed in the sexual act.[52]

However, the writing of Abu Dhakir gave this tradition a new turn.[53] His text is quite distinct from the type of book that used sexuality and sexual exploits either for humorous or for pornographic ends in which Arabic literature abounds precisely because of its personal and intimate nature; it is distinct because he was writing about his own experience, and because of the sophistication of his analysis of himself and his attempts to find psychological remedies to ease his pains, physical, sexual, and moral.

At seventy, he searched ways to ease the agony of this frustration, even weeping at times in self-pity. But there were other remedies, notably the act of writing, which was an outlet that relieved his inner pain. The sexual story that he wrote took him back to happier times and he could temporarily forget the present. This short piece ends with a *mathal* to the effect that if you cannot have the meat then dip your bread in the gravy (*illi ma yuhasil al lahm ya fitt fi-l maraq*). Abu Dhakir gives poignant explanations for the reasons that led him to write. In narrating some of the details of his life, Abu Dhakir had found an outlet for his most private agonies. He wrote, he tells us, because it was a method of expression that helped to relieve his inner agony, that helped him to support the solitude, the loneliness of old age. Writing was a remedy for his anxieties and for his feeling of helplessness in the face of daily problems he was not always able to confront or solve. He found a psychological remedy, temporary but soothing, for his pains.

This kind of personal narrative, in which Abu Dhakir combined a great intimacy and a deep concern for inner life with the problems of old age that any person who reached seventy would have to face, which exposed the innermost concerns a person could face, is one of the elements closest to a "modernity" that only much later developed and became widespread; it is one of the elements that contrast most starkly with the dominant forms of writing of his times, such as the *'ulama'* biographies that provided an entirely different perspective on a person, concentrating on his schooling, his teachers, the books he read and those he authored, his intellectual or other achievements, and so on. One narrative provided the public image that the writer wished to project to his reader; the other was private and intimate. The projection of a public image rested on conformity to certain norms; the personal one created its own norms.

The personal narratives, though never as prevalent as other biographical genres, nevertheless attained a certain popularity during this period, not only in Egypt but in Syria and in Anatolia. Cemal Kafadar and Suraiya Faroqhi have identified a number of first-person narratives in Istanbul and Anatolia. Abu Dhakir was roughly contemporary with another figure who wrote a first-person narrative with a very personal element, the Shaykh al-Islam Fayzalla Afandi (d. 1703), head of the Ottoman *'ulama'* hierarchy. He wrote about his own career as well as those of his close friends, about marriage arrangements and career advancements.[54] The relative popularity of the personal narrative over a wide geographical region was in all probability, in part, due to similar reasons, although other factors still to be explored must certainly have played a role as well.

Abu Dhakir's Last Years

Abu Dhakir's final years coincided with 'Ali Bey al-Kabir's coming to power. Developments in the last decades of the century—the political control of 'Ali Bey al-Kabir and his successors, who imposed unprecedented levels of taxation, and the unfavorable market conditions for local production—led to an impoverishment of the urban middle class and a reduction of its cultural sphere. As a result of the increasingly difficult conditions faced by the urban population, the volume and the scope of middle-class cultural production retracted. Few texts like the ones discussed above seem to have been written during the ending decades of the eighteenth century. The various economic crises had directed the energies of the ordinary person toward survival. Abu Dhakir, in some of the last words that he wrote toward the end of his life (1178/1765), expressed the helplessness of aging, the agony of having to face bodily disintegration, and his anxiety about the way society was developing around him and about the critical conditions that the ordinary person would have to confront from then onward for some time to come. The reality that he saw made him conclude that "[T]he poor will be poor forever and the rich likewise; there is no running away from this truth."[55] The words that Abu Dhakir had articulated expressed both his own private anxieties and those of his generation and his class.

These findings challenge the views of some modern historians of Middle East studies. Abu Dhakir and the trend he represented show that rather than consider the eighteenth century one in which religious culture dominated and the nineteenth century one in which secular culture emerged, we find a basis for modern culture in an earlier period and among the middle ranks rather than the elites. His articulate antiestablishment approach and the style and language he used to express this approach show that those who were trained in religious establishments, as he was, could develop in different intellectual directions. His text, which expressed authentic opinions and inner views, was a personal narrative of the kind that modern historians have sometimes preferred to neglect, considering the self-narrative to be a "new and revolutionary" way of telling lives that was discovered by the West, and that Muslims were introduced to methods of writing modern biography largely by Orientalists.[56] Relying on an approach based on the dynamic West as opposed to a passive East, such views continue to persist in the study of Islamic or Arab societies, with regard to the personal narrative as well as numerous other subjects. The volumes of research, on Islamic societies or on Ottoman societies, that have shown the contrary have not been able as yet to dislodge this framework. It continues to privilege "Islam" and "Muslim" as a category of analysis above and beyond any material conditions or historical processes that had a bearing on any particular theme or subject.

In the final analysis, however, one concludes that in the course of two centuries the culture of the urban middle class had undergone significant developments. Trade and commercial capitalism had granted to many of them space, resources, and opportunity. The crises that the middle class faced as the eighteenth century progressed had complex consequences. The years of prosperity had resulted in a certain type of middle-class culture; the adverse conditions of the later period had introduced a new awareness, a social and political dimension, to their culture. These conditions had also produced, albeit in a few exceptional writers, a way of looking at and of understanding the inner self that went beyond the ideals that dominated the society of the times.

The main lines of eighteenth-century history, in Egypt as well as in the other Ottoman provinces, are fairly well known to historians. The provinces of the Ottoman state were controlled more and more by local elites, the resources of the Imperial Treasury more and more by local rulers. What is less known is the history of the social layer below these rulers, those who were outside the power structure but who, as the previous pages show, were not only part of the changes that were taking place, but were also the initiators of certain trends. By recognizing them as part of the historical process and part of the cultural history of the period, in their own terms and with their ups and downs, we can better understand the period as a whole.

7

Conclusion

THE PRESENT study has explored trends that brought about the visible emergence of a middle-class culture and allowed its significant expression through the written word, providing a picture of seventeenth- and eighteenth-century culture different from the generally accepted one. Not only does the study suggest that a middle-class culture existed and can be identified, but it also demonstrates that the culture had a role to play both in relation to the contemporary scene and to subsequent developments.

The emergence of an educated culture among some members of the urban middle class, developing independently of the establishment culture of their own period and of the state policies that directed the educational system of the nineteenth century, is a testimony both to the dynamism of these people and to the importance of their culture as a basis for later developments. In some features, middle-class culture constituted one of the foundations of the "modernity" upon which the nineteenth century rested. The complex conditions of the seventeenth and eighteenth centuries had created significant elements of modernity in their culture, manifested in an approach to knowledge that tended to be wide, inclusive, practical, realistic, and accessible; in their interest in the individual, in the ordinary person, and in the banalities of everyday life; in the emergence of personal and inner life as a valid reference and a valid source of knowledge for the educated person quite independent of any mystical implication.

Why not see a link between the antiestablishment writing of Muhammad b. Hasan Abu Dhakir in the first part of the eighteenth century and people like 'Abdalla Nadim at the end of the nineteenth century? Both were educated, both were left out of the benefits that the upper echelons were achieving, both had social concerns. Moreover, 'Abdalla Nadim's interest in the ordinary person, his concern for social issues, his critical outlook toward certain social groups who imitated Europeans in their dress and in their food, and his open disapproval of the behavior of other groups such as Sufis can be linked to the culture of the previous century insofar as he wrote about the social realities that he observed around him and had political concerns and a critical view toward those in power. Likewise Ya'qub Sannu', who was active in the 1870s, made use of colloquial language and was very critical of the establishment, so much so that the theater where his plays were performed was closed. Yet critics have not made a connection between these men and their eighteenth-century precursors.

One of the most significant features of the period studied was the new acceptance of local culture as a point of reference, developing as a result of geopolitical transformations. The manifestations of this local character were evident in the use of local vernacular, local expressions, and very often local concerns. Seen from this dimension the emergence in the written word of a language close to the spoken one during the seventeenth century goes beyond the study of language and of class, and becomes one of the manifestations of geopolitical transformations affecting Egypt as they did other regions at various times from the sixteenth through the eighteenth centuries. These changes created commonalities between rather different cultural groups—the Mamluks and the middle class, for instance—and were one of the sources of what was to become the "national culture" that was to develop at the end of the nineteenth century. Thus "national culture" need not be seen as only the result of state policy or of elite formulations, but as having other dimensions as well. The study's demonstration that the culture that the middle class developed was local in nature, far from the "universal" culture of Islamic scholars, illustrates a trend that emerged in other regions of the Ottoman state, probably for the same reasons.

All these features, expressed in a relatively small number of works, experienced a much fuller development in the nineteenth century. Eighteenth-century middle-class culture was thus a foundation for later cultural developments. Taking this progression into consideration makes modern culture look less flat, more diverse, and more complex than it is usually thought to be. This progression means that there is some historical depth to modern culture, that it was not entirely molded from above, either by a ruler's whims or through state policies, and that, finally, it was not only the result of following Western models. We need to rethink what is meant by the nineteenth-century renaissance. It is not enough to consider the roles of elites, states, and state policies, because these constitute only one level of reality, not the totality. A fuller comprehension is gained by considering the less visible, less prominent layers of reality that formed a significant foundation for these roles.

Another basis for developments that were to occur as a result of Muhammad 'Ali's policies was the emergence of educated middle-class individuals who were distinct in their cultural contours from scholars and academicians. Modernization under Muhammad 'Ali was linked to his reforms in state and administrative structures, in the military, in health and education. To function on a day-to-day basis, all these reforms required a larger civil administration than had existed in the previous century. But would such drastic reforms have been possible had not the people who implemented them already been exposed to a certain openness, a receptivity to new ideas?

There are some aspects of the developments of the nineteenth century about which we know little, yet about which it is interesting to speculate. Regarding the new administration that was set up by Muhammad 'Ali and that employed large numbers of people in different ranks within the structure, it is not difficult to imagine that members of the middle class, with more or less education, may have had a role of some significance in making the new administration function and consequently in the implementation of a modern state structure. We know that middle-ranking employees in a government administration bear a good part of the burden of making things work. Whereas members of the religious establishment may have viewed some of these changes with suspicion, partly because they were excluded and partly because they had tense relations with Muhammad 'Ali, the members of the impoverished middle class would on the contrary welcome the possibilities for employment in an expanding bureaucracy. Thus the middle-ranking employee could make the difference between a structure that ran smoothly and one that did not.

Likewise, the construction of new schools in the nineteenth century could not alone bring about educational reforms unless there existed some level of consent and collaboration by those for whom these schools were founded. When Muhammad 'Ali elaborated his policies of state education, the reaction among the population was ambivalent. On the one hand, the policy met resistance because the new schools were unfamiliar and because families did not like the fact that children were taken away from their homes as boarders, which reminded people of the military service. Moreover, as far as the children themselves were concerned, the state schools were much more rigid than the system of *kuttab* with which they were familiar, because they were divided into different classes with different levels, and because they had to have examinations and were required to take many more subjects. On the other hand, there was receptivity for the school system for the obvious reason that people eventually saw that the new system led to greater job possibilities than they had had before. A large number of families had long accepted the fact that children must be educated. Moreover, the creation of new schools required a detachment from the *'ulama'* approach that emphasized empiricism and observation. As such the new schools may well have integrated important elements of the educated middle-class culture. Here again, the foundation had already been laid by a fairly widespread educational system and a middle-class cultural grounding.

To try to understand the changes taking place in the nineteenth century, therefore, with no consideration of the historical context that helped to prepare their groundwork, is to make nineteenth-century history appear flat and superficial. For this reason, understanding the developments that took place in the eighteenth century are essential for our understanding of the later period.

Thus the culture of the nineteenth century cannot be understood only as the foundation of museums, of opera houses, of theaters, of the spread of newspapers. Important as all these innovations were, they represent one trend rather than the totality of nineteenth-century culture. Moreover, with the exception of the newspaper, this trend was associated with the top social layers. It cannot be understood as representative of society or as an expression of its different social groups. These new and important nineteenth-century cultural developments were part of a more complex picture that was made up of a number of trends and dimensions, and these too must be considered in order to fully understand the developments of the nineteenth century.

Knowledge of the early modern middle-class culture therefore adds a dimension to our understanding of the culture of the nineteenth century, making the global cultural spectrum more diverse and richer, and giving it new depth. By including the culture of the educated urban dweller in the picture, we get a more comprehensive view of the totality. Terms like "traditional" culture or "religious" culture, sometimes used to describe the eighteenth century, are in fact totally inadequate, only serving to make a rich and complex picture look simple and easy to understand, but depriving it of its depth and complexity.

Including this culture makes a social comment on the contemporary scene in a way that the study of social, political, and economic history has not been able to do. Sources on middle-class culture are not as plentiful as those on economic and political history, yet an understanding of the cultural developments of the middle class can shed important light on the social context and show dimensions not evident through social history. Likewise, studying these middle-class developments allows us to understand the social scene from a different angle. By considering the culture of this period as part of a process of change and as closely related to society and to shifting social structures, without passing judgment on abstract qualities of the cultural production, the role of culture in the process of change can better be observed as part of a larger context of historical transformation.

Furthermore, this study provides an argument, if additional arguments are still needed, against the decline paradigm. Rather than considering the use of colloquial language to be a decline in proper Arabic, or the spread of poor calligraphy to be a decline in artistic writing, these and other features can on the contrary be understood to be manifestations of middle-class culture emerging as a new force in shaping the production and content of books.

The study has concentrated on the culture of the middle class in Cairo. This focus does not mean that it was a unique development or that Cairo was unique or that it was radically different from other major cities like Aleppo or Istanbul. Trends found in Cairo could be observed in cities in France and Italy as well as in cities like Istanbul, Damascus, and Aleppo in the Ottoman state. The reduction in the production costs of paper, for instance, a European invention, was an incentive to paper traders wherever they were; regardless of political borders, cheap paper was an attractive commodity. As a result private libraries spread among members of the middle class, with a slightly different chronology, in several cities north and south of the Mediterranean.

What this study suggests is that the whole issue of how to understand Ottoman culture is problematic. Much more research is required in this direction. One of the conclusions of the study is in a sense an obvious one, notably that the notion of "Ottoman" culture is not useful in the present context insofar as it suggests and has in the past been used as a term covering overall trends. As far as culture was concerned, the geographical framework was of great importance, yet it was both complex and changing. The various dimensions that make up a particular culture—religion, economy, education, and so on—do not all fall within the same physical borders. The borders of Islamic culture, universal in nature, encompassed many different political entities and social groups. The borders of commercial capitalism followed other borders, those of political authority still others, with different degrees of overlapping, of convergence or divergence, operating at all these levels.

Rather than an "Ottoman" culture with its center in Istanbul and its periphery in the provinces, we need another method of understanding the cultural history of the region, and one which is still not developed. One of the major features of Istanbul culture was the presence of a strong and wealthy court and court culture, with court writers, painters, and calligraphers that set models for others to follow; the presence of a highly hierarchical and bureaucratized religious educational structure that produced and consumed large numbers of books; and so on. It represented a type of culture that for obvious reasons would not be found in other cities.

Of the culture of the middle ranks, we have yet to fully explore its manifestations, its relations to the cultural structure mentioned above, the possibilities for its oral or written expression. Possibly conditions in Cairo were more favorable to the middle ranks because they were not overwhelmed by strong hierarchical structures for much of the period and because of certain cultural or historical specificities. Only in-depth studies in Istanbul and other cities can help us understand the global picture. The field of Ottoman studies is one of the fastest-growing fields of Middle Eastern history; many monographs are being produced that deal with particular regions, cities, and towns. Perhaps one day in the not-too-distant future we can expect to see studies that take regional trends into consideration not on the basis of a core periphery model, which is an adaptation of the old Orientalism that measures one region according to the achievements of another, but on the basis of monographic studies that provide an in-depth look at the way a given society functioned. Such studies can form the basis for an overall view of the region that examines how, why, and where particular trends, such as those with which this book is concerned, spread; where there were similarities or differences in chronology, in the way the trends were realized, in how social groups related to them, and so on. In other words, this book is a call to start moving Ottoman studies in a new and more far-reaching direction.

The culture of the urban middle class developed over the course of the three Ottoman centuries studied, expanding, then retracting, but without quite disappearing. It was still leaving its mark on culture a hundred years later, in some of the directions in which nineteenth-century culture developed. In the meantime, its history during those hundred years is still waiting to be written.

Notes

Glossary

Bibliography

Index

Notes

Abbreviations

References to court cases are abbreviated as follows: an abbreviated form for the name of the court, followed by the number of the volume, the case number, the date, and the page. The system of double dating is used when the original documents provide the date in *hijiri*, according to the Islamic calendar in use at the time.

BA   Court of Bab 'Ali, the main court of Cairo
Q. *'Ask*   Qisma 'Askariyya, the court handling inheritances of the military
Q. *'Arab* Qisma 'Arabiyya, the court handling inheritances of civilians

1. Introduction

1. Raymond Williams, *The Sociology of Culture* (New York: Schocken Books, 1982), 12.
2. Ehud Toledano, *State and Society in Mid-Nineteenth-Century Egypt* (Cambridge, U.K.: Cambridge Univ. Press, 1990); Jane Hathaway, *The Politics of Households in Ottoman Egypt: The Rise of the Qazdaglis* (Cambridge, U.K.: Cambridge Univ. Press, 1997).
3. See the numerous references to their work in the bibliography.
4. Georg Lukács, *History and Class Consciousness: Studies in Marxist Dialectics*, trans. Rodney Livingstone (London: Merlin Press, 1971), 56–57.
5. Ralf Dahrendorf, *Class and Class Conflict in an Industrial Society* (1959; reprint, London: Routledge and Kegan Paul, 1972), 5–6.
6. Peter Burke, *Popular Culture in Early Modern Europe* (New York: New York Univ. Press, 1978), 23, 28.
7. Robert Darnton, *The Great Cat Massacre and Other Episodes in French Cultural History* (New York: Vintage Books, 1985), 3–4.
8. Robert Muchembled, *Culture populaire et culture des élites dans la France moderne (XVe–XVIIIe siècle)* (Paris: Flammarion, 1978), 182–83.
9. Peter Burke, *A Social History of Knowledge: From Gutenberg to Diderot* (Cambridge, U.K.: Cambridge Univ. Press, 2000), 14–15.

10. Suraiya Faroqhi, *Subjects of the Sultan: Culture and Daily Life in the Ottoman Empire* (London: I.B. Tauris, 2000).

11. Muhammad Hakim, "Coptic Scribes and Political Arithmetic: The Case of Mu'allim Ghali Serjius" (paper given to the Seminar on Control, Mobility and Self-Fulfillment: Learning and Culture in the Islamic World Since the Middle Ages, American Univ. in Cairo, Apr. 13–15, 2000).

12. Peter Gran, *Beyond Eurocentrism: A New View of Modern World History* (Syracuse, N.Y.: Syracuse Univ. Press, 1996), 3–6.

13. José Antonio Maravall, *Culture of the Baroque: Analysis of a Historical Structure*, trans. Terry Cochran (Minneapolis: Univ. of Minnesota Press, 1986), 8–9.

14. Nelly Hanna, *Making Big Money in 1600: The Life and Times of Isma'il Abu Taqiyya, Egyptian Merchant* (Syracuse, N.Y.: Syracuse Univ. Press, 1998); Fernand Braudel, *The Mediterranean and the Mediterranean World in the Age of Philip II*, 2 vols., trans. Sian Reynolds (New York: Harper Colophon, 1972); Peregrine Horden and Nicholas Purcell, *The Corrupting Sea: A Study of Mediterranean History* (Oxford, U.K.: Blackwell Publishers, 2000).

15. Ariel Salzmann, "Towards a Comparative History of the Ottoman Empire, 1450–1850," *Archiv Orientalni* 66, supplement 8, 351–66; Daniel Goffman, *The Ottoman Empire and Early Modern Europe* (New York: Cambridge Univ. Press, 2002).

16. Joseph Fletcher, "Integrative History: Parallels and Interconnections in the Early Modern Period, 1500–1800," *Journal of Turkish Studies* 9 (1985): 37–40.

17. Gran, *Beyond Eurocentrism*, 3.

18. J. Brugman, *An Introduction to the History of Modern Arabic Literature in Egypt* (Leiden, Netherlands: Brill, 1984), 3.

19. James Heyworth-Dunne, *An Introduction to the History of Education in Modern Egypt* (London: Luzac and Co., 1939), 13.

20. Jonathan Dollimore and Alan Sinfield, eds., *Political Shakespeare: New Essays in Cultural Materialism* (Ithaca, N.Y.: Cornell Univ. Press, 1985); Cedric C. Brown and Arthur F. Marotti, *Texts and Cultural Change in Early Modern England* (London: Macmillan Press, 1997).

21. Sabry Hafez, *The Genesis of Arabic Narrative Discourse: A Study in the Sociology of Modern Arabic Literature* (London: Saqi Books, 1993), 10–12.

2. Society, Economy, and Culture

1. Harry A. Miskimin, *The Economy of Later Renaissance Europe, 1460–1600* (Cambridge, U.K.: Cambridge Univ. Press, 1977), 139–49.

2. Ilkay Sunar, "State and Economy in the Ottoman Empire," in *The Ottoman Empire and the World Economy*, ed. Huri Islamoglu-Inan (Cambridge, U.K.: Cambridge Univ. Press, 1987), 64.

3. Suraiya Faroqhi, *Towns and Townsmen of Ottoman Anatolia: Trade, Crafts, and Food Production in an Urban Setting, 1520–1650* (Cambridge, U.K.: Cambridge Univ. Press, 1984), 2.

4. See Hanna, *Making Big Money in 1600*, 44 and the references therein.

5. Ibid., 43–48.

6. Ibid., 83.

7. André Raymond, *Artisans et commerçants au Caire au XVIIIe siècle* (Damascus: Institut français de Damas, 1973), 1:204–5, 1:229–31.

8. Ibid., 2:405.

9. K. N. Chaudhuri, *Trade and Civilisation in the Indian Ocean: An Economic History from the Rise of Islam to 1750* (Cambridge, U.K.: Cambridge Univ. Press, 1985), 210–11.

10. Halil Inalcik, "Capital Formation in the Ottoman Empire," *Journal of Economic History* 29, no. 1 (Mar. 1969): 102–4.

11. Subhi Labib, "Capitalism in Medieval Islam," *Journal of Economic History* 29, no. 1 (Mar. 1969): 81–87. Some of these arguments are outlined in Nelly Hanna, "Merchants and the Economy in Cairo, 1600–1650," in *Etudes sur les villes du Proche-Orient XVIe-XIX siècle, hommage à André Raymond,* ed. Brigitte Marino (Damascus: Institut français d'études arabes de Damas, 2001b), 225–36.

12. Peter Gran, "Late Eighteenth-Early Nineteenth Century Egypt: Merchant Capitalism or Modern Capitalism?" in *L'Egypte du XIXe siècle* (Paris: Centre national de la recherche scientifique, 1982), 268.

13. Chaudhuri, *Trade and Civilisation,* 102–8.

14. Suraiya Faroqhi, "Merchant Networks and Ottoman Craft Production (Sixteenth–Seventeenth Centuries)," in *Urbanism in Islam: The Proceedings of the International Conference on Urbanism in Islam,* vol. 1 (Tokyo: Institute of Oriental Studies, Univ. of Tokyo, 1989), 114–20.

15. Fernand Braudel, "The Mediterranean Economy in the Sixteenth Century," in *Essays in European Economic History, 1500–1800,* ed. Peter Earle (Oxford, U.K.: Clarendon Press, 1974), 8–10.

16. Raymond, *Artisans,* 1:207–10; André Raymond, *Le Caire des Janissaires* (Paris: CNRS Editions, 1995), 53.

17. Raymond, *Artisans,* 1:181.

18. Peter Gran, *Islamic Roots of Capitalism: Egypt 1760–1840,* 2d ed. (Syracuse, N.Y.: Syracuse Univ. Press, 1998), 21. Republished by the American Univ. Cairo, 1999.

19. Fernand Braudel, *Civilization and Capitalism, Fifteenth–Eighteenth Century,* vol. 3, *The Perspectives of the World,* trans. Sian Reynolds (New York: Harper and Row, 1984), 130–31.

20. Sevket Pamuk, "Money in the Ottoman Empire, 1324–1914," in *An Economic and Social History of the Ottoman Empire,* vol. 2, *1600–1914,* ed. Halil Inalcik with Donald Quataert (Cambridge, U.K.: Cambridge Univ. Press, 1994), 958–59.

21. Bruce Masters, *The Origins of Western Economic Dominance in the Middle East: Mercantilism and the Islamic Economy in Aleppo, 1600–1750* (New York: New York Univ. Press, 1988), 48–49; Establet and Pascual, *Familles et Fortunes à Damas: 450 Foyers Damascans en 1700* (Damascus: Institut français de Damas, 1994), 96–101.

22. Roland Jennings, "Loans and Credit in Early Seventeenth-Century Ottoman Judicial Records: The Sharia Court of Anatolian Kayseri," *Journal of the Economic and Social History of the Orient* 16, parts 2–3 (1973): 174–75.

23. Court of Bab 'Ali (hereafter *BA*) 100, 224 (1026/1617), 28; *BA* 100, 241 (1026/1617), 31.

24. Raymond, *Artisans,* 2:392.

25. Nelly Hanna, *Habiter au Caire, Les Maisons moyennes et ses habitants aux XVIIe et XVIIIe siècles* (Cairo: Institut français d'archéologie orientale, 1991), 54–58.

26. Terence Walz, *Trade Between Egypt and Bilad al-Sudan* (Cairo: Institut français d'archéologie orientale, 1978), 94–95.

27. Raymond, *Artisans*, 1:238.

28. Ira Lapidus, *Muslim Cities in the Later Middle Ages* (Cambridge, Mass.: Harvard Univ. Press, 1967), 108–10.

29. 'Abdul Rahman Al-Jabarti, *'Abd al-Rahman al-Jabarti's History of Egypt, 'Aja'ib al-Athar fi al-tarajim wa'l akhbar*, ed. Thomas Phillip and Moshe Perlmann (Stuttgart: Franz Steiner Verlag, 1994), 2:298, 2:279–80.

30. Muhammad Amin Al-Muhibbi, *Khulasat al-Athar fi A'yan al-Qarn al-Hadi 'Ashar*, 4 vols. (Cairo: Al-Matba'a al-Wahabiyya, 1284/1867), 4:49.

31. André Raymond, "Soldiers in Trade: The Case of Ottoman Cairo," *Brismes* 17, no. 2 (1991): 25–26.

32. Raymond, *Artisans*, 2:422–23.

33. Afaf Lutfi Al-Sayyid Marsot, "A Socio-Economic Sketch of the 'Ulama' in the Eighteenth Century," in *Colloque international sur l'histoire du Caire* (Grafenhainichen, Germany: General Egyptian Book Organization, 1972a), 314–18.

34. Stanford Shaw, *The Financial and Administrative Organization and Development of Ottoman Egypt, 1517–1798* (Princeton, N.J.: Princeton Univ. Press, 1962), 117, 131.

35. Raymond, *Artisans*, 2:814–17.

36. Gran, *Islamic Roots of Capitalism*, 23.

37. Raymond, *Artisans*, 1:28.

38. André Raymond, "Pouvoir politique, autonomies urbaines et mouvements populaires au Caire au XVIIIe siècle," in *Etats et pouvoirs en Méditerranée, mélanges offerts à André Nouschi* (Nice, France: Univ. de Nice, n.d.), 8–9.

3. Culture and Education of the Middle Class

1. Nelly Hanna, "Culture in Ottoman Egypt," in *The Cambridge History of Egypt*, vol. 2, ed. Martin Daly (Cambridge, U.K.: Cambridge Univ. Press, 1998b), 101–2.

2. Robert Mantran, *Istanbul au siècle de Soliman le Magnifique* (Paris: Hachette, 1994), 230–34.

3. Abraham Marcus, *The Middle East on the Eve of Modernity: Aleppo in the Eighteenth Century* (New York: Columbia Univ. Press, 1989).

4. *BA* 130, 595 (1062/1651), 595; *BA* 130, 1204 (1062/1651), 301.

5. Muhammad ibn Hasan Abu Dhakir, untitled manuscript, Bibliothèque Nationale, Paris, fonds arabe 4643, 44a.

6. Ministry of Waqf, "Waqf 'Uthman Katkhuda Mustahfazan," no. 2215, dated 1149, 234.

7. Jonathan Bloom, *Paper Before Print: The History and Impact of Paper in the Islamic World* (New Haven, Conn.: Yale Univ. Press, 2001), 74. Ra'if Georges Khoury mentions a couple of deeds dating from the thirteenth century in *Chrestomathie de papyrologie arabe: Documents relatifs à la vie privée, sociale et administrative des premiers siècles islamiques*, préparée par Adolf Grohmann, retravaillée et élargie par Ra'if Georges Khoury (Leiden, Netherlands: Brill, 1993), 22–26.

8. Mutsuo Kawatoko, "Coffee Trade in al-Tur Port, South Sinai," in *Le commerce du café avant*

l'ère des plantations coloniales, ed. Michel Tuscherer (Cairo: Institut français d'archéologie orientale, 2001), 52.

9. Carlo M. Cipolla, *Literacy and Development in the West* (Harmondsworth, U.K.: Penguin Books, 1969), 41.

10. Margaret L. Meriwether, *The Kin Who Count: Family and Society in Ottoman Aleppo, 1740–1840* (Austin: Texas Univ. Press, 1999), 22–24.

11. Carlo Ginzburg, *The Cheese and the Worms: The Cosmos of a Sixteenth-Century Miller*, trans. John and Anne Tedeschi (Baltimore, Md.: Johns Hopkins Univ. Press, 1992), 28–30.

12. Dror Ze'evi, *An Ottoman Century: The District of Jerusalem in the 1600s* (Albany, N.Y.: SUNY Press, 1996), 32.

13. Meropi Anastassiadou, "Livres et 'bibliothèques' dans les inventaires après décès de Salonique au XIX siècle," in *Livres et lecture dans le monde ottoman, Revue des mondes musulmans et de la Méditerranée* 87–88 (1999): 138.

14. Frederic C. Lane, "The Mediterranean Spice Trade: Further Evidence of Its Revival in the Sixteenth Century," *American Historical Review* 45, no. 3 (Apr. 1940): 580–90.

15. Ibn Hajar al-Haythami, "Tahrir al-Maqal fi Adab wa Ahkam yahtaj ilayha mu'addib al-atfal," manuscript in Dar al-Kutub al-Misriyya, Majami' 143, pp. 146–67.

16. Al-Haythami, "Tahrir al-Maqal," 163.

17. André Raymond, "L'activité architecturale au Caire," 346. Elementary schools normally were a floor above public fountains' *sabils*. See also Mahmud Hamed al-Husaini, *Al-Asbila al-'Uthmaniyya bi madinat al-Qahira 1517–1798* (Cairo: Maktabat Madbuli, 1988).

18. Raymond, "L'activité architecturale," 347.

19. Saad El Khadem, "Quelques reçus de commerçants et d'artisans du Caire des XVIIe et XVIIe siècles," in *Colloque international sur l'histoire du Caire* (Grafenhainichen, Germany: General Egyptian Book Organization, 1972), 269.

20. El Khadem, "Quelques reçus de commerçants," 276.

21. Raymond, *Artisans*, 1:294.

22. Ibid., 1:20–25.

23. Al-Jabarti, *Al-Jabarti's History of Egypt*, 2:3–4.

24. Al-Muhibbi, *Khulasat al-Athar fi A'yan*, 2:72–73, 2:328.

25. Elizabeth Eisenstein, *The Printing Revolution in Early Modern Europe* (Cambridge, U.K.: Cambridge Univ. Press, 1983), 6.

26. André Raymond, "Une liste des corporations de métiers au Caire en 1801," *Arabica* 4 (1957): 150–63. The guild of "those who tell stories in coffee houses and other locations in Cairo" is listed under no. 147. That this guild exercised its profession in other cities in Egypt is proven by a reference dated 1065/1654 to the storytellers (*hakawiyun*) of coffeehouses in Dimyat paying their taxes to the *multazim*: Court of Dimyat, register 105, case 292, p. 152.

27. *BA* 135, case 394 (1068/1657), 101.

28. Johann Wild, *Voyages en Egypte de Johann Wild (1606–1610)*, trans. Oleg Volkoff (Cairo: Institut français d'archéologie orientale, 1973), 130.

29. Edward William Lane, *An Account of the Manners and Customs of the Modern Egyptians* (1836; reprint, London: East-West Publications, 1989), 386, 395, 408.

30. Al-Muhibbi, *Khulasat al-Athar fi A'yan*, 3:321.

31. Marcus, *The Middle East on the Eve of Modernity*, 43–44.

32. Ibid., 226.

33. Khurashi, manuscript of *Fatwas*, title page missing, dated 1155/1742, copied 1187/1773, no pagination.

34. Nelly Hanna, "Coffee and Coffee Merchants in Cairo, 1580–1630," in *Le commerce du café avant l'ère des plantations coloniales, espaces réseaux, sociétés (XVe–XIXe siècles)*, ed. Michel Tuscherer (Cairo: Institut français d'archéologie orientale, 2001c), 95. Al-Jabarti writes of a shaykh who was criticized by his peers for going to coffeehouses (*Al-Jabarti's History of Egypt*, 1:684, 1:636).

35. Muhammad Khalil al-Muradi, *Silk al-Durar fi a'yan al-qarn al-thani 'ashar* (n.p., 1883), 1:98.

36. Hanna, "Culture in Ottoman Egypt," 106.

37. Saad El Khadem, "Quelques reçus de commerçants," 269–70.

38. Antonio Gramsci, *The Gramsci Reader: Selected Writings 1916–1935*, ed. David Forgacs (New York: New York Univ. Press, 2000), 53, 300–301.

39. Cornell Fleischer, *Bureaucrat and Intellectual in the Ottoman Empire: The Historian Mustafa Ali (1541–1600)* (Princeton, N.J.: Princeton Univ. Press, 1986), 36, 202.

40. Karen Barkey, *Bandits and Bureaucrats: The Ottoman Route to State Centralization* (Ithaca, N.Y.: Cornell Univ. Press, 1994), 156–63.

41. Heyworth-Dunne, *An Introduction to the History of Education*, 27–28.

42. Ahmad 'Izzat 'Abdul-Karim, *Tarikh al-Ta'lim fi 'Asr Muhammad 'Ali* (Cairo: Maktabat al-Nahda al-Misriyya, 1938), 10; Heyworth-Dunne, *An Introduction to the History of Education*, 37.

43. Heyworth-Dunne, *An Introduction to the History of Education*, 17–18.

44. These figures are provided by Heyworth-Dunne, *An Introduction to the History of Education*, 28–29.

45. Gamal El-Din El-Shayyal, "Some Aspects of Intellectual and Social Life in Eighteenth-century Egypt," in *Political and Social Change in Modern Egypt*, ed. P. M. Holt (London: Oxford Univ. Press, 1968), 117.

46. Al-Muradi, *Silk al-Durar*, 2:219.

47. Al-Muhibbi, *Khulasat al-Athar*, 2:276; al-Jabarti, *Al-Jabarti's History of Egypt*, 1:314, 1:334, 1:325, 1:341.

48. 'Abdul-Ghani al-Nabulsi, *Al-Haqiqa wal-Majaz fi Rihla ila Bilad al-Sham wa Misr Wal-Hijaz*, ed. Ahmad 'Abd al-Majid al-Haridi (Cairo: Hay'at al-Kitab, 1986), 181, 205, 273–74.

49. M. Peled, "Nodding the Necks: A Literary Study of Shirbini's *Hazz al-Quhuf*," *Die Welt des Islams* 26 (1986): 62.

50. Yusuf al-Maghribi, *Raf' al-Isar 'an kalam ahl Misr*, ed. 'Abdul-Salam Ahmad 'Awwad (Moscow: Soviet Academy of Sciences, 1968), 28; see also p. 40.

51. Fleischer, *Bureaucrat and Intellectual in the Ottoman Empire*, 22–23.

52. Abu Dhakir, untitled manuscript, 13a–16a.

53. Norbert Elias, *La civilization des moeurs*, trans. Pierre Kamnitzer (Paris: Kalman Levy, 1973), 121 ff.

54. Abu Dhakir, untitled manuscript, 200b.

55. Manuscript in the Bibliothèque Nationale, Paris, fonds arabe 3568, p. 95. Although the

catalogue of this library dates the manuscript to the seventeenth century, references to Shaykh 'Abd al-Khaliq al-Sadat, who according to al-Jabarti died in 1161/1741, indicate an eighteenth-century dating.

56. Mari'i Yusef al-Maqdisi, "Qala'id al-'Uqyan fi Fada'il Al-'Uthman," manuscript in Suhaj Municipal Library, Tarikh 60 (1031/1621), 104–5.

57. Yusuf al-Shirbini, *Hazz al-Quhuf fi Sharh Qasida Abu Shaduf* (Bulaq, Egypt: National Press, 1857), 39.

58. Abu Dhakir, untitled manuscript, 124a.

4. Books and the Middle Class

1. Roger Chartier, *Culture écrite et société, l'ordre des livres (XIVe–XVIIIe siècles)* (Paris: Bibliothèque Michel Albin, 1996), 28–29.

2. Burke, *Popular Culture in Early Modern Europe*, 250–59.

3. *BA* 114, 38 (1141/1728), 11.

4. Colette Establet, "Les inventaires après-décès, sources d'histoire culturelle (Damas)," in *Etudes sur les villes du Proche-Orient XVIe-XIXe siècle, Hommage à André Raymond*, ed. Brigitte Marino (Damascus: Institut français d'études arabes de Damas, 2001), 81–90; Colette Establet and Jean-Paul Pascual, "Les livres des gens à Damas vers 1700," *Livres et lecture dans le monde ottoman, Revue des mondes musulmans et de la Méditerranée* 87–88 (1999): 143–72.

5. Bernard Heyberger, "Livres et pratiques de la lecture chez les chrétiens (Syrie, Liban), XVII-XVIIIe siècle," in "Livres et lecture dans le monde ottoman," ed. Frederic Hitzel, in *Revue des mondes musulmans et de la Méditerranée* 87–88 (1999): 209–24.

6. David King, *A Catalogue of the Scientific Manuscripts in the Egyptian National Library* (Cairo: General Egyptian Book Organization in collaboration with the American Research Center in Egypt and the Smithsonian Institution, 1981).

7. Bibliothèque Nationale, France, *Catalogue des manuscripts arabes de la bibliothèque nationale par le Baron de Slane* (Paris: Imprimerie nationale, 1883–95), 542–45, 546–75.

8. Magdi Girgis, "Athar al-Arakhina 'ala Awda' al-Qibt fil qarn al-thamin 'ashar," *Annales Islamologiques* 34, no. 2 (2000): 36–37.

9. Nabil Selim Atalla, *Illustrations from Coptic Manuscripts* (Cairo: Lenhert and Landrock, 2000), 14–15, 35–41.

10. Jean Irigoin, "Papiers orientaux et papiers occidentaux," in *Colloques internationaux du centre national de la recherche scientifique no. 559, La paléographie grecque et byzantine* (Paris: Editions du CNRS, 1977), 45, 54.

11. Dard Hunter, *Papermaking: The History and Technique of an Ancient Craft* (New York: Dover Publications, 1978), 153, 162–63.

12. Raymond, *Artisans*, 1:174, 183, 343.

13. Nasir 'Uthman, "Ta'ifa al-Sahhafin fil qarn al-sabi' 'ashir," in *Al-Tawa'if al-Mihaniyya wal-Ijtima'iyya fi Misr fil 'asr al-'uthmani*, ed. Nasir Ibrahim, Markaz al-Buhuth wal Dirasat al-Ijtima'iyya (Cairo: Egyptian Society for Historical Studies, 2003), 64–65.

14. *Qisma 'Askariyya* (hereafter Q. *'Ask*) 99, 112 (1118/1706), 72; Q. *'Ask* 29, 52 (1019/1610), 29.

15. Bloom, *Paper Before Print*, 84.

16. *BA* 119, 466 (1048/1638), 83; Raymond, "Une liste."

17. *Q. 'Ask* 134, 66 (1144/1731), 41.

18. Colette Establet and Jean-Paul Pascual, "Les livres des gens à Damas vers 1700," *Livres et lecture dans le monde ottoman, Revue des mondes musulmans et de la Méditerranée* 87–88 (1999): 147.

19. Alexander Russell, *The Natural History of Aleppo*, 2 vols., 2d ed. rev. (1794; reprint, Westmead, U.K.: Gregg International Publishers, 1969), 2:95.

20. Frederic Hitzel, "Manuscripts, livres et culture livresque à Istanbul," in *Livres et lecture dans le monde ottoman, Revue des mondes musulmans et de la Méditerranée* 87–88 (1999): 24–26.

21. Al-Jabarti, *Al-Jabarti's History of Egypt*, 1:643, 1:603–4.

22. Ibid., 1:479–80, 1:360, 1:461, 1:364.

23. Ibid., 1:265, 1:276, 2:298, 2:279–80.

24. A. Mingana, *Catalogue of Arabic Manuscripts in the John Rylands Library, Manchester* (Manchester, U.K.: Univ. of Manchester Press, 1934), 441, 445.

25. Muhibb al-Din al-Muhibbi, "Kitab Nuzhat al-Nufus wal-Albab fi Mukatabat al-Muhibb lil-Ahbab," manuscript in al-Azhar Library, Cairo, no. 7116, Abaza 520, p. 47. This work is a compilation of al-Muhibbi's correspondence.

26. Ibid., 34.

27. *Q. 'Ask* 147, 25 (1152/1739), 17–34.

28. *BA* 225, 247 (1155/1742), 247.

29. Nelly Hanna, "The Chronicles of Ottoman Egypt: History or Entertainment?" in *The Historiography of Islamic Egypt (c. 950–1800)*, ed. Hugh Kennedy (Leiden, Netherlands: Brill, 2001a), 244–45.

30. *Q. 'Arab* 78, 165 (1121/1709), 109–10; *Q. 'Arab* 79, 195 (1122/1710), 116.

31. Heyworth-Dunne, *An Introduction to the History of Education*, 10–11.

32. A large number of copies have survived. Many of them list no author. In some of them, the author is named as Muhammad b. Sulayman B. Da'ud b. Bishr al-Salami al-Shadhli.

33. Al-Jabarti, *Al-Jabarti's History of Egypt*, 1:643, 1:603–4, 1:2, 1:86, 1:403, 2:96, 2:447.

34. Jihane Tate, *Une waqfiyya du XVIIIe siècle à Alep: La waqfiyya d'al Hagg Musa al-Amiri* (Damascus: Institut français de Damas, 1990), 152.

35. *Q. 'Ask* 146, 322 (1151/1738), 246; and 658 (1151/1738), 491.

36. Edward Brown, *Le voyage en Egypte d'Edward Brown, 1673–74*, trans. Marie-Therese Breant (Cairo: Institut français d'archéologie orientale, 1974), 53–54.

37. Boaz Shoshan, "On Popular Literature in Medieval Cairo," *Poetics Today* 14, no. 2 (1993): 350.

38. Elizabeth Sartain, *Jalal al-Din al-Suyuti: Biography and Background* (Cambridge, U.K.: Cambridge Univ. Press, 1975), 74; see also p. 123.

39. 'Ali b. Hasan al-'Attas Ba 'Alawi, *Kitab al-'Atiya al-Haniya wal Wasiya al-Murdiya wal Hadhwa al-Mudiya* (Cairo: Muhammad Abdul Wahid al-Tubi Press, 1325/1907), 19.

40. "Kitab Anis al-Jalis," Bibliothèque Nationale, Paris, fonds arabe 3453 (1187/1773), 4a–b.

41. Muhammad al-Mahdi, *Contes du Cheykh El-Mohdy*, trans. J. J. Marcel (Paris: Imprimerie de Felix Locquin, 1833), 1:45–46.

42. Pierre Aquilon, "Petites et moyennes bibiothèques, 1480–1530," in *Histoire des biblio-*

thèques françaises, ed. André Vernet (Paris: Promodis Editions du Cercle de la Librairie, 1989), 286–87.

43. Q. *'Ask* 139, 457 (1147/1734), 354; Q. *'Ask* 140, 130 (1148/1735), 91.

44. Q. *'Ask* 163, 437 (1166/1752), 294; Q. *'Ask* 139, 439 (1147/1734), 337.

45. Roger Chartier, *Culture écrite et société,* 219.

5. Shaping a Culture of the Middle Class

1. Cemal Kafadar, "The Question of Ottoman Decline," *Harvard Middle Eastern and Islamic Review* 4, nos. 1–2 (1997–98): 57.

2. This section on Copts relies heavily on the excellent work that Magdi Girgis has done on the Coptic community in the seventeenth and eighteenth centuries and on the many discussions I have had with him on this subject. I therefore extend him herewith my acknowledgments. See his "Athar al-Arakhina 'ala awda' al-Qibt fil qars al-thamin 'ashir," in *Annales Islamologiques* 34 (2000).

3. Adam Fox, *Oral and Literate Culture in England, 1500–1700,* Oxford Studies in Social Sciences (Oxford, U.K.: Oxford Univ. Press, 2000), 112–14.

4. Hanna, "Culture in Ottoman Egypt," 104.

5. Al-Muhibbi, *Khulasat al-Athar,* 2:412–16.

6. 'Abdul-Ra'uf al-Munawi, *Kitab Al-Nuzha al-Zahiyya fi Ahkam al-Hammam al-Shar'iyya wal-Tibiyya,* ed. 'Abdul-Hamid Salih Hamdan (Cairo: Dar Al-Misriyya al-Lubnaniyya, 1987), 15.

7. Al-Maghribi, *Raf' al-Isar,* 156–59; al-Muhibbi, *Khulasat al-Athar,* 4:501–3.

8. Al-Muhibbi, *Khulasat al-Athar,* 2:289–91.

9. Muhammad 'Abdul-Mu'ti Al-Ishaqi, *Lata'if Akhbar al-Uwal fiman Tasarrafa fi Misr min Arbab al-Duwal* (Cairo: Maktabat al-Miliji, 1897), 11.

10. Ibid., 12.

11. Ibid., 146.

12. Al-Shirbini, *Hazz al-Quhuf,* 4.

13. Shihab al-Din Al-Khafaji, *Rihana al-Alibba wa zahrat al-Hayah al-Dunya* (Cairo: Al-Matba'a al-Amiriyya, 1273/1856), 222, 263, 270, 273–76; 280–81.

14. Ahmad al-Budayri al-Hallaq, *Hawadith Dimishq al-Yawmiyya, 1154–1175 (1741–1762),* ed. Ahmad 'Izzat 'Abdul-Karim (Cairo: Egyptian Society for Historical Studies, 1959), 24–25, 62–63.

15. Ibid., 150–51.

16. Ibid., 24–25, 35, 39.

17. Doris Behren-Abouseif, "Une polémique anti-ottomane par un artisan au Caire du XVIIe siècle," in *Etudes sur les villes du Proche-Orient XVIe–XIXe siècle, Hommage à André Raymond,* ed. Brigitte Marino (Damascus: Institut français d'études arabes de Damas, 2001), 55.

18. "Kitab Anis al-Jalis," 84–85.

19. A. Mingana, *Catalogue of Arabic Manuscripts,* 894.

20. Al-Shirbini, *Hazz al-Quhuf,* 212. An example of a Juha joke in *Anis al-Jalis* (pp. 84–85) narrates how Juha came home one day to find his father making love to his mother. Upset by what he saw, he stormed upstairs to his grandmother's room, threw himself on her, and tried to make love to her. Her screams brought his father running up to see what was happening and to forcibly

pull him away, while Juha shouted at him angrily, "If you make love to *my* mother, I will make love to *your* mother."

21. Madiha Doss, "Military Chronicles of Seventeenth-Century Egypt as an Aspect of Popular Culture" (paper presented to the Colloquium on Logos, Ethos and Mythos in the Middle East and North Africa, Budapest, Sept. 18–22, 1995a), 73–76; Madiha Doss, "Some Remarks on the Oral Factor in Arabic Linguistics," in *Dialectica Arabica, A Collection of Articles in Honour of the Sixtieth Birthday of Professor Heikki Palva* (Helsinki: Finnish Oriental Society, 1995b), 49–61.

22. The index of proverbs is on p. 311.

23. Abu Dhakir, untitled manuscript, 16b, 19a, 19b, 28a, 175a.

24. Charles Taylor, *Sources of the Self: The Making of the Modern Identity* (Cambridge, Mass.: Harvard Univ. Press, 2001), 211–15.

25. "Nuzhat al-Qulub wal-Nawadhir fi Ghara'ib al-Hikayat wal-Nawadir," manuscript, Bibliothèque Nationale, Paris, fonds arabe 3577, datable to eighteenth century.

26. "Kitab al-Dhakha'ir wal-Tuhaf fi Bir al-Sanayi' wal- Hiraf," manuscript Orient A 963, Gotha Library, Leiden, Netherlands.

27. "Kitab Anis al-Jalis," 149–58.

28. Al-Maghribi, *Raf' al-Isar*, 50, 56, 132, 133, 137.

29. Ibid., 32, 154.

30. Ibid., 63, 227.

31. Abu Dhakir, untitled manuscript, 42a; El-Said Badawi and Martin Hinds, *A Dictionary of Egyptian Arabic, Arabic-English* (Beirut: Librairie du Liban, 1986), 640. My acknowledgments to Elizabeth Sartain for providing me with this reference.

32. Al-Maghribi, *Raf' al-Isar*, 24–27.

33. Ibid., 100.

34. Al-Shirbini, *Hazz al-Quhuf*, 110.

35. Ibid., 64, 109.

36. Hanna, *Making Big Money*, 150–51.

37. The court of *Al-Zahid* has many of these cases because it was located in a district of the city where textiles were produced; see court of *Al-Zahid* 671, case 800, p. 220; case 852, p. 232; case 874, p. 237; case 1310, p. 378, dated 1148/1735.

38. Abu Dhakir, untitled manuscript, 248a and b.

39. 'Ali b. 'Umar Al-Batanuni al-Abusiri, "Kitab al-'Unwan fi Makayid al-Nisa'," manuscript in the Bibliothèque Nationale, Paris, fonds arabe 3565 (1133/1720), 2–5.

40. Al-Batanuni al-Abusiri, *Kitab al-'Unwan*, 85a, 105a.

41. Bibiliothèque Nationale, fonds arabe 3564, 3565, 3566, 3567, dated between 1684 and 1756.

42. Muhammad al-Makki Ibn Khanqah, *Tarikh Hums*, ed. Umar Najib al-Umar (Damascus: Institut français de Damas, 1987), 70.

43. Ibn Khanqah, *Tarikh Hums*, 28.

44. Ibid., 223.

45. Ibid., 219–20.

46. Al-Maghribi, *Raf' al-Isar*, 198.

47. Ibid., 91.

48. Amira El-Azhary Sonbol, *The New Mamluks: Egyptian Society and Modern Feudalism* (Syracuse, N.Y.: Syracuse Univ. Press, 2000), 216.

49. Al-Muhibbi, *Qasd al-Sabil fima fil-lugha al-'arabiyya min al-dakhil*, ed. 'Uthman Mahmud al-Sini (Riyadh: Maktabat al-Tawba, 1994); see, for instance, 1:185, 1:194, 1:199, 1:203.

50. Ra'if Georges Khoury, *Chrestomathie de papyrologie arabe*, 165–71.

51. Ahmad Rushdi Salih, *Al-Adab al-Sha'bi*, 3d ed. (Cairo: Maktabat al-Nahda al-Misriyya, 1971), 1:41–50

52. Guy Demerson, *Livres populaires du XVIe siècle: Répertoire sud-est de la France* (Lyon: Centre national de la recherche scientifique, 1986), 22–23.

53. Arnoud Vrolijk, *Bringing a Laugh to a Scowling Face: A Study and Critical Edition of the Nuzhat al-Nufus wa Mudhik al-'abus by 'Ali Ibn Sudun al-Bashbughawi* (Leiden, Netherlands: Centre for Non-Western Studies, Leiden Univ., 1998), 137–38.

54. Al-Maghribi, *Raf' al-Isar*, 69, 127, 135, 143, 198, 228.

55. Abu Dhakir, untitled manuscript, 41a, 87a.

56. Al-Maghribi, *Raf' al-Isar*, 30.

57. Abu Dhakir, untitled manuscript, 174a.

58. Baber Johansen, "Coutumes locales et coutumes universelles aux sources des règles juridiques en droit musulman hanefite," *Annales Islamologiques* 27 (1993): 30; Baber Johansen, *The Islamic Law on Land Tax and Rent: The Peasants' Loss of Property Rights as Interpreted in the Hanafite Legal Literature of the Mamluk and Ottoman Periods* (Beckenham, Kent, U.K.): Croom Helm Ltd, 1988), 85–90; Ibn Nujaym, *Al-Ashbah wal-Nadha'ir*, 93–98.

59. Muhammad Siraj, "Tatawwur al-fiqh fil 'asr al-'uthmani," in *Al-'Adala bayn al-Shari'a wal-Waqi'*, ed. Nasir Ibrahim and 'Imad Hilal (Cairo: Markaz al-Buhuth wal Dirasat al-Ijtima'iyya, Cairo Univ., in collaboration with the Egyptian Society for Historical Studies, 2002), 69–70.

60. Nelly Hanna, "Cultural Life in Mamluk Households (Late Ottoman Period)," in *Mamluks in Egyptian Society and Politics*, ed. Thomas Philipp and Ulrich Haarman (Cambridge, U.K.: Cambridge Univ. Press, 1998), 198.

61. 'Abdalla al-Shabrawi, *Kitab 'Unwan al-Bayan wa Bustan al-Adhhan wa Majmu' Nasa'ih fil Hikam* (Cairo: Matba'at al-Hajar, 1275/1858), 9, 19.

62. Ahmad al-Damanhuri, "Sabil al-Rashad ila Naf' al-'Ibad," manuscript in Dar al-Kutub al-Misriyya, Ijtima' Taymur, 32.

63. Ibid., 48.

64. Ibid., 66.

6. Radical Intellectuals: A Culture of Crisis

1. Raymond, *Artisans*, 2:653–57.

2. Abu Dhakir, untitled manuscript, 184b.

3. Fleischer, *Bureaucrat and Intellectual in the Ottoman Empire*, 22–24.

4. Al-Jabarti, *Al-Jabarti's History of Egypt*, 1:10–11, 14.

5. Ahmad al-Damanhuri, *Al-Naf' al-Ghazir fi Salah al-Sultan wal Wazir*, ed. Fuad 'Abdul-Mun'im Ahmad (Alexandria, Egypt: Mu'assasat Shabab al-Jami'a, 1992), 65.

6. "Raha al-Rawh wa Salwa al-Qalb al-Majruh," manuscript in Dar al-Kutub al-Misriyya, Cairo, Akhlaq Taymur, no. 1214, no date, 7, 11.

7. Gilbert Delanoue, *Moralistes et politiques Musulmans dans l'Egypte du XIXe siècle (1798–1882)* (Cairo: Institut français d'archéologie orientale, 1982), 1:14–16.

8. Al-Jabarti, *Al-Jabarti's History of Egypt*, 1:314, 1:325, 1:552–69, 1:587–611.

9. Al-Muhibbi, *Khulasat al-Athar*, 4:415.

10. Al-Jabarti, *Al-Jabarti's History of Egypt*, 2:86–87.

11. James Heyworth-Dunne, "Arabic Literature in Egypt in the Eighteenth Century with Some Reference to Poetry and Poets," *Bulletin of the School of Oriental and African Studies, London Univ.* 9 (1937–39): 684.

12. Muhammad Sayyid Kilani, *Al-Adab al-Misri fi Dhill al-Hukm al-'Uthmani* (Cairo: Dar Al-Firjani, 1984), 217–22.

13. Hanna, *Habiter au Caire*, 72–78.

14. Al-Jabarti, *Al-Jabarti's History of Egypt*, 4:266, 301.

15. Ellis Cashmore and Chris Rojek, *Dictionary of Cultural Theorists* (London: Arnold Press, 1999), 478–79; Michael Lowy, "Against the Grain: The Dialectical Conception of Culture in Walter Benjamin's Thesis of 1940," in *Walter Benjamin and the Demands of History*, ed. Michael Steinberg (Ithaca, N.Y.: Cornell Univ. Press, 1996), 206–10.

16. André Raymond, "Pouvoir Politique," 8–9.

17. John Gascoigne, "The Universities and the Scientific Revolution: The Case of Newton and Restoration Cambridge," in *Science, Politics, and Universities in Europe, 1600–1800*, Variorum Collected Studies Series (Aldershot, U.K.: Ashgate Publishing, 1998), 392–95.

18. Richard B. Sher and Andrew Hook, "Introduction: Glasgow and the Enlightenment," in *The Glasgow Enlightenment*, ed. Andrew Hook and Richard B. Sher (East Lothian, Scotland: Tuckwell Press, 1995), 11.

19. Abu Dhakir, untitled manuscript, 30a, b.

20. Elisabeth Badinter, *Les passions intellectuelles*, vol. 1, *Désirs de gloire (1735–1751)* (Paris: Fayard, 1999), 9–10.

21. Hisham Sharabi, *Arab Intellectuals and the West: The Formative Years, 1875–1914* (Baltimore, Md.: Johns Hopkins Univ. Press, 1970), 2–3.

22. Raymond Williams, *Problems in Materialism and Culture* (London: Verso Editions and NLB, 1980), 37–38.

23. Al-Jabarti, *Al-Jabarti's History of Egypt*, 1:132, 1:147–48; Abu Dhakir, untitled manuscript, 166a.

24. Al-Jabarti, *Al-Jabarti's History of Egypt*, 1:121, 1:137–38.

25. Abu Dhakir, untitled manuscript, 113b.

26. Mikhail Bakhtin, *Rabelais and His World*, trans. Helene Iswolsky (Bloomington: Indiana Univ. Press, 1984), 157–58.

27. Ibid., 3 ff.

28. Goeff Eley, "Nations, Publics and Political Cultures: Placing Habermas in the Nineteenth Century," in *Habermas and the Public Sphere*, ed. Craig Calhoun (Cambridge, Mass.: MIT Press, 1999), 320–25.

29. Abu Dhakir, untitled manuscript, 158a–60b.

30. Ibid., 116a, b.
31. Ibid., 120b.
32. André Raymond, *Artisans*, 1:86–97.
33. Al-Shirbini, "Kitab Tarh al-Madad li-Hall al-'Ala' wal-Durar," manuscript in Dar al-Kutub al-Misriyya, Majami' Tal'at no. 578, copy dated 1327/1909, 5–6, 13.
34. Al-Jabarti, *Al-Jabarti's History of Egypt*, 1:411–14, 1:401–3.
35. André Raymond, "Quartiers et mouvements popularies au Caire au XVIIIe siècle," in *Political and Social Change in Modern Egypt*, ed. Peter M. Holt (London: Oxford Univ. Press, 1968), 112–13.
36. Al-Jabarti, *Al-Jabarti's History of Egypt*, 1:127–29, 1:143.
37. Abu Dhakir, untitled manuscript, 115b, 116a.
38. Raymond, *Artisans*, 1:239, 556.
39. Abu Dhakir, untitled manuscript, 182b.
40. Ibid., 36, 51.
41. Ibid., 15b
42. Ibid., 85b.
43. Ibid., 39a.
44. Al-Jabarti, *Al-Jabarti's History of Egypt*, 2:359–60, 2:332–33.
45. Abu Dhakir, untitled manuscript, 34a.
46. Burke, *A Social History of Knowledge*, 13–15.
47. Mustafa b. 'Abdalla Hajji Khalifa, *Kashf al-Dhunun 'an Asami al-Kutub wal-Funun* (Beirut: Dar al-Kutub al-'Ilmiyya, 1992), 1:12–13.
48. Abu Dhakir, untitled manuscript, 117b.
49. 'Abdalla al-Shabrawi, "Kitab 'Arus al-Adab wa Furjat al-Albab," manuscript in Dar al-Kutub al-Misriyya, Cairo, Adab Tal'at no. 4489, dated 1154/1741, 6, 12–13. The title of the present book is taken from a chapter entitled "In Praise of Books" in al-Shabrawi's book.
50. Abu Dhakir, untitled manuscript, 122b.
51. Ibid., 247b.
52. Hajji Khalifa, *Kashf al-Dhunun*, 1:218–19.
53. Abu Dhakir, untitled manuscript, 170a–73a.
54. Cemal Kafadar, "Self and Others: The Diary of a Dervish in Seventeenth-century Istanbul and First-Person Narratives in Ottoman Literature," *Studia Islamica* 69 (1989): 121–50; Suraiya Faroqhi, *Approaching Ottoman History: An Introduction to the Sources* (Cambridge, U.K.: Cambridge Univ. Press, 1999), 163–66.
55. Abu Dhakir, untitled manuscript, 249b.
56. Martin Kramer, ed., *Middle Eastern Lives: The Practice of Biography and Self-Narrative* (Syracuse, N.Y.: Syracuse Univ. Press, 1991), 1–2.

Glossary

adab: literature.
afandi: bureaucrat.
'alim: (pl. *'ulama'*): religious scholar.
'amma: commoners.
dhikr: Sufi ritual.
fatwa: a non-binding religious opinion.
fiqh: jurisprudence.
fuqaha: scholars in jurisprudence.
fusha: classical Arabic.
hadith: prophetic traditions.
iltizam: tax farm.
'ilm: religious sciences.
khassa: elites.
madrasa: religious college.
majlis (pl. *majalis*): literary salon.
maktab (same as *kuttab*): elementary school.
mathal (pl. *amthal*): proverb.
mufti: a religious scholar who has the competence to give a legal opinion.
nisf: the smallest silver coin.
qadi: magistrate.
sabil: public fountain.
shaykh: a person who studied religious sciences; also a person of a certain age.
shari'a: Islamic law.
tafsir: Quranic explanation.
tariqa: a Sufi brotherhood.
tujjar: merchants.
ujaq: member of an Ottoman regiment.
'ulama' (sing. *'alim*): religious scholars.
'urf: usage.
waqf: pious foundation.

Bibliography

Court Records

Court records are in bound and numbered volumes. The following registers from the various courts of Cairo were consulted.
Court of Bab 'Ali *(BA)*, the main court of Cairo.
Court of Dimyat.
Court of Al-Zahid.
Ministry of Waqf.
Qisma 'Askariyya *(Q. 'Ask)*, the court handling inheritances of the military.
Qisma 'Arabiyya *(Q. 'Arab)*, the court handling inheritances of civilians.

Books and Articles

'Abdul-Karim, Ahmad 'Izzat. *Tarikh al-Ta'lim fi 'Asr Muhammad 'Ali*. Cairo: Maktabat al-Nahda al-Misriyya, 1938.
'Abdul-'Ati, 'Abdul-Ghani Mahmud. *Al-Ta'lim fi Misr zaman al-Ayyubiyyin wal-Mamalik*. Cairo: Dar al-M'rif, 1984.
Abu Dhakir, Muhammad ibn Hasan. Untitled manuscript. Bibliothèque Nationale, Paris, fonds arabe 4643.
Anastassiadou, Meropi. "Livres et 'bibliothèques' dans les inventaires après décès de Salonique au XIX siècle." In *Livres et lecture dans le monde ottoman, Revue des mondes musulmans et de la Méditerranée* 87–88 (1999): 111–42.
Aquilon, Pierre. "Petites et moyennes bibiothèques, 1480–1530." In *Histoire des bibliothèques françaises*, edited by André Vernet, 285–310. Paris: Promodis Editions du Cercle de la Librairie, 1989.
Atalla, Nabil Selim. *Illustrations from Coptic Manuscripts*. Cairo: Lenhert and Landrock, 2000.
Al-'Attas Ba 'Alawi, 'Ali b. Hasan. *Kitab al-'Atiya al-Haniya wal Wasiya al-Murdiya wal Hadhwa al-Mudiya*. Cairo: Muhammad Abdul Wahid al-Tubi Press, 1325/1907.

Badawi, El-Said, and Martin Hinds. *A Dictionary of Egyptian Arabic, Arabic-English.* Beirut: Librairie du Liban, 1986.

Badawi, Muhammad Mustafa, ed. *Modern Arabic Literature.* Cambridge, U.K.: Cambridge Univ. Press, 1992.

Badinter, Elisabeth. *Les passions intellectuelles.* Vol. 1, *Désirs de gloire (1735–1751).* Paris: Fayard, 1999.

Baer, Gabriel. "Shirbini's Hazz al-Quhuf and Its Significance." In *Fellah and Townsman in the Middle East: Studies in Social History.* London: Frank Cass, 1982.

Bakhtin, Mikhail. *Rabelais and His World.* Translated by Helene Iswolsky. Bloomington: Indiana Univ. Press, 1984.

Barkey, Karen. *Bandits and Bureaucrats: The Ottoman Route to State Centralization.* Ithaca, N.Y.: Cornell Univ. Press, 1994.

Basha, 'Umar Musa. *Tarikh al-Adab al-'Arabi, al-'Asr al-'Uthmani.* Beirut: Dar al-Fikr al-Mu'asir, 1986.

Al-Batanuni al-Abusiri, 'Ali b. 'Umar. "Kitab al-'Unwan fi Makayid al-Nisa'." Manuscript in Bibliothèque Nationale, Paris, fonds arabe 3565 (1133/1720).

Behrens-Abouseif, Doris. "Une polémique anti-ottomane par un artisan au Caire du XVIIe siècle." In *Etudes sur les villes du Proche-Orient XVIe–XIXe siècle, Hommage à André Raymond,* edited by Brigitte Marino, 55–63. Damascus: Institut français d'études arabes de Damas, 2001.

Berkey, Jonathan. *The Transmission of Knowledge in Medieval Cairo: A Social History of Islamic Education.* Princeton, N.J.: Princeton Univ. Press, 1992.

Bibliothèque Nationale (France). *Catalogue des manuscripts arabes de la bibliothèque nationale par le Baron de Slane.* Paris: Imprimerie nationale, 1883–95.

Bloom, Jonathan. *Paper Before Print: The History and Impact of Paper in the Islamic World.* New Haven, Conn.: Yale Univ. Press, 2001.

Braudel, Fernand. *The Mediterranean and the Mediterranean World in the Age of Philip II,* 2 vols., trans. Sian Reynolds (New York: Harper Colophon, 1972).

———. "The Mediterranean Economy in the Sixteenth Century." In *Essays in European Economic History, 1500–1800,* edited by Peter Earle, 45–88. Oxford, U.K.: Clarendon Press, 1974.

———. *Civilization and Capitalism, Fifteenth–Eighteenth Century.* Vol. 3, *The Perspectives of the World.* Translated by Sian Reynolds. New York: Harper and Row, 1984.

Brown, Cedric C., and Arthur F. Marotti, eds. *Texts and Cultural Change in Early Modern England.* London: Macmillan Press Ltd, 1997.

Brown, Edward. *Le voyage en Egypte d'Edward Brown, 1673–74.* Translated by Marie-Therese Breant. Cairo: Institut français d'archéologie orientale, 1974.

Brugman, J. *An Introduction to the History of Modern Arabic Literature in Egypt.* Leiden, Netherlands: Brill, 1984.

Al-Budayri al-Hallaq, Ahmad. *Hawadith Dimishq al-Yawmiyya, 1154–1175 (1741–*

1762). Edited by Ahmad 'Izzat 'Abdul-Karim. Cairo: Egyptian Society for Historical Studies, 1959.

Burke, Peter. *Popular Culture in Early Modern Europe.* New York: New York Univ. Press, 1978.

———. *A Social History of Knowledge: From Gutenberg to Diderot.* Cambridge, U.K.: Cambridge Univ. Press, 2000.

Cashmore, Ellis, and Chris Rojek, eds. *Dictionary of Cultural Theorists.* London: Arnold Press, 1999.

Chartier, Roger. *Culture écrite et société, l'ordre des livres (XIVe-XVIIIe siècles).* Paris: Bibliothèque Michel Albin, 1996.

Chaudhuri, K. N. *Trade and Civilisation in the Indian Ocean: An Economic History from the Rise of Islam to 1750.* Cambridge, U.K.: Cambridge Univ. Press, 1985.

Cipolla, Carlo M. *Literacy and Development in the West.* Harmondsworth, U.K.: Penguin Books, 1969.

Dahrendorf, Ralf. *Class and Class Conflict in Industrial Society.* 1959. Reprint, London: Routledge and Kegan Paul, 1972.

Al-Damanhuri, Ahmad. "Sabil al-Rashad ila Naf' al-'Ibad." Manuscript in Dar al-Kutub, Ijtima' Taymur 32.

———. *Al-Naf' al-Ghazir fi Salah al-Sultan wal-Wazir.* Edited by Fuad 'Abdul-Mun'im Ahmad. Alexandria, Egypt: Mu'assasat Shabab al-Jami'a, 1992.

Dankoff, Robert. "The Languages of the World According to Evliya Celebi." *Journal of Turkish Studies* 13 (1989): 23–32.

Darnton, Robert. *The Great Cat Massacre and Other Episodes in French Cultural History.* New York: Vintage Books, 1985.

Delanoue, Gilbert. *Moralistes et politiques musulmans dans l'Egypte du XIXe siècle (1798–1882).* 2 vols. Cairo: Institut français d'archéologie orientale, 1982.

Demerson, Guy. *Livres populaires du XVIe siècle: Répertoire sud-est de la France.* Lyon, France: Centre national de la recherche scientifique, 1986.

Dollimore, Jonathan, and Alan Sinfield, eds. *Political Shakespeare: New Essays in Cultural Materialism.* Ithaca, N.Y.: Cornell Univ. Press, 1985.

Doss, Madiha. "Military Chronicles of Seventeenth-Century Egypt as an Aspect of Popular Culture." Paper presented to the Colloquium on Logos, Ethos, and Mythos in the Middle East and North Africa, Budapest, Sept. 18–22, 1995a, 67–79.

———. "Some Remarks on the Oral Factor in Arabic Linguistics." In *Dialectica Arabica, A Collection of Articles in Honour of the Sixtieth Birthday of Professor Heikki Palva,* 49–61. Helsinki: Finnish Oriental Society, 1995b.

Eisenstein, Elizabeth. *The Printing Revolution in Early Modern Europe.* Cambridge, U.K.: Cambridge Univ. Press, 1983.

Eley, Geoff. "Nations, Publics, and Political Cultures: Placing Habermas in the Nineteenth Century." In *Habermas and the Public Sphere*, edited by Craig Calhoun, 289–339. Cambridge, Mass.: MIT Press, 1999.

Elias, Norbert. *La civilisation des moeurs.* Translated by Pierre Kamnitzer. Paris: Kalman Levy, 1973.

Establet, Colette. "Les inventaires après-décès, sources d'histoire culturelle (Damas)." In *Etudes sur les villes du Proche-Orient XVIe–XIXe siècle, Hommage à André Raymond*, edited by Brigitte Marino, 81–90. Damascus: Institut français d'études arabes de Damas, 2001.

Establet, Colette, and Jean-Paul Pascual. *Familles et fortunes à Damas: 450 foyers damascains en 1700*. Damascus: Institut français de Damas, 1994.

———. "Les livres des gens à Damas vers 1700." *Livres et lecture dans le monde ottoman, Revue des mondes musulmans et de la Méditerranée* 87–88 (1999): 143–72.

Faroqhi, Suraiya. *Towns and Townsmen of Ottoman Anatolia: Trade, Crafts and Food Production in an Urban Setting, 1520–1650*. Cambridge, U.K.: Cambridge Univ. Press, 1984.

———. "Merchant Networks and Ottoman Craft Production (Sixteenth–Seventeenth Centuries)." In *Urbanism in Islam: The Proceedings of the International Conference on Urbanism in Islam*. Vol. 1, 85–132. Tokyo: Institute of Oriental Studies, Univ. of Tokyo, 1989.

———. *Approaching Ottoman History: An Introduction to the Sources*. Cambridge, U.K.: Cambridge Univ. Press, 1999.

———. *Subjects of the Sultan: Culture and Daily Life in the Ottoman Empire*. London: I. B. Tauris, 2000.

Febvre, Lucien, and Henri-Jean Martin. *L'apparition du livre*. Paris: Editions Michel Albin, 1971.

Fleischer, Cornell. *Bureaucrat and Intellectual in the Ottoman Empire: The Historian Mustafa Ali (1541–1600)*. Princeton, N.J.: Princeton Univ. Press, 1986.

Fletcher, Joseph. "Integrative History: Parallels and Interconnections in the Early Modern Period, 1500–1800." *Journal of Turkish Studies* 9 (1985): 37–57.

Fox, Adam. *Oral and Literate Culture in England, 1500–1700*. Oxford Studies in Social Sciences. Oxford, U.K.: Oxford Univ. Press, 2000.

Gascoigne, John. "The Universities and the Scientific Revolution: The Case of Newton and Restoration Cambridge." In *Science, Politics, and Universities in Europe, 1600–1800*. Variorum Collected Studies Series, 391–434. Aldershot, U.K.: Ashgate Publishing, 1998.

Ginzburg, Carlo. *The Cheese and the Worms: The Cosmos of a Sixteenth-Century Miller.* Translated by John and Anne Tedeschi. Baltimore, Md.: Johns Hopkins Univ. Press, 1992.

Girgis, Magdi. "Athar al-Arakhina 'ala Awda' al-Qibt fil qarn al-thamin 'ashar" *Annales Islamologiques* 34 (2000): 23–44.

Goffman, Daniel. *The Ottoman Empire and Early Modern Europe*. New York: Cambridge Univ. Press, 2002.

Goody, Jack. *Literacy in Traditional Societies*. Cambridge, U.K.: Cambridge Univ. Press, 1968.

Gramsci, Antonio. *The Gramsci Reader: Selected Writings 1916–1935*. Edited by David Forgacs. New York: New York Univ. Press, 2000.

Gran, Peter. "Late Eighteenth–Early Nineteenth Century Egypt: Merchant Capitalism or Modern Capitalism?" In *L'Egypte du XIXe siècle*, 267–81. Paris: Centre national de la recherche scientifique, 1982.

———. *Beyond Eurocentrism: A New View of Modern World History*. Syracuse, N.Y.: Syracuse Univ. Press, 1996.

———. *Islamic Roots of Capitalism: Egypt, 1760–1840*. 2d ed. Syracuse, N.Y.: Syracuse Univ. Press, 1998. Republished by the American Univ. Cairo, 1999.

Hafez, Sabry. *The Genesis of Arabic Narrative Discourse: A Study in the Sociology of Modern Arabic Literature*. London: Saqi Books, 1993.

Hajji Khalifa, Mustafa b. 'Abdalla. *Kashf al-Dhunun 'an Asami al-Kutub wal-Funun*. 2 vols. Beirut: Dar al-Kutub al-'Ilmiyya, 1992.

Hakim, Muhammad. "Al-A'tab wal-Ru'us: Al-Takwin al-Ijtima'I lil Raqam fi Misr ma bayn 1821–1824." *Mutun 'Asriyya til 'Ulum al-Ijtima'iyya* 1 (winter–spring 2000): 89–106.

———. "Coptic Scribes and Political Arithmetic: The Case of Mu'allim Ghali Serjius." Paper given to the Seminar on Control, Mobility and Self-Fulfillment: Learning and Culture in the Islamic World Since the Middle Ages, American Univ. Cairo, Apr. 13–15, 2000.

Hanna, Nelly. *Habiter au Caire, Les maisons moyennes et leurs habitants aux XVIIe et XVIIIe siècles*. Cairo: Institut français d'archéologie orientale, 1991.

———. *Making Big Money in 1600: The Life and Times of Isma'il Abu Taqiyya, Egyptian Merchant*. Syracuse, N.Y.: Syracuse Univ. Press, 1997.

———. "Cultural Life in Mamluk Households (Late Ottoman Period)." In *Mamluks in Egyptian Society and Politics*, edited by Thomas Philipp and Ulrich Haarman, 196–204. Cambridge, U.K.: Cambridge Univ. Press, 1998.

———. "Culture in Ottoman Egypt." In *The Cambridge History of Egypt*. Vol. 2. Edited by Martin Daly, 87–112. Cambridge, U.K.: Cambridge Univ. Press, 1998.

———. "The Chronicles of Ottoman Egypt: History or Entertainment?" In *The Historiography of Islamic Egypt (c. 950–1800)*, edited by Hugh Kennedy, 237–50. Leiden, Netherlands: Brill, 2001.

———. "Merchants and the Economy in Cairo, 1600–1650." In *Etudes sur les villes du Proche-Orient XVIe–XIX siècle, Hommage à André Raymond*, edited by Brigitte Marino, 225–36. Damascus: Institut français d'études arabes de Damas, 2001.

———. "Coffee and Coffee Merchants in Cairo, 1580–1630." In *Le commerce du café avant l'ère des plantations coloniales, espaces réseaux, sociétés (XVe–XIXe siècles)*, edited by Michel Tuscherer, 91–102. Cairo: Institut français d'archéologie orientale, 2001.

Hathaway, Jane. *The Politics of Households in Ottoman Egypt: The Rise of the Qazdaglis.* Cambridge, U.K.: Cambridge Univ. Press, 1997.

Al-Haythami, Ibn Hajar. "Tahrir al-Maqal fi Adab wa Ahkam yahtaj ilayha mu'addib al-atfal." Manuscript in Dar al-Kutub al-Misriyya, Majami' 143, pp. 146–67.

Heyberger, Bernard. "Livres et pratiques de la lecture chez les Chrétiens (Syrie, Liban), XVII–XVIIIe siècles." Edited by Frederic Hitzel, in *Livres et lecture dans le monde Ottoman, Revue des mondes musulmans et de la Méditerranée* 87–88 (1999): 209–24.

Heyworth-Dunne, James. "Arabic Literature in Egypt in the Eighteenth Century with Some Reference to Poetry and Poets." *Bulletin of the School of Oriental and African Studies, London Univ.* 9 (1937–39): 675–89.

———. *An Introduction to the History of Education in Modern Egypt*. London: Luzac and Co., 1939.

Hitzel, Frederic. "Manuscripts, livres et culture livresque à Istanbul." *Livres et lecture dans le monde ottoman, Revue des mondes musulmans et de la Méditerranée* 87–88 (1999): 19–38.

Horden, Peregrine, and Nicholas Purcell. *The Corrupting Sea: A Study of Mediterranean History*. Oxford, U.K.: Blackwell Publishers, 2000.

Hunter, Dard. *Papermaking: The History and Technique of an Ancient Craft*. New York: Dover Publications, 1978.

Al-Husayni, Mahmud Hamid. *Al-Asbila al-'Uthmaniyya bi-madinat al-Qahira 1517–1798*. Cairo: Maktabat Madbuli, 1988.

Ibn al-Khanqah, Muhammad al-Makki. *Tarikh Hums*. Edited by Umar Najib al-Umar. Damascus: Institut français de Damas, 1987.

Ibn Nujaym, Zayn al-'Abidin. *Al-Ashbah wal Nadha'ir*. Beirut: Dar al-Kutub al-'Ilmiyya, 1985.

Ibn al-Siddiq, Hasan. *Ghara'ib al-Bada'I wa 'Aja'ib al-Waqai*. Edited by Yusuf Nu'aysa. Damascus: Dar al-Ma'rifa, 1988.

Inalcik, Halil. "Capital in the Ottoman Empire." *Journal of Economic History* 29, no. 1 (Mar. 1969): 97–140.

Irigoin, Jean, "Papiers orientaux et papiers occidentaux." In *Colloques internationaux du centre national de la recherche scientifique no. 559, La paléographie grecque et byzantine*. Paris: Editions du CNRS, 1977.

Al-Ishaqi, Muhammad 'Abdul-Mu'ti. *Lata'if Akhbar al-Uwal fiman Tasarrafa fi Misr min Arbab al-Duwal*. Cairo: Maktabat al-Miliji, 1897.

Al-Jabarti, 'Abdul Rahman. *'Abd al-Rahman al-Jabarti's History of Egypt, 'Aja'ib al-Athar fi al-tarajim wa'l akhbar*. 2 vols. Edited by Thomas Phillip and Moshe Perlmann. Stuttgart, Germany: Franz Steiner Verlag, 1994.

Jennings, Roland. "Loans and Credit in Early Seventeenth-Century Ottoman Judicial Records: The Sharia Court of Anatolian Kayseri." *Journal of the Economic and Social History of the Orient* 16, parts 2–3 (1973): 168–216.

Johansen, Baber. *The Islamic Law on Land Tax and Rent: The Peasants' Loss of Property Rights as Interpreted in the Hanafite Legal Literature of the Mamluk and Ottoman Periods.* Beckenham, Kent, U.K.: Croom Helm Ltd., 1988.

———. "Coutumes locales et coutumes universelles aux sources des règles juridiques en droit musulman hanefite." *Annales Islamologiques* 27 (1993): 29–35.

Kafadar, Cemal. "Self and Others: The Diary of a Dervish in Seventeenth-Century Istanbul and First-Person Narratives in Ottoman Literature." *Studia Islamica* 69 (1989): 121–50.

———. "The Question of Ottoman Decline." *Harvard Middle Eastern and Islamic Review* 4, nos. 1–2 (1997–98): 30–75.

Kaplan, Steven, ed. *Understanding Popular Culture: Europe from the Middle Ages to the Nineteenth Century.* Hawthorne, N.Y.: Mouton Publishers, 1984.

Kawatoko, Mutsuo. "Coffee Trade in the al-Tur Port, South Sinai." In *Le commerce du café avant l'ère des plantations coloniales*, edited by Michel Tuscherer, 51–68. Cairo: Institut français d'archéologie orientale, 2001.

El Khadem, Saad. "Quelques reçus de commerçants et d'artisans du Caire des XVIIe et XVIIIe siècles." In *Colloque international sur l'histoire du Caire*, 269–276. Grafenhainichen, Germany: General Egyptian Book Organization, 1972.

Al-Khafaji, Shihab al-Din. *Rihana al-Alibba wa zahrat al-Hayah al-Dunya.* Cairo: Al-Matba'a al-Amiriyya, 1273/1856.

Khoury, Ra'if Georges. *Chrestomathie de papyrologie arabe: Documents relatifs à la vie privée, sociale et administrative des premiers siècles islamiques.* Préparée par Adolf Grohmann, retravaillée et élargie par Ra'if Georges Khoury. Leiden, Netherlands: Brill, 1993.

Kilani, Muhammad Sayyid. *Al-Adab al-Misri fi Dhill al-Hukm al-'Uthmani.* Cairo: Dar Al-Firjani, 1984.

King, David. *A Catalogue of the Scientific Manuscripts in the Egyptian National Library.* Cairo: General Egyptian Book Organization in collaboration with the American Research Center in Egypt and the Smithsonian Institution, 1981.

"Kitab Anis al-Jalis." Bibliothèque Nationale, Paris, fonds arabe 3453, dated 1187/1773.

"Kitab al-Dhakha'ir wal-Tuhaf fi Bir al-Sanayi' wal- Hiraf." Manuscript Orient A 963, Gotha Library, Leiden, Netherlands.

"Kitab Nuzhat al-'Ashiqin wa Ladhat al-Sami'in." Manuscript in the Bibliothèque Nationale, Paris, fonds arabe 3568, datable to seventeenth century.

Kramer, Martin, ed. *Middle Eastern Lives: The Practice of Biography and Self-Narrative.* Syracuse, N.Y.: Syracuse Univ. Press, 1991.

Labib, Subhi. "Capitalism in Medieval Islam." *Journal of Economic History* 29, no. 1 (Mar. 1969): 73–96.
Lane, Edward William. *An Account of the Manners and Customs of the Modern Egyptians*. First published in 1836. London: East-West Publications, 1989.
Lane, Frederic C. "The Mediterranean Spice Trade: Further Evidence of Its Revival in the Sixteenth Century." *American Historical Review* 45, no. 3 (Apr. 1940): 580–90.
Lapidus, Ira. *Muslim Cities in the Later Middle Ages*. Cambridge, Mass.: Harvard Univ. Press, 1967.
Lowy, Michael. " 'Against the Grain': The Dialectical Conception of Culture in Walter Benjamin's Thesis of 1940." In *Walter Benjamin and the Demands of History*, edited by Michael Steinberg, 206–14. Ithaca, N.Y.: Cornell Univ. Press, 1996.
Lukács, Georg. *History and Class Consciousness: Studies in Marxist Dialectics*. Translated by Rodney Livingstone. London: Merlin Press, 1971.
Al-Maghribi, Yusuf. *Rafʿ al-Isar ʿan kalam ahl Misr*. Edited by ʿAbdul-Salam Ahmad ʿAwwad. Moscow: Soviet Academy of Sciences, 1968.
Al-Mahdi, Muhammad. *Contes du Cheykh El-Mohdy*. 3 vols. Translated by Jean-Joseph Marcel. Paris: Imprimerie de Felix Locquin, 1833.
Mantran, Robert. *Istanbul au siècle de Soliman le Magnifique*. Paris: Hachette, 1994.
Manuscript in the Bibliothèque Nationale, Paris, *fonds arabe* 3568.
Al-Maqdisi, Mariʿi Yusuf. "Kitab Muniyat al-Muhibbin wa Bughiyat al-ʿAshiqin." Manuscript in Dar al-Kutub al-Misriyya (Egyptian National Library), Cairo, Adab Talʿat, no. 4648.
———. "Qalaʾid al-ʿUqyan fi Fadaʾil Al-ʿUthman." Manuscript in Suhaj (Egypt) Municipal Library, Tarikh 60, 1031/1621.
———. "Ghidhaʾ al-Arwah bil Muhadatha wal-Mizah." Manuscript in Dar al-Kutub al-Misriyya, Cairo, Adab Taymur, no. 666.
Al-Maqdisi, Mariʿi Yusuf, and Hasan al-ʿAttar. *Inshaʾ Marii wa Inshaʾ al-ʿAttar*. Constantinople: Matbaʾat al-Jawaʾib, 1299/1881.
Maravall, Jose Antonio. *The Culture of the Baroque: Analysis of a Historical Structure*. Translated by Terry Cochran. Minneapolis: Univ. of Minnesota Press, 1986.
Marcus, Abraham. *The Middle East on the Eve of Modernity: Aleppo in the Eighteenth Century*. New York: Columbia Univ. Press, 1989.
Marsot, Afaf Lutfi Al-Sayyid. "A Socio-Economic Sketch of the 'Ulama' in the Eighteenth Century." In *Colloque international sur l'histoire du Caire*, 313–19. Grafenhainichen, Germany: General Egyptian Book Organization, 1972.
———. "The 'Ulama' of Cairo in the Eighteenth and Nineteenth Centuries." In *Scholars, Saints and Sufis: Muslim Religious Institutions in the Middle East Since 1500*, edited by Nikki R. Keddie, 149–65. Berkeley: Univ. of California Press, 1972.
Masters, Bruce. *The Origins of Western Economic Dominance in the Middle East: Mercantil-*

ism and the Islamic Economy in Aleppo, 1600–1750. New York: New York Univ. Press, 1988.
Meriwether, Margaret L. *The Kin Who Count: Family and Society in Ottoman Aleppo, 1740–1840*. Austin: Texas Univ. Press, 1999.
Mingana, A. *Catalogue of Arabic Manuscripts in the John Rylands Library, Manchester.* Manchester, U.K.: Univ. of Manchester Press, 1934.
Miskimin, Harry A. *The Economy of Later Renaissance Europe, 1460–1600*. Cambridge, U.K.: Cambridge Univ. Press, 1977.
Muchembled, Robert. *Culture populaire et cultures des élites dans la France moderne (XVe–XVIIIe siècle)*. Paris: Flammarion, 1978.
Al-Muhibbi, Muhammad Amin. *Qasd al-Sabil fima fil-lugha al-'arabiyya min al-dakhil*. 2 vols. Edited by 'Uthman Mahmud al-Sini. Riyadh: Maktabat al-Tawba, 1994.
Al-Muhibbi, Muhibb al-Din. "Kitab Nuzhat al-Nufus wal-Albab fi Mukatabat al-Muhibb lil-Ahbab." Manuscript in al-Azhar Library, Cairo, no. 7116, Abaza 520.
———. *Khulasat al-Athar fi A'yan al-Qarn al-Hadi 'Ashar.* 4 vols. Cairo: Al-Matba'a al-Wahabiyya, 1284/1867.
Al-Munawi, 'Abdul-Ra'uf. "Al Radd al-Mandur fi dhamm al-Bukhl wa Madh Al Jawd." Manuscript in Dar al-Kutub al-Misriyya, Cairo, adab 256, dated 1047/1637.
———. *Kitab al-Nuzha al-Zahiyya fi Ahkam al-Hammam al-Shar'iyya wal-Tibiyya.* Edited by 'Abdul-Hamid Salih Hamdan. Cairo: Dar Al-Misriyya al-Lubnaniyya, 1987.
Munck, Thomas. *The Enlightenment: A Comparative Social History, 1721–1794*. London: Arnold Publishers, 2000.
Al-Muradi, Muhammad Khalil. *Silk al-Durar fi a'yan al-qarn al-thani 'ashar.* 4 vols. N.p., 1883.
Nabulsi, 'Abdul-Ghani. *Al-Haqiqa wal-Majaz fi Rihla ila Bilad al-Sham wa Misr Wal-Hijaz*. Edited by Ahmad 'Abd al-Majid al-Haridi. Cairo: Hay'at al-Kitab, 1986.
"Nuzhat al-Qulub wal-Nawadhir fi Ghara'ib al-Hikayat wal-Nawadir." Manuscript in the Bibiliothèque Nationale, Paris, fonds arabe 3577, datable to eighteenth century.
Ostle, Robin, ed. *Marginal Voices in Literature and Society: Individual and Society in the Mediterranean Muslim World*. Aix-En-Provence, France: Maison Méditerranéenne des Sciences de l'Homme, 2000.
Pamuk, Sevket. "Money in the Ottoman Empire, 1326–1914." In *An Economic and Social History of the Ottoman Empire*. Vol. 2, *1600–1914*, edited by Halil Inalcik with Donald Quataert, 945–80. Cambridge, U.K.: Cambridge Univ. Press, 1994.
Peled, M. "Nodding the Necks: A Literary Study of Shirbini's *Hazz al-Quhuf*." *Die Welt des Islams* 26 (1986): 57–75.
Piterberg, Gabriel. "Speech Acts and Written Texts: A Reading of a Seventeenth-

Century Ottoman Historiographic Episode." *Poetics Today* 14, no. 2 (summer 1993): 387–418.

Rafeq, Abdul-Karim. "The Law Court Registers of Damascus, with Special Reference to Craft Corporations During the Second Half of the Eighteenth Century." In *Les Arabes par leurs archives (XVIe–XXe siècles)*. Edited by Jacques Berques and Dominique Chevallier, 141–59. Paris: CNRS, 1976.

———. *Buhuth fil Tarikh al-Iqtisadi wal-lijtima'i li Bilad al-Sham fil 'Asr al-Hadith* (Damascus: N.p., 1985).

———. "Craft Organization, Work Ethics, and the Strains of Change in Ottoman Syria." *Journal of the American Oriental Society* 111, no. 3 (1991): 495–511.

"Raha al-Rawh wa Salwa al-Qalb al-Majruh." Manuscript in Dar al-Kutub al-Misriyya, Cairo, Akhlaq Taymur no. 1214.

Raymond, André. "Une liste des corporations de métiers au Caire en 1801." *Arabica* 4 (1957): 150–63.

———. "Quartiers et mouvements populaires au Caire au XVIIIe siècle." In *Political and Social Change in Modern Egypt*, edited by Peter M. Holt, 104–16. London: Oxford Univ. Press, 1968.

———. *Artisans et commerçants au Caire au XVIIIe siècle*. 2 vol. Damascus: Institut français de Damas, 1973/1974.

———. "Le Caire, économie et société urbaines à la fin du XVIIIe siècle." In *L'Egypte au XIXe siècle*, 121–39. Paris: Centre national de la recherche scientifique, 1982.

———. "L'activité architecturale au Caire à l'époque ottomane (1517–1798)." *Annales Islamologiques* 25 (1990): 343–59.

———. "Soldiers in Trade: The Case of Ottoman Cairo." *Brismes* 17, no. 2 (1991): 16–37.

———. *Le Caire des Janissaires*. Paris: CNRS Editions, 1995.

———. "Pouvoir politique, autonomies urbaines et mouvements populaires au Caire au XVIIIe siècle." *Etats et pouvoirs en Méditerranée, mélanges offerts à Andre Nouschi*, 1–18. Nice, France: Univ. de Nice, n.d.

Russell, Alexander. *The Natural History of Aleppo*. 2d ed. rev. 2 vols. 1794; reprint, Westmead, U.K.: Gregg International Publishers, 1969.

Salama, Ibrahim. *L'enseignement islamique en Egypte, son évolution, son influence sur les programmes modernes*. Cairo: National Printing Press, 1938.

Salih, Ahmad Rushdi. *Al-Adab al-Sha'bi*. 3d ed. 2 vols. Cairo: Maktabat al-Nahda al-Misriyya, 1971.

Salzmann, Ariel. "Towards a Comparative History of the Ottoman Empire, 1450–1850." *Archiv Orientalni* 66, supplement 8, 351–66.

Sartain, Elizabeth. *Jalal al-Din al-Suyuti: Biography and Background*. 2 vols. Cambridge, U.K.: Cambridge Univ. Press, 1975.

Al-Sayyid Murtada al-Zabidi. *Taj al-'Arus min Jawahir al-Qamus*. Edited by 'Abdul-Sattar Ahmad Farraj. Kuwait: Al Turath al-'Arabi, 1965.

Al-Shabrawi, 'Abdalla. "Kitab 'Arus al-Adab wa Furjat al-Albab." Manuscript in Dar al-Kutub al-Misriyya, Cairo, Adab Tal'at no. 4489, dated 1154/1741.

——. *Kitab 'Unwan al-Bayan wa Bustan al-Adhhan wa Majmu' Nasa'ih fil Hikam.* Cairo: Matba'at al-Hajar, 1275/1858.

Al-Shabrawi, Ahmad. *Kitab Rawdat Ahl al-Fukaha.* Cairo: Al-Matba'a al-'Amira al-Sharafiyya, 1317/1899.

Shafiq, Ahmad Pasha. *Mudhakarati fi Nisf Qarn.* 4 vols. Cairo: al-Hay'a al-Misriyya lil-Kitab, 1999.

Sharabi, Hisham. *Arab Intellectuals and the West: The Formative Years, 1875–1914.* Baltimore, Md.: Johns Hopkins Univ. Press, 1970.

Al-Sha'rani, 'Abd al-Wahab. *Lata'if al-Minan.* Cairo: 'Alam al-Fikr, 1976.

Shaw, Stanford. *The Financial and Administrative Organization and Development of Ottoman Egypt, 1517–1798.* Princeton, N.J.: Princeton Univ. Press, 1962.

El-Shayyal, Gamal El-Din. "Some Aspects of Intellectual and Social Life in Eighteenth-Century Egypt." In *Political and Social Change in Modern Egypt*, edited by Peter M. Holt, 117–132. London: Oxford Univ. Press: 1968.

Sher, Richard B., and Andrew Hook. "Introduction: Glasgow and the Enlightenment." In *The Glasgow Enlightenment*, edited by Andrew Hook and Richard B. Sher, 1–20. East Lothian, Scotland: Tuckwell Press, 1995.

Al-Shirbini, Yusuf. *Hazz al-Quhuf fi Sharh Qasida Abu Shaduf.* Bulaq, Egypt: National Press, 1857.

——. "Kitab Tarh al-Madad li-Hall al-'Ala' wal-Durar." Manuscript in Dar al-Kutub al-Misriyya, Majami' Tal'at no. 578, copy dated 1327/1909.

Shoshan, Boaz. "High Culture and Popular Culture in Medieval Islam." *Studia Islamica* 83 (1991): 67–107.

——. "On Popular Literature in Medieval Cairo." *Poetics Today* 14, no. 2 (1993): 349–65.

Shuman, Mohsen. "The Beginnings of Urban *Iltizam* in Egypt." In *The State and Its Servants: Administration in Egypt from Ottoman Times to the Present*, edited by Nelly Hanna, 17–31. Cairo: American Univ. in Cairo Press, 1995.

Siraj, Muhammad. "Tatawwur al-fiqh fil 'asr al-'uthmani." In *Al-'Adala bayn al-Shari'a wal-Waqi'*, edited by Nasir Ibrahim and 'Imad Hilal, 61–77. Cairo: Markaz al-Buhuth wal Dirasat al-Ijtima'iyya, Cairo Univ., in collaboration with the Egyptian Society for Historical Studies, 2002.

Sonbol, Amira El-Azhary. *The New Mamluks: Egyptian Society and Modern Feudalism.* Syracuse, N.Y.: Syracuse. Univ. Press, 2000.

Street, Brian V. *Literacy in Theory and Practice.* Cambridge, U.K.: Cambridge Univ. Press, 1984.

Sunar, Ilkay. "State and Economy in the Ottoman Empire." In *The Ottoman Empire and the World Economy*, edited by Huri Islamoglu-Inan, 63–87. Cambridge, U.K.: Cambridge Univ. Press, 1987.

Tate, Jihane. *Une waqfiyya du XVIIIe siècle à Alep: La waqfiyya d'al Hagg Musa al-Amiri.* Damascus: Institut français de Damas, 1990.

Taylor, Charles. *Sources of the Self: The Making of the Modern Identity.* Cambridge, Mass.: Harvard Univ. Press, 2001.

Toledano, Ehud. *State and Society in Mid-Nineteenth-Century Egypt.* Cambridge, U.K.: Cambridge Univ. Press, 1990.

'Uthman, Nasir. "Ta'ifa al-Sahhafin fil qarn al-sabi' 'ashir." In *Al-Tawa'if al-Mihaniyya wal-Ijtima'iyya fi Misr fil 'asr al-'uthmani,* edited by Nasir Ibrahim, Markaz al-Buhuth wal Dirasat al-Ijtima'iyya, 64–65. Cairo: Egyptian Society for Historical Studies, 2003.

Vernet, André, ed. *Histoire des bibliothèques françaises, les bibliothèques médiévales du VIe siècle à 1530.* Paris: Promodis, Editions du Cercle de la Librairie, avec le concours du CNRS, 1989.

Vrolijk, Arnoud, *Bringing a Laugh to a Scowling Face: A Study and Critical Edition of the Nuzhat al-Nufus wa Mudhik al-'abus by 'Ali Ibn Sudun al-Bashbughawi.* Leiden, Netherlands: Centre for Non-Western Studies, Leiden Univ., 1998.

Walz, Terence. *Trade Between Egypt and Bilad al-Sudan.* Cairo: Institut français d'archéologie orientale, 1978.

Wild, Johann de. *Voyages en Egypte de Johann Wild (1606–1610).* Translated by Oleg Volkoff. Cairo: Institut français d'archéologie orientale, 1973.

Williams, Raymond. *Problems in Materialism and Culture.* London: Verso Editions and NLB, 1980.

———. *The Sociology of Culture.* New York: Schocken Books, 1982.

Ze'evi, Dror. *An Ottoman Century: The District of Jerusalem in the 1600s.* Albany, N.Y.: SUNY Press, 1996.

Index

'Abdul-Karim, Ahmad 'Izzat, 71
'Abdullah, 'Umar b., 128
'Abdul-Rahman, Isma'il b., 95
Abu Dhakir, Muhammad Ibn Hasan:
	ambivalence to leaders, 154, 155;
	appearance of women in works of,
	125–26; concern with material life, 159;
	distancing from dominant view, 163–69;
	on education, 53; identity of, 149–50,
	152; last years of, 169–71; literary text of,
	1–2; on *majalis*, 75, 76; on
	money/poverty, 160–62; Nadim and,
	172; personal narrative of, 167–69; on
	polygamy, 126; as source material, 20;
	type of knowledge acquired by, 77; use of
	colloquial language, 134, 157–58; use of
	proverbs, 121, 162
Abu Zayd al-Hilali, 67
administrative culture, 13
Afandi, al-Islam Fayzalla, 169
Afandi, Isma'il, 95
Ahmad, Shihabi, 38
'Aja'ib al-Athar (al-Jabarti), 141
al-Ajhuri, 'Atiya, 64
Aleppo: book production in, 88–89, 95;
	education in, 53; investments in trade in,
	38; trade/industry of, 30, 34
*Al-Fawa'ih al-Jinaniyya fi Mada'ih
	al-Ridwaniyya* (al-Idkawi), 143
Allah, Daud b. Shaykh Makram, 100–101

Anatolia, 28–29, 58, 59, 169
al-'Anbuti, 'Amir, 150
Anis al-Jalis, 97, 119, 123
Anwar, Muhammad Abul, 144
Aquilon, Pierre, 99
Arabization, 131–32
al-'Arayshi, Muhammad, 31
*Artisans et commerçants au Caire au XVIIe
	siècle* (André), 31, 35
Azhar: influence on society, 9–10;
	intellectuals educated in, 152; language
	used in, 158; number of students at, 71;
	origin of *'ulama'* of, 114; prominence of,
	106
al-Azhari, Muhammad, 123

al-Badawi, al-Sayyid, 68
Badinter, Elisabeth, 151
al-Badri, Hasan, 150, 152, 154, 160
Bakhtin, Mikhail, 155–56
al-Bakri, Zayn al-'Abidin, 73–74
Barkey, Karen, 70
Barsbay (sultan of Egypt), 30
al-Batanuni al-Abusiri, 'Ali b. Umar, 127
Baybars, al-Dhahir, 67
al-Bazzazi (early jurist), 135
before/after approach, 51–52
Benjamin, Walter, 145
Bey, Murad, 137

209

Bibliothèque Nationale, *Fonds arabe*, 83–84
biographical dictionaries, 25, 122
biographies, 21–22
book culture: consequences of, 112, 166–67; development of, 12, 58, 80; material conditions contributing to, 80–86; as method of knowledge diffusion, 14; price/availability of paper and, 20; sources of information on, 22; spread of colloquial and, 157
books: commercial use of, 94; consequences of spread of, 98–101, 166–67; decline paradigm and, 176; diversity in quality of, 89–92; number/value of, 86, 101; ownership of, 58, 88, 93–94; price of, 17, 91–93; printing press institution and, 101; production of, 12; reading habits and, 96–98; reasons for increase in, 101; spread of, 79–86; subject matter of, 102–3; of Sufism, 93, 94–96
book trade, 42
Braudel, Fernand, 35, 37
brotherhoods, 13, 69–70
Brown, Edward, 96
Burke, Peter, 10, 11, 80, 165

Cairo: accessibility of books in, 79, 80; book production in, 89; comparative studies of, 15–19; complexity of monetary system in, 63; copying of manuscripts in, 83–84; culture of, 140–44, 176; deteriorating importance of, 47; development of oral tradition in, 65–66; economy in eighteenth century, 6; educational system in, 51, 52–53, 54, 61, 70–71, 106, 110; history of written word in, 19; investments in trade in, 38–39; in later period, 46–47; literacy in, 59–60; *majalis* and, 73–74, 75; marriage alliances in, 43–44; middle-class writers in, 118; population involved in trade, 31; price of books in, 91; reading habits in, 96; role of *'ulama'* in, 41–42; trade/industry of, 28–30, 34, 35, 39, 59–60

Catalogue of the Scientific Manuscripts in Egyptian National Library, A (King), 83
catalogues of Arabic manuscripts, 22–23
centralized power structure. *See* state power structures
Chabrol, 71
Chartier, Robert, 79
Chaudhuri, K. N., 32, 34
Chauvin, Victor, 71
Chelebi, Evliya, 31
chronicles: appearance of ordinary man in, 127–28; descriptions of poverty in, 161; development of popular style of, 94; language of, 119–20; middle-class culture in, 115–16, 118; shortcomings of, 21–22
Cipolla, Carlo M., 57
civilizing process, 75–76
class, use of term, 7–8
coffeehouses, 14, 65–68, 120, 186n. 34
coffee merchants, 28, 31, 35
collective reading, 96–97
colloquial language: early use of in written word, 19; in literature, 24–25, 115, 119–20, 122, 173; Mamluk reading of, 137; middle-class writers' use of, 157–58; spread of, 128–36
commercial capitalism: borders of, 176; comparative studies of, 15; impact on economy, 32–36; middle-class development and, 7, 26–33, 27, 51; middle-class investments in, 37–39; spread of books and, 80, 94, 100; spread of literacy and, 57–64. *See also* economic context; trade
commercial centers, 34
commercial culture, 13
Copts, 13, 53, 64, 84, 107–8
copyists, 89–90
court records: appearance of women in, 125; financial arrangements revealed in,

37–38; increase in middle-class use of, 62–64; information gathered from, 18, 20–21, 22, 84–85; paper categories listed in, 87; recent research on, 5; use of paper documents, 81–82. *See also* probate records; *waqf* deeds

culture: categorization of, 5–6, 10–13; democratization of, 24; dimensions of, 13; economic context and, 6; of establishment, 10–12; expressed in chosen literature, 4–5; influence of trade on, 26; of Islam, 176; of Istanbul, 19, 176; local vs. universal, 135–36, 173; of nineteenth century, 175; of Ottoman state, 176–77; as part of context of literary works, 2–3, 115–16; of ruling class in eighteenth century, 140–44; studies of, 11; taxation system and, 8–9, 26–27, 36–40, 139–40; of *'ulama'*, 12, 51, 105–6; *'ulama'* control of, 105; written word and, 64. *See also* book culture; middle-class culture; national culture; oral culture; scholarly culture

Culture of the Baroque, The (Maravall), 16

Dala'il al-Khairat, 92, 94–96, 188n. 32
al-Damanhuri, Ahmad, 107, 137–38, 141
Damascus, 42, 67
al-Damurdashi, 22
Darnton, Robert, 10
decline paradigm, 176
Delanoue, Gilbert, 142
Demerson, Guy, 133
Description de l'Egypte, 31
Dhahab, Muhammad Bey Abul, 141
dictionaries, 115, 128, 129–31, 134
Doss, Madiha, 119–20
dramatic performances, 66–67

Early Modern Literature in History series, 24

economic context: commercial capitalism, 31–36; comparative studies of, 15–17; cultural context and, 6–8, 26–27; cultural significance of, 110, 170–71; of eighteenth century, 144; impact on literature, 158–63; investments and, 37–39; in later period, 44–47; response to crises in, 147; role of *'ulama'* in, 41; soldiers' role in, 42–43; spread of literacy and, 57. *See also* commercial capitalism; trade

education: approach to study of, 53–54; changes necessary for middle-class development, 6; elite control of, 9–10, 12, 27; history of written word in Egypt and, 55–57; leadership potential and, 70–77; means of obtaining, 13–14, 51–53; of middle class, 49, 50–52, 54–69, 77–78; new reading habits and, 102; nineteenth-century reforms in, 174–75; oral culture as part of, 64–69; oral reading and, 96–97; over-extension of, 70–71; reevaluation of, 3; religious control over, 105–6; rise of intellectuals and, 151–52; role in social change, 147–48; role of *majalis* in, 74–76; spread of literacy, 57–64; *'ulama'* as link between hierarchy and lower classes, 41–42; use of biographies for study of, 21–22

Egypt: Arab conquest of, 130–31; availability/price of paper in, 86–88; copying of manuscripts in, 84; cultural exchange between classes, 106–7; education in, 52–53; history of written word in, 19, 55–57; in later period, 46–47; personal narratives of, 166–69; reading habits in, 96; spread of books in, 79; spread of literacy in, 57–58, 59; sugar production in, 30–31, 35; textile production in, 34–35; trade/industry of, 28–29, 30–31, 35; weakened central power structures in, 104–5

Eisenstein, Elizabeth, 65

Elias, Norbert, 75
elites: control of society, 9–10, 12, 27; control over education/culture, 105; enrichment of, 45–46; *majalis* and, 74–75; of middle class, 69–74, 76–77; middle class vs. during early period, 36–40. *See also 'ulama'*
El-Shayyal, Gamal El-Din, 71
Erasmus, 112
Establet, Colette, 38, 82, 88
establishment culture, 10–12
Europe: comparative studies of, 15–16; debate on knowledge in, 165; papermaking in, 86; shift in trade and, 15, 28–29; spread of books in, 79, 80, 99, 103; spread of literacy in, 57–58; universities and cultural change in, 148

al-Falaki, Mustafa, 41
Faroqhi, Suraiya, 5, 11, 35, 169
fatwa (legal opinion), 163–65
finance, 7, 30, 37–39, 42, 44, 47
Firuzabadi, 130
Fleischer, Cornell, 70, 140
Fletcher, Joseph, 18–19
Fox, Adam, 112

Gascoigne, John, 148
geopolitical transformation, 173
Ghara'b al-Bada''i (al-Siddiq), 118
al-Ghayti, Najm al-Din, 113
Ginzburg, Carlo, 58
Girgis, Magdi, 84
Gramsci, Antonio, 9, 69
Gran, Peter, 16, 19, 24
Grohman, Adolf, 131
guilds: of book merchants, 93; of copyists, 89; investments and, 38; literary texts concerning, 123; movement between crafts, 41–43; of paper production, 88; social/political concerns and, 7, 40; of storytellers, 185n. 26

Habermas, Jürgen, 156
Hafez, Sabry, 24
Hajji Khalifa, Mustafa b. 'Abdalla, 166, 168
al-Hakim, 'Abdul-Rahman al-Shami, 94
Hakim, Muhammad, 13
Hamidi, 117
al-Hanbali, Muhammad al-Maqdisi b. Ya'qub, 101
Al-Hariri, Muhammad, 42
Hashish, Ahmad, 118
Hathaway, Jane, 5
al-Haythami, Ibn Hajar, 60–61
Hazz al-Quhuf (al-Shirbini), 74, 116, 119, 122, 134, 158–59
Heyberger, Bernard, 82
Heyworth-Dunne, James, 23, 71, 94
al-Hijazi, Hasan al-Badri, 154
historical context, 105
historical process: challenges to hegemony in, 152–53; fuller understanding of, 175–76; influence on culture, 6–15; literary texts and, 2, 145; spread of colloquial as, 128–29; viewing of through culture, 3; writers as part of, 150–51
historical studies: before/after approach, 51–52; bias of, 21–22, 170; challenges to Ottoman studies, 17–18; comparative approach to, 15–16; on dissent of lower classes, 146–47; generalization in, 59; hindrances to, 59; on oral vs. written traditions, 65, 66; on spread of books, 82–83; trends in, 5, 10–12; of *'ulama'*, 111; use of literary sources for, 109. *See also* methodology; Ottoman studies

Ibn al-Karaki, 97
Ibn al-Siddiq, 118
Ibn Danyal, 133

Ibn Iyas, 133, 134
Ibn Jawziyya, 141
Ibn Khanqah, Muhammad al-Makki, 127–28
Ibn Nujaym, 135
Ibn Sudun, 133, 134
Ibn Taymiyya, 141
al-Idkawi, 'Abdalla, 142, 143
illustrations, 129
iltizam system. *See* taxation system
Inalcik, Halil, 32
al-'Inani, 'Abdul-Rahman, 100
Industrial Revolution, 7
intellectual leadership, 69–74, 76–77
intellectuals, 150–71, 174
international commerce. *See* commercial capitalism; trade
investments, 37–39, 47
al-Ishaqi, 'Abdul-Mu'ti, 113, 115–16
al-Iskandar, Abdul-Rahman, 98
Islam: culture of, 176; educational system of, 54–55; oral contracts and, 81–82; view of education, 52
Islamic Roots of Capitalism, Egypt, 1760–1840 (Gran), 24
Islamic scholarship, 129, 163–66
Istanbul: control of taxation system, 8–9, 44–45; culture of, 19, 176; education in, 52–53, 106; libraries in, 89; *majalis* in, 74–75; personal narratives of, 169; spread of literacy in, 58; trade/industry of, 30, 34; weakened power structures in, 104–5

al-Jabarti, 'Abdul Rahman: on astronomers, 13; on book copying, 90; on books, 89, 95; culture described by, 110; literary value of work of, 21–23; on lower classes, 48; on *majalis*, 72–73, 137, 140; male-dominated chronicles of, 124, 125, 126–27; on Mamluk lifestyle, 144; necrology of al-Ajhuri, 64; on number of *madrasas*, 71; panegyrics in works of, 143; on patrons of coffeehouses, 186n. 34; on poverty, 161; on shaykhs, 96–97; on social structure, 141; as source material, 20; on *'ulama'*, 154–55; use of personal narrative, 167
al-Jabarti, Hasan, 73, 96–97
al-Jalfi, Ridwan Katkhuda, 73, 137, 140–41, 142–43
al-Jawli, Muhammad 'Ali, 43
Jennings, Roland, 38
Jerusalem, 59
Jews, 53, 56
Johansen, Baber, 135
Juda jokes, 119, 153, 189–90n. 20

al-Kabir, 'Ali Bey, 45, 47, 139, 169–70
Kafadar, Cemal, 169
Karimi merchants, 30
Kashf al-Dhunun (Hajji Khalifa), 168
Katkhuda, 'Abdul-Rahman, 45, 141
Katkhuda, 'Uthman, 45, 55, 93
El Khadem, Saad, 63, 68–69
al-Khafaji, Ahmad, 113
al-Khafaji, Shihab al-Din, 117
al-Khaliq al-Sadat, 'Abd, 187n. 55
al-Khalwati Muhammad b. Salim al-Hifnawi al-Shafi'i, 89
al-Khayyat, Mustafa, 90
Khedive Abbas II, 130
al-Kilani, Muhammad Sayyid, 23
King, David, 83
Kitab al-Dhakha'ir wal-Tuhaf fi Bir al-Sanayi' wal-Hiraf, 118, 123
Kitab al-'Unwan fi Makayid al-Nisa (al-Batanuni al-Abusiri), 127
Kitab 'Arus al-Adab wa Furjat al-Albab (al-Shabrawi), 167, 193n. 49
Kitab Nuzhat al-'Ashiqin wa Ladhat al-Sami'in, 76, 186n. 55
Kitab Tarh al-Madad li-Hall al-'Ala' wal-Durar (al-Shirbini), 159–60
al-Kiwani, Ahmad, 68

knowledge: debate on, 163–69; elite control of, 9–10, 12; *majalis* and, 74–76; means of transmitting, 13–14, 50–53, 65, 110; middle-class approach to, 172; oral traditions and, 64–69; spread of books and, 79, 102; written word and, 55–57. *See also* education
Koprulu, Mehmed Pasha, 89

Labib, Subhi, 32
Lane, Edward William, 67, 71
Lane, Frederic, 60
language: colloquial dictionary, 115; of eighteenth-century writers, 157–58; as field of conflict, 130–31; interest in ordinary man and, 122; political changes and, 135; of seventeenth-century chronicles, 119–20; spread of colloquial terms, 128–36; used in Azhar, 158
Leur, Jacob Cornelis van, 30
literacy: class status and, 10–11; connection to trade, 57–64; consequences of spread of, 93–94; international trade and, 16; religious schools contribution to, 54–55; spread of books and, 80; spread of colloquial and, 132–33
literary salons. *See majalis*
literary texts: aimed at middle class, 111–13; as cultural product, 2; emergence of ordinary person in, 121–23; of middle class, 77; nature/use of, 23–25; reactions to changing cultural conditions in, 145–46; work context of, 123–28
literature: appearance of women in, 124–26; contribution of coffeehouses to, 66–67; contribution of *majalis* to, 74; democratization of, 111; development of personal narrative, 166–68; effects of spread of books, 103; eighteenth-century style/language of, 157; ideal social structure repeated in, 141; of *majalis*, 72–73; middle-class contribution to, 68–69, 117–18, 148–56; of middle class in later Ottoman period, 49, 140, 144–48, 150–51, 155–56; subject matter of, 158–63, 166, 168; types of manuscripts copied, 83–84; use of colloquial in, 128–36, 158; use of for social history, 109; writing of oral tradition, 119–21
local culture, 135–36, 173
local power structures: control of taxation system, 8–9, 27, 44–47, 104–5, 139–40; influence on society, 9; Ottoman conquest and, 36; regional histories and, 18; relationship with middle class, 36–37; shaping of middle-class culture and, 104–5; *'ulama'* as link to lower classes, 41–42. *See also* Mamluk ruling class; *'ulama'*

al-Maghribi, Yusuf: dictionary of colloquial language, 128, 133–34, 157; on *majalis*, 74; methodology of, 129–30; use of household terms, 124; use of proverbs, 121; use of work context, 123; works by, 113, 114–15
al-Mahalli, Husayn, 41
Mahammad, Shaykh, 94
al-Mahdi, Muhammad, 45–46, 98, 137, 155
majalis (literary salons), 14, 72–76, 140–41, 168
maktab. *See* education
al-Maliki, Ibrahim al-'Abidi, 74
al-Maliki, Shanan Muhammad, 154–55
Mamluk ruling class: collections of books of, 90–91, 93; control of taxation system, 8–9, 27, 44–47, 104–5, 139–40; Copts' links to, 107–8; culture of in eighteenth century, 140–44; education of, 136–37; impact on education, 62; lifestyle of, 45, 144; *majalis* and, 75; Ottoman conquest and, 36; relationship with populace, 47–48, 139

Mantran, Robert, 52–53
manuscripts, 83–84, 89–90
al-Maqdisi, Mari'i, 77
Maravall, José Antonio, 16
Marcel, J. J., 98
Marcus, Abraham, 52–53
marginalization, 17–18, 21, 46
marriage alliances, 43–44
Marsot, Afaf, 45
Marxism, 7
Masters, Bruce, 38
material conditions, 6, 26, 27–40, 80–86. *See also* economic context; taxation system; trade
Mediterranean, 15–19, 32–36, 37–39, 57–59
Mehmet the Conqueror, 106
Menoccio (sixteenth-century miller), 58
merchant class, 31–32, 34
methodology: of al-Maghribi, 129–30; application to this study, 57–58; comparative approach to commercial capitalism, 33–36; comparative framework, 15–19; cultural categorization and, 10; singular perspective of, 21, 111. *See also* historical studies
middle Arabic. *See* colloquial language
middle class: characteristics of, 3; contours of, 40; core/periphery of, 40–44; education of, 48–49, 50–52, 54–69, 70, 77–78; elites vs. during later period, 44–49; impoverishment of, 27, 40, 49, 61–62, 160–62; as initiators of trends, 171; investments of, 37–39, 42, 47; lifestyle of, 31, 39; link to ruling class, 41–43, 47, 49, 107–8; *majalis* attendance, 75–76; Mamluk control of taxes and, 44–47; polarization of classes and, 143–45; potential for intellectual leadership, 69–74; reaction to crises of eighteenth century, 47–48, 144–47; relationship with ruling class, 27, 36–37, 48; spread of books to, 79–101; taxation as control of, 8–9, 26–27, 36–40; *'ulama'* literature aimed at, 111–13; writers from, 118, 148–56
middle-class culture: categorization of, 4; comparative framework for understanding, 15–17; development of, 4–20, 105–6; economic/cultural contexts of, 6–8, 26–49; of eighteenth century, 136–38, 144–48; elite members of, 76–77; elites vs. during early period, 36–40; emergence of, 172–74; identity of, 156–63; impact of, 172–77; impact of al-Kabir's control on, 169–70; impact of trade on, 32–36; impact on written word, 111–19; influence on upper classes, 113–16; literary classes of, 23–24; *majalis* and, 75–76; material conditions underlying, 26–33, 48–49; nature of, 2–3, 50–51; nonreligious perspective of, 4, 12–15, 107–8, 148, 151–52; oral aspect of, 64–69; political context of, 104–5; presence in written word, 108–19; regional/local power structures and, 8–12; religious culture vs., 50–51; sources of information concerning, 20–25; spread of books and, 98–101, 102
military: control of taxation system, 8–9, 27, 44–47; development of middle class and, 114–16; as link between ruling and middle classes, 43; as periphery of middle class, 41; trade activities of, 42–43. *See also* Mamluk ruling class
al-Misri, Ahmad 'Abdalla al-Rumi, 95
al-Misri, 'Uthman Efendi ibn Ahmad al-Safa'i, 162
modernity: Abu Dhakir and, 169; expression of in middle-class literary works, 3–4; middle-class contribution to, 5–6, 53–54, 69, 172
modernization, 174
monetary system, 37–38, 63
Mubarak, 'Ali, 54

Muhammad, Hajj, 38
Muhammad 'Ali, 51–52, 81, 101, 174
al-Muhibbi, Muhibb al-Din: on book production, 92; dictionary of non-Arabic words, 131; literary value of works of, 20, 21–23; on *majalis*, 73; on patronage, 143; on power structures, 41; on price of books, 91; use of colloquial language, 128; work in coffeehouses, 67
al-Munawi, 'Abdul-Ra'uf, 113
al-Muradi, Muhammad Khalil, 68, 72
Mustafa Ali, 140–41
Mutafariqqa, Hasan, 43

al-Nabulsi, 'Abdul-Ghani, 73–74, 118
Nadim, 'Abdalla, 54, 147, 172–73
national culture, 173
nonreligious perspective: of Abu Dhakir, 164–65; conditions shaping, 12–15; development of, 53, 148; of middle-class writers, 4; rise of intellectuals and, 151–52; spread of books and, 102; structural basis for, 107–8; in *'ulama'* works, 137
Nuzhat al-Qulub, 122

oral contracts, 81–82
oral culture: nature of, 64–69; popular culture as, 10; spread of books and, 102; writing of, 68–69, 81, 119–21, 128
oral reading, 96
ordinary person, 22, 25, 121–36, 172–73
oriental despotism model, 10–11
Ottoman state: centralization of power structures of, 104–5, 139–40; conquest of Egypt, 36–40; control of taxation system, 8–9; culture of, 176–77; education in, 52–53, 70–71; investments in trade, 37; oral tradition in, 65–66; ruling structures of, 7–8; social hierarchy of, 141–42; spread of books in, 82–83; spread of literacy in, 58–59; trade policies, 29; weakened central power structure of, 104–5
Ottoman studies, 5, 15–20, 176–77. *See also* historical studies

Pamuk, Sevket, 37–38
panegyrics, 22, 143
paper: availability/price of, 16–17, 86–88, 176; growth of writing and, 20; new attitudes about reading and, 97–98; oral tradition and, 68; use of for legal documents, 81–82
Pascual, Jean-Paul, 38, 82, 88
patronage, 93, 142–43
pepper, 30, 35
personal narrative, 166–69
poetry, 67–69, 73, 117, 123, 142–43
political context, 102–3, 104–5, 114–15, 135, 139–40. *See also* local power structures; power structures; state power structures
political identity, 156–63
polygamy, 126
Popular Culture in Early Modern Europe (Burke), 10
pornography, 168
power structures: centralization of, 139; influence on middle-class culture, 8–9, 26–27, 105–6; shift from regional to local, 104–5, 171; spread of colloquial and, 135. *See also* local power structures; state power structures
printing press, 79–81, 86–87, 99, 101–3
private libraries: development of, 20, 176; listed in probate records, 85–86; of Mamluks, 93, 137; owners of, 98–101; price of books in, 92; reasons for increase in, 86–90; as sources of information, 22; spread of books and, 96
private reading, 97–98
probate records, 21
professional structures, 7, 38, 40

proverbs, 120–21, 122, 124, 137–38, 153, 162
putting-out system, 33, 34

Qasd al-Sabil firma fillugha al-'arabiyya min al-dakhil (al-Muhibbi), 131
Qazudghli household, 44–45

Rabelais, 155
radical intellectuals, 148–71
Raf' al-Isar (al-Maghribi), 74
Rafeq, Abdul-Karim, 5
"Raha al-Rawh wa Salwat al-Qalb al-Majruh," 141
al-Rahman, 'Atiyat, 125
al-Raqabawi, Muhammad b. Ahmad, 143
Raymond, André: on economic crises, 159; economic study of Cairo, 6–7, 21; on merchants/artisans, 35; on middle class in Cairo, 39; on military, 43; on monetary system, 63; on other *'ulama'*, 41; on paper-related guilds, 88; on school construction, 61; on taxation system, 46; on trade in Cairo, 29, 31; on urban wealth, 47–48; on written correspondence, 63
reading habits, 96–98
religion: academic book production of, 25; elite control of, 27; function of *majalis* in, 72–74; influence of Azhar on society, 9–10; influence on literary works, 4; influence on social structure, 8; middle-class culture vs., 50–51; nonreligious perspective of middle class vs., 12–15; as source of education, 52–55, 71–72; *'ulama'* as link to lower classes, 41–42
religious leaders. *See 'ulama'*
revolt, 47–48, 70, 145–46, 160
Rihana al-Alibba (al-Khafaji), 117
ruling class. *See* Mamluk ruling class; military; *'ulama'*

Russell, Alexander, 88–89
al Ruwi'i, Ahmad Khattab, 38

Sabil al-Rashad ila Naf' al-'Ibad, 137–38
saj', 120
salon culture, 20. *See also majalis* (literary salons)
al-Sanablawi, Ahmad, 41–42
Sannu', Ya'qub, 147, 173
Sartain, Elizabeth, 97
scholarly culture, 2, 9–10
scientific culture, 13
al-Shabrawi, 'Abdalla, 107, 137, 143, 167, 193n. 49
al-Shafi'i, 'Amir al-Anbuti, 160
al-Shafi'i, Husayn al-Mahalli, 89
Shalabi, 'Abdul-Ghani, 161
Shalabi, Ahmad, 22
Shanan, Ahmad Bey, 154
Sharabi, Hisham, 151
al-Shara'ibi, Qasim, 31
al-Sha'rani, 'Abd al-Wahab, 92, 112
al-Sharaybi, Khawaja Ahmad, 73
al-Sharqawi, 'Abdulla, 45–46, 155
al-Sharshuhi, Ahmad b. Sulayman, 100
Shaw, Stanford, 46
shaykhs, 69–70, 71, 96–97
Shihata, Salama b., 66
al-Shirbini, Yusuf: attitude of, 150; concern with material life, 158–60; education of, 152; interest in ordinary people, 122; *majalis* and, 74; on middle-class elite, 77; motivations of, 116; on *'ulama'*, 155; use of colloquial language, 124, 134; use of Juda jokes, 119; use of proverbs, 121
Shoshan, Boaz, 96
Siraj, Muhammad, 135
social context: of coffeehouses, 67–68; cultural exchange between classes, 107; in eighteenth century, 139, 144; impact of trade on, 32; introduction to in *maktab*, 55; *majalis* and, 72–73, 75–76;

social context (*cont.*)
oral culture as part of, 65; polarization of, 45–46, 49; relationship between elite and middle class, 36–37, 40–49; as seen in literary texts, 145–46, 153; spread of books and, 100, 102; spread of colloquial and, 131, 134–35; viewing of through culture, 3–4; writers and, 150–51
social history, 109
Social History of Knowledge, A (Burke), 11, 165
Sonbol, Amira El-Azhary, 130
sources, 20–25, 109–10
spice merchants, 31
State and Society in Mid-Nineteenth-Century Egypt (Toledano), 5
state power structures: development of middle-class culture and, 7–8; loosening of control, 44–47; middle-class development and, 26–27; policy on international trade, 29; '*ulama*' as link to lower classes, 41–42
Steensgaard, Neils, 30
storytellers, 66–67, 120, 185n. 26
stratum, use of term, 7–8
street riots, 47–48, 70, 145–46, 160
Subjects of the Sultan: Culture and Daily Life in the Ottoman Empire (Faroqhi), 11
Sufism, 13, 73, 94–96, 113
Sufi *tariqas*. *See* brotherhoods
sugar production, 28, 30–31, 35, 40, 44
Sulayman, Shihada b., 81–82
Sulayman the Magnificent, 106
al-Suyuti, Jalal al Din, 97
Syria: domination of scholarly families in, 106; education in, 70; literacy in, 58, 59; middle-class writers in, 118; ordinary man in literature of, 127–28; personal narratives of, 169

al-Tahtawi, Rifa'a, 54, 71
tariqas. *See* brotherhoods

taxation system: impact on education, 61; impact on eighteenth-century literature, 160; influence on middle-class culture, 8–9, 26–27, 36–40, 139–40; Mamluk control of, 8–9, 27, 44–47, 104–5, 139–40
Taylor, Charles, 121
textile production: competition for, 44; educated workers in, 71–72; European imports and, 27; income of workers in, 40; increased demand for, 28; information available on, 35–36; putting-out system in, 33, 34–35; significance of, 31
Toledano, Ehud, 5
trade: changes in early modern period, 30–31; changes in later period, 44–47; comparative studies of, 16–17; development of middle class and, 7; financial mechanisms for, 7, 30, 37–39, 42, 44; growth of writing and, 20; impact on economy as a whole, 32; influence on culture, 26; role of soldiers in, 42–43; shift toward northern Europe, 28–29; spread of books and, 80, 100; spread of literacy and, 16, 57–64

'*ulama*': amassing of wealth, 154–55; attitudes of middle class toward, 146; as book owners, 59, 93; control over education/culture, 105; culture of, 12, 51, 105–6, 110; debate over knowledge and, 163–66; educational reforms and, 175; enrichment of the elite, 45–46; expression of middle-class views of, 154; function of scholarship of, 129; image of, 22; influence on society, 9–10; methodology of, 120; middle-class connections with, 41–42, 105; middle-class elite vs., 76–77, 78; oral culture of, 65; origins of, 114; polarization within community, 44, 46; recognition of

middle class by, 111–13; relationship with Mamluks, 27; role as leaders, 69; social standing of, 141–42; as teachers at Azhar, 71; use of biographical dictionaries, 109
'Umar, Hajj, 38
al-'Umari, Abi Bakr, 67
urban population: impoverishment of, 27; Mamluk relationship with, 46–49, 144; reaction to crises of eighteenth century, 145–46
urban spaces, 47, 65–69
'Uthman, Nasir, 87

Venice, 34, 37
Vrolijik, Arnoud, 133

Walz, Terence, 40
waqf deeds, 20–21, 60–61
Wild, Johann de, 66
Williams, Raymond, 2, 145, 152–53
women, 39, 53, 124–27, 164
writers: eighteenth-century style/language of, 157; of middle class, 118, 148–56; motivations of, 168–69; portrayal of ordinary man, 121–26, 153; response to crises, 171; subject matter of, 158–69; use of colloquial language, 115, 117–20, 128–36, 157–58. *See also individual writers*
written word: by/for/about middle class, 49, 108–19; commercial need for, 62–64; consequences of middle-class influence on, 119–36; consolidation of Mamluk social ideology by, 141; democratization of, 24–25, 153; elite control of, 12; history of, 55–57; impact of middle class on, 111–19; oral culture and, 64; paper trade and, 20, 68; spread of colloquial and, 131–32. *See also* book culture; books; literature

Yuhanna, Mariam b., 81–82
Yusuf, 'Abdul-Fattah b., 94
Yusuf, Lutfalla b., 108

al-Zabidi, Murtada, 73
al-Zayyat, Muhammad Badr al-Din, 117

Nelly Hanna is professor and chair of the Department of Arabic Studies at the American University of Cairo. She is the author of a number of books, including *Making Big Money in 1600: The Life and Times of Ismai'l Abu Taqiyya, Egyptian Merchant*, also published by Syracuse University Press.